GW01221003

Spire Studies in Architectural History
Volume 2

The Practice of Architecture
eight architects, 1830-1930

edited by Christopher Webster

For Sophie and Ted
with thanks for a special gift

The Practice of Architecture
eight architects, 1830-1930

edited by Christopher Webster

Spire Books Ltd
PO Box 2336, Reading RG4 5WJ
www.spirebooks.com

Spire Books Ltd
PO Box 2336, Reading RG4 5WJ
www.spirebooks.com

Copyright © 2012 Spire Books Ltd, Christopher Webster and the authors

All rights reserved

CIP data: a catalogue record for this book is available from the British Library

Designed by John Elliott

Printed by Berforts Information Press Ltd

ISBN 978-1-904965-35-0

CONTENTS

	Introduction *Christopher Webster*	9
1	Henry Roberts (1803-76): architect and housing reformer: Evangelical, family and other connections *James Stevens Curl*	15
2	William Culshaw (1807-74) and Henry Sumners (1825-95): rebuilding Victorian Liverpool *Joseph Sharples*	49
3	The rewards for diligence and prudence: the exemplary career of William Hill (1827-1889) *Christopher Webster*	79
4	Acrobatic Gothic, freely treated: the rise and fall of Bassett Keeling (1837-86) *James Stevens Curl*	107
5	Edward Schroeder Prior (1852-1932): rogue architect? *Stewart Abbott*	145
6	Harold A. Peto (1854-1933): architect, interior designer, collector, and aesthete *Hilary J. Grainger*	169
7	Artist in the craft of building: the architectural work of Hugh Thackeray Turner (1853-1937) *Robin Stannard*	207
	Notes on the contributors	237

Portsmouth Town Hall, William Hill, 1886-90. (*Building News*, 51, 1886, after p. 456.)

Introduction

Christopher Webster

In its first volume of *Transactions*, published in 1836, the recently formed Institute of British Architects had, heading its Regulations, 'Its Object': architectural education, the 'promotion' of architecture and the 'establish[ment] of uniformity and respectability in the profession'.[1] These were all laudable objectives and long overdue in this country, yet as the essays in this book reveal, 'uniformity and respectability' were not to be quickly or easily achieved.

The architects who are the subjects of this book are all of interest in their own right; indeed several of them reached the very top of the profession. However, perhaps this is a case of 'the sum being greater than the parts' for collectively, the careers of these men provide important insights into the still neglected subject of what it meant to be an architect in the first hundred years of the Institute's existence. Despite Frank Jenkins' claim that in the second half of the eighteenth century, the architectural profession began to emerge as 'something approaching ... the pattern which we accept today,'[2] even for the two generations that followed 1850, architectural practice could encompass a huge range of activity in terms of employment, building types, styles, clients and geographical spread. As Robert Macleod concluded, 'The single most dominant characteristic of Victorian architecture was its diversity',[3] and Professor Curl chose to place 'diversity' in the title of his most recent work on the period.[4]

The establishment of the IBA in 1834 is a convenient peg on which to hang notions of a coherent and properly regulated profession, yet complaints about the conduct of competitions, fees charged or offered, education and unscrupulous conduct – complaints that came from within and beyond the profession – continued unabated for the rest of the century. And, until well into the twentieth century, it was still possible for anyone, regardless of training or competence, to open an architect's office.

Nothing better illustrates the breadth of activity encompassed by the word 'architect' at the beginning of our period than a brief consideration of some of the 23 practices listed in the White's Leeds *Directory* of 1853.[5] History would tend to award the crown to Cuthbert Brodrick who had just arrived in the town after winning the hugely prestigious competition for the new town hall in 1852, 'an essay in civic pride, if ever there was one'.[6] Despite having only a handful of years of largely unremarkable experience when he entered the competition, the commission should have been the foundation of a spectacular career, yet it represented its pinnacle; Brodrick's career had peaked. However, the dream of repeating such a transformational victory must have spurred on many an ambitious young architect; the twenty-one year old Giles Gilbert Scott's victory for the Liverpool Cathedral competition in 1903 was even more the stuff of fairy tales.

Immediately above Brodrick's name in the *Directory* is one George Askey about whom absolutely nothing is known and who appears not to have obtained a single commission. And immediately below Brodrick is John B. Chantrell, who no doubt hoped to capitalise on the family name,[7] but who, like Askey, appears to have had no success, despite the thorough training and other advantages supplied by his father, long since retired from Leeds. Perhaps both clung to the unlikely ambition of repeating a competition victory as Brodrick had done. Further down the list was William Hill, whose known work by 1853 comprised nothing more glamorous than rows of workers' houses, yet as Chapter 3 reveals, he ended his career with two of the outstanding monuments of the age. But most remarkable of the architects in Leeds around 1850 was John West Hugall, remarkable that is, in the context of his background. By the time of his retirement, he could look back on a career as a designer and restorer of churches rewarded by fellowship of the RIBA in 1872 when his proposers were J.L. Pearson, Ewan Christian and Owen Jones, just about as eminent a trio of architects as could be assembled then. Yet Hugall's preparation for this apparently glittering career involved nothing more than several years as a wine merchant. No doubt he had long held an *interest* in medieval churches – he was a founder member of the Yorkshire Architectural Society in 1842 – but in 1847, he simply announced his entry to the profession 'which was more in accordance with [my] taste',[8] without, apparently, any training whatsoever.

The picture in Leeds was, in essence, a microcosm of the national scene in which the exceptionally accomplished vied with the untrained, untried or simply incompetent, for work.[9] One would like to think that

Introduction

building committees were able to spot the difference and award contracts accordingly, although the papers of the Incorporated Church Building Society include worryingly frequent occurrences of half-built churches needing to be strengthened or even demolished. And instances of disgruntled shareholders feeling they had been seduced by showy perspective drawings and unrealistically low estimates, are legion.

Even when the inept, the unscrupulous and would-be architects are removed from all those claiming membership of the national profession, those left are far from a coherent group. This variety is, on the one hand, perplexing, and certainly suggests that any claim for a coherent profession even by the end on the nineteenth century is premature. But it is also indicative that architectural practice encompassed a fascinatingly wide set of activities, performed by designers with an equally diverse set of interests and opinions about what constituted sound practice; and there were many who saw this as providing the profession with a welcomed vibrancy that was certainly not unhealthy.

Ruskin attacked 'the idea of an independent architectural profession' as 'a mere modern fallacy',[10] and subsequently expressed the wish 'to see the profession of architecture united, not with that of the engineer, but [with that] of the sculptor.'[11] Later in the century, several eminent architects – most of whom had shunned membership of the RIBA – publicly expressed the view that the practice of architecture was not a profession at all, but a branch of the fine arts. Painters were not subject to qualifications obtained by competitive examination and subject to rules of conduct; why should they be? Regulation, they argued, would do nothing to encourage creativity.[12] The anti-registration group set out its case in *Architecture, a Profession or an Art?* in 1892 of which the following gives a flavour.[13]

> To answer a few dozen questions would not have been considered as any test of knowledge of design in any of the arts [in the past]. Nor can it now [Bodley].[14]
> An original genius may not be recognised, and his work may offend the judges; while tame commonplace work, mere repetitions of stale truisms, or accepted ideas of others, would infallibly come to the front [Pearson].[15]

The eight men who are the focus of this book could all claim a thorough architectural education but, as will be revealed, their careers developed along very different paths, although all but Culshaw eventually joined the RIBA; even Prior, despite being one of the contributors to *Architecture, a Profession or an Art?*, was a member.

Henry Roberts (1803-76), whose career began before Victoria's accession, enjoyed a number of advantages: a string of titled clients, association with Prince Albert, commendable social housing projects and he was a luminary of the London scene. Yet while architecture had provided him with a decent living, his fall from grace – a combination of events which included the wrath of the Ecclesiologists, expressing opinions which antagonising some of his paymasters, and impropriety with 'a member of the lower orders' – is cautionary. For his near contemporary, William Culshaw (1807-74), hard work and astute business dealings provided his practice with a solid, if unspectacular, reputation in the rapidly expanding town of Liverpool – and enabled this son of a builder to elevate himself to the ranks of the middle class. In partnership with Henry Sumner (1825-95), he played a significant role in the development of what was essentially a new building type: the well-lit, multi-storey, commercial office, much in demand by the town's mercantile community. Twentieth-century technological advances eclipsed them, and most were either demolished or neglected. The essay here is thus an important account a type of a practice that fulfilled a crucial role in Britain's industrial supremacy, yet has hitherto been largely marginalized by scholarship.

William Hill (1827-89) and Bassett Keeling (1837-86) are another pair of near contemporaries, both had useful Nonconformist connections and both trained in Leeds; probably, they knew each other. And both provided a wide range of building types for their clients. However, while Hill started modestly, and remained in Leeds, Keeling left for the opportunities of a London office. Yet it was Hill whose career took him around the country supervising projects, not Keeling's, and Hill who ended his days with a national reputation. His advantage was not at the drawing board – the two might reasonably be ranked as equals on that score – but in terms of his financial acumen and organisational ability, factors of crucial importance for those seeking long-term success, but easily overlooked in surveys of architectural practice.

For architects born in the 1850s, practice often involved an additional range of issues; regulation of the profession and formal education leading to examinations have already been touched upon. In addition, the role of traditional crafts and materials in a rapidly developing world of building, and the protection of ancient buildings they were called upon to repair or extend exercised many. Edward Prior (1852-1932) played an important role in the last two of these. He was a founder member of the St George's Art Society – forerunner of the Art Workers' Guild – and long-time secretary of the Arts and Crafts Exhibition Society. Yet, somewhat surprisingly, he was also a member of the RIBA and a designer keen to exploit the possibilities of concrete. He would have had much in common with Thackeray Turner (1853-1937), a committed member of the SPAB and for many years its secretary. In addition, he produced a number of thoughtfully designed churches and medium-sized houses which reflected the more conservative end of the current stylistic trends. For Harold Peto (1854-1933) – best known for his domestic work for the wealthy while in partnership with Ernest George, and who was himself from a privileged background – the practice of architecture involved more than designing buildings and often included specification of their furnishings and decoration, the purchase of exquisite antiques, and later their garden settings too. He also designed the first-class interiors of several liners.

These essays should reminded us that architectural practice is a neglected subject – even among those at the top of the profession, there are important gaps in our knowledge, and for the layers of the profession below it, we know very little. It is a subject that would repay further research.

Notes
1. *Transactions of the Institute of British Architects of London, Session 1835-6*, John Weale, 1836, x.
2. F. Jenkins, *Architect and Patron*, Oxford U.P., 1962, 91.
3. R. Macleod, *Style and Society Architectural Ideology in Britain 1835-1914*, RIBA Publications, 1971, 123.
4. J.S. Curl, *Victorian Architecture Diversity and Invention*, Spire Books, 2007.
5. W. White, *Directory and Gazetteer of Leeds ...* , William White, 1853, 216.
6. K. Grady, 'From Medieval Borough to Great Victorian City' in C. Webster (ed.), *Building a Great Victorian City*, Northern Heritage Publications in association with the Victorian Society, 2011, 22.
7. For J.B. Chantrell's father, see C. Webster, *R.D. Chantrell (1793-1872) and the Architecture of a Lost Generation*, Spire Books, 2010.
8. *Leeds Mercury*, 29 June 1850. He was not even a *successful* wine merchant and in 1850, sued his shop manager for embezzlement, a process which revealed useful details of Hugall's architectural ambitions.
9. For the provincial scene generally, much insightful material – along with useful statistics – can be found in G. Brandwood, 'Many and Varied: Victorian Provincial Architects in England and Wales' in K. Ferry (ed.), *Powerhouses of Provincial Architecture*, The Victorian Society, 2009, 3-14.
10. J. Ruskin, *Seven Lamps of Architecture*, Smith Elder, 2nd ed., 1855, xii.
11. J. Ruskin, address to the RIBA, 1865, quoted in S. Kostof, *The Architect*, Oxford U.P., 1977, 200.
12. The best account appears in Macleod [n. 3], 123-36.
13. N Shaw & T.G. Jackson (eds), *Architecture, a Profession or an Art?*, John Murray, 1892.
14. G.F. Bodley, 'Architectural Study and the Examination Test' on Shaw & Jackson [n. 13], 68.
15. T.G. Jackson, 'Introductions', in Shaw & Jackson [n. 13], xxii.

1.1: Henry Roberts: from a pencil-and-wash drawing on paper by Daniel Maclise, 1828. (*Author's collection.*)

1

Henry Roberts (1803-76) architect and housing reformer Evangelical, family, and other connections

James Stevens Curl

Henry Roberts[1] was born on 16 April 1803 in Philadelphia, PA, U.S.A., the son of Josiah (1773-1846), a London merchant who had an address at 212 South 3rd Street in that city. The family returned to England in 1804 or 1805. In 1818 Roberts was articled to Charles Fowler (1792-1867 – who had just established his independent architectural practice),[2] and in 1824 won two medals of the Society of Arts.[3] In 1825 he joined the office of Robert Smirke (1780-1867), 'whose tastes, habits, modes of construction, and method of making working drawings, he ... thoroughly imbibed',[4] then, on Smirke's advice, entered, on 28 November 1825, the Royal Academy Schools,[5] when his address was recorded as 10 Camberwell Terrace.

In 1824 Roberts was one of six invited to participate in an architectural competition to design buildings for the Protestant Dissenters' Grammar School, Mill Hill, Middlesex: the others were William Tite (1798-1873 – who won in 1825), William Ford (c. 1790-1876), James Field (fl. 1816-42), 'W. Brooke' (presumably William Brooks [1786-1867 – a zealous anti-Papist]),

CHAPTER 1

and 'J. Griffith' (probably John Griffith of Finsbury [1796-1888]).[6] It might seem surprising that one so young should be invited, but the key is the school, founded in 1807 to provide a first-rate education for those debarred from establishments run by the Anglican Church: the Roberts and Clayton[7] families (who were related)[8] were connected with the School, with several of the personalities running it, with the Clapham Sect, and, through the Congregationalist Minister, John Clayton (1780-1865),[9] with the London Missionary Society which maintained links with Evangelical Churches in Russia, especially in St Petersburg: this association was important for Roberts.

It was through the Royal Academy Schools that Roberts met the Cork-born Daniel Maclise (1806-70),[10] who had arrived in London in 1827 and rapidly made a reputation as a portraitist: Roberts sat for him in 1828 (**1.1**).[11] Shortly afterwards, Roberts set out to tour the Continent. His visit to Naples proved to be of lasting importance, because he saw the Albergo di Poveri, or Reclusorio, begun in 1753 under the ægis of King Charles III (reigned 1734-59) to designs by Ferdinando Fuga (1699-1782): this provided shelter and employment for 8,000 persons. It was one of Roberts's first tastes of philanthropic housing.[12]

Early independent practice, success, and connections

Roberts was back in London by 1830, and established himself in Suffolk Street: in 1831 his opportunity came with the new Hall for the Fishmongers' Company of the City of London. The construction of London Bridge

1.2: Fishmongers' Hall, London (1832-5), lithographed by Louis Haghe (1806-85), inscribed 'Henry Roberts Architect', printed by Day & Haghe. (*Author's collection.*)

Henry Roberts (1803-76)

(designed by John Rennie [1761-1821] and realised under the direction of his son, John [1794-1874]) and its approaches necessitated the demolition of the old Hall, so the Company's Surveyor, Richard Suter (1797-1883),[13] prepared details of the site, and it was decided to offer premiums for the three best designs in an architectural competition. There were 83 entries, and early in 1832 these were exhibited: in February the winning Greek Revival scheme was revealed as by Roberts, of 23 Suffolk Street, Pall Mall; the second premium was won by John Davies (1796-1865); and the third by Lewis Nockalls Cottingham (1787-1847).[14] Roberts's scheme was cleverly planned, and the architecture was influenced by the work of Smirke: throughout the Hall the utmost Grecian refinement was apparent. Construction was innovative: the building sits on a concrete raft; the floor between the warehouse-podium and the Hall proper was constructed of brick arches springing from cast-iron bearers spaced by tie-rods; hollow bricks (a favourite Roberts material) were used for internal work; and there was much iron, both cast and wrought. Fishmongers' Hall was completed in 1840 (**1.2**): Roberts was never again to design a building of such splendour.[15]

Roberts then employed an assistant, George Gilbert Scott (1811-78 – who described the foundations of the structure in a paper given at the Institute of British Architects),[16] and in the autumn moved to 18 Adam Street, Adelphi. Scott was only eight years younger than Roberts, and spent two years with him, claiming to have made 'all the working drawings of this considerable public building, from the foundation to the finish'.[17] Scott, the 'only clerk in the office' described Roberts as of 'independent circumstances', and as 'gentlemanly, religious, precise, and quiet':[18] he wrote of his time with Roberts as 'almost a blank' in his memory 'from its even and uneventful character',[19] yet he regarded the older man as his 'very excellent friend'.[20]

In 1834 Roberts made Scott clerk of the works for the Collegiate School in Camberwell, an essay in Gothic, completed 1835: Scott 'superintended' this 'throughout its erection' (which was 'very rapid'), an arrangement 'more beneficial' to him than to the building,[21] the most agreeable feature of which was the arcaded entrance (**1.3**). Roberts probably got the job through his Evangelical connections, and the headmaster, John Allen Giles (1808-84),[22] was later (1838) one of his proposers for election as a Fellow of the Society of Antiquaries of London.[23]

Roberts received the Soane Medallion in 1834, was a founder-member of the Institute of British Architects (he became a Fellow in 1837), but more important for his career was his connection with the Revd Baptist Wriothesley Noel (1799-1873 – tenth son of Sir Gerard Noel Noel, 2nd

CHAPTER I

1.3: Camberwell Collegiate School, London (1834-5), lithographed by Frederick Mackenzie (*c.* 1787-1854), inscribed 'Henry Roberts Archt 1834'. (*Author's collection.*)

Baronet [1759-1838], and his wife, Diana [1762-1823 – *née* Middleton, *suo jure* Baroness Barham from 1813 – Evangelical patroness], of Exton Park, Rutland), whose brother, Charles (1781-1866), was created 1st Earl of Gainsborough in 1841. Baptist Noel himself was a charismatic Evangelical Anglican clergyman who denounced Tractarianism as a 'serious offence'.[24] When State-Church tensions grew to breaking point with the Gorham case,[25] Noel abandoned the Established Church in 1848 and became a Baptist in 1849.[26] Deeply concerned with both the physical and moral welfare of the poor, his influence was behind the appointment of Roberts as Honorary Architect to the Destitute Sailors' Asylum, Ensign Street (formerly Well Street), Whitechapel, which opened in 1835, a forerunner of many model lodging-houses.[27] So, by the mid-1830s, Roberts was a young, successful architect, with a major building being completed in the City, and with excellent contacts.[28] His friendship with Noel was to attract clients among clergy, landed gentry, and aristocracy.

Various commissions followed. First was the Glebe House, Southborough, Kent, a handsome building in a Græco-Italianate style, the contract-drawings for which survive.[29] Then came the north aisle of St Peter's parish church, Yoxford, Suffolk (**1.4**): the mural tablets commemorating the Davy and Clayton[30] families therein provide clues as to why Roberts was appointed. The Claytons, as noted above, were involved with the school at Mill Hill

For the Enlargement of Yoxford Church.

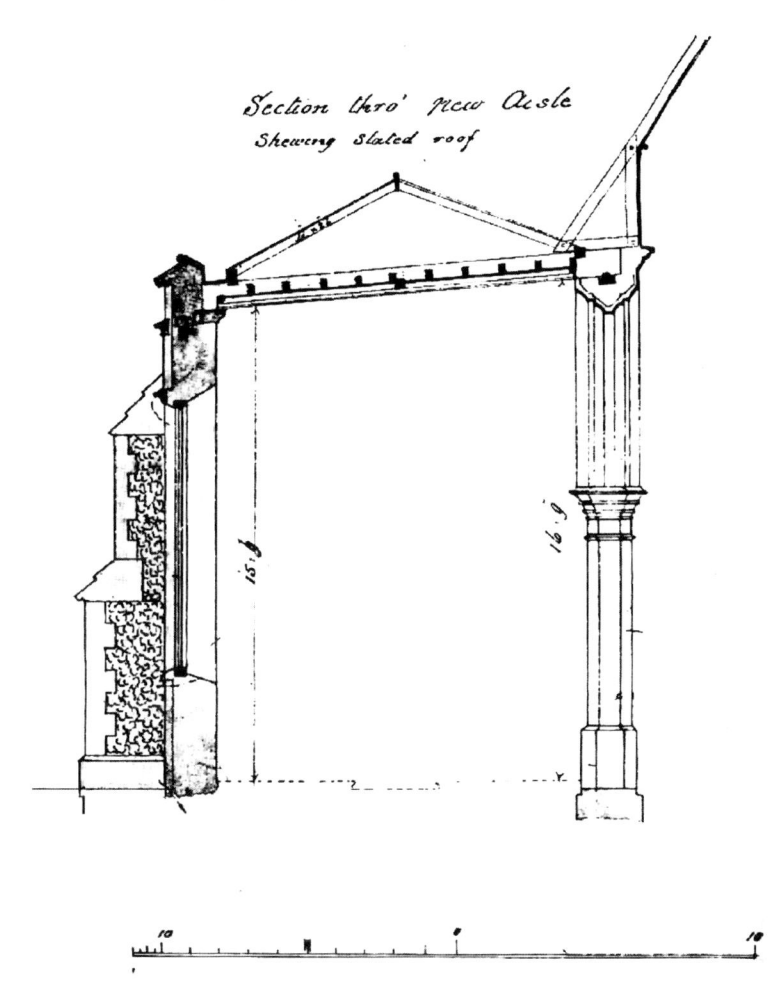

*Section thro' new Aisle
Shewing Slated roof*

1.4: Roberts's drawing signed 'Adam St Adelphi June 1837' for the 'Enlargement of Yoxford Church'. Below is a 'Detail of Roof timbers' Roberts repeated the East Anglian octagonal pier elsewhere, regardless of location. (*Lambeth Palace Library.*)

and with the King's Weigh House Chapel in London with which Baptist Noel was also to have connections. The Evangelical Davy family was related to Roberts, for one of his daughters had Davy among her names: two of the memorial tablets commemorate Eleazar Davy (d.1803 – of Yoxford, High Sheriff of the County of Suffolk in 1770) and his nephew, the antiquary David Elisha Davy (1769-1851 – who had been curate of Yoxford, but resigned in 1795). In addition, Samuel Thomas Roberts[31] was instituted to the living at Yoxford on 23 February 1837, and it was he who wrote (3 April 1837) to the Incorporated Society for Promoting the Enlargement, Building, and Repairing of Churches and Chapels recommending the appointment of a 'first-class Architect from London' whose services were acquired 'at the cost of a friend'.[32] At Yoxford a Robert Henry Cooper (d.1851) is also commemorated, and the Coopers were related by marriage to the Roberts family.

Roberts designed the Scotch Presbyterian Reformed Church, Grosvenor Square, Chorlton-on-Medlock, Manchester (long since demolished), drawings of which he exhibited at the Royal Academy in 1838, and this was followed by Escot House (also exhibited at the RA) and church, Devon, in 1838-40, commissions again gained through his Evangelical connections, this time for Sir John Kennaway (1797-1873 – 2nd Baronet from 1836). The Kennaways were related by marriage to the Noel family, were Anglican Evangelicals, supporters of the Church Missionary Society, and participants in the Church Association. Escot House is a handsome Neo-Classical-Italianate building (**1.5**) with fine Greek-inspired fire-surrounds (**1.6**) identical to those in other Roberts buildings,[33] but the Church of St Philip and St James in the grounds is dull Gothic Revival (interestingly, surviving drawings by Roberts for non-Classical buildings seem hesitant compared with those for Classical works). Baptist Noel would seem to be the likely

1.5: Terrace-garden front of Escot House, Devon (1838), showing the assured handling of solids and voids. (*Author.*)

HENRY ROBERTS (1803-76)

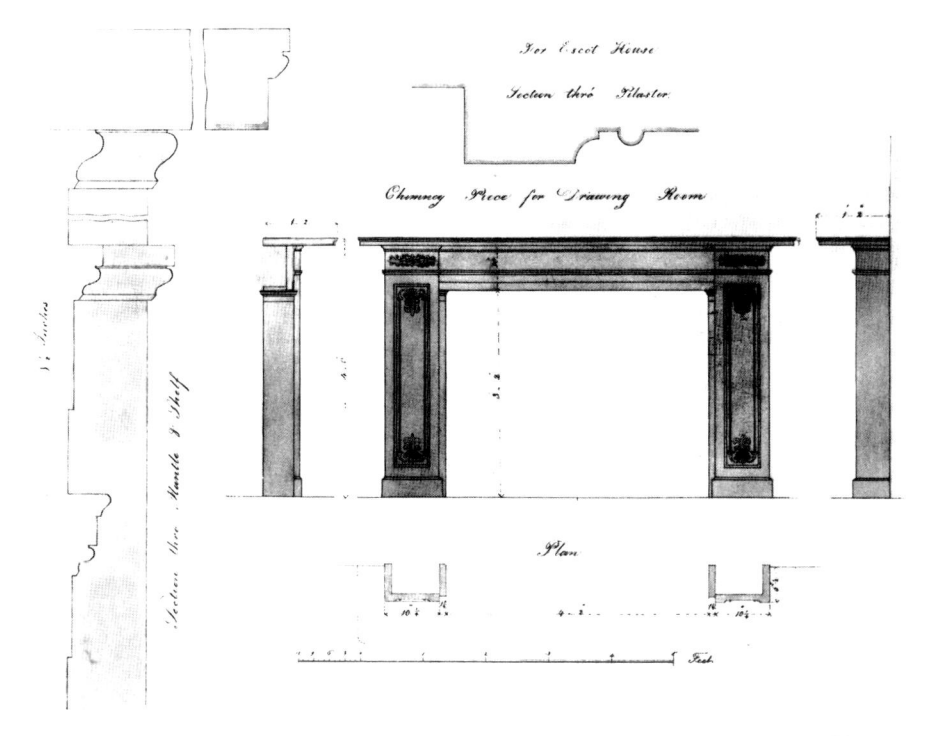

1.6: Design by Roberts for a drawing room chimney-piece at Escot House, Devon (1838): an identical specimen was provided at Toft Hall, Cheshire. Drawing by Roberts. (*Devon County Record Office, Exeter, 961 M/add.1/E29.*)

link between Roberts and Kennaway,[34] but there was also a Devonian connection through Charles Fowler, who hailed from Cullompton. Such a link was important for another reason: the stonemason engaged at Escot House and church was Henry Gullett (1810-84), who came from Shaugh Prior, Devon, but in 1838-40 was living with his family at Talaton, near Ottery St Mary. Gullett was to work as chief stonemason on several of Roberts's schemes, moving to addresses in various parts of England for this purpose.[35]

Titled clients seem to have consulted Roberts thereafter, for in 1839-40 he designed works at Claydon House, Buckinghamshire, for Sir Harry Verney (1801-94 – 2nd Baronet from 1826, whose mother-in-law was the daughter of the 8th Baron Kinnaird). Arthur Fitzgerald Kinnaird (1814-87 – 10th Lord Kinnaird of Inchture and 2nd Baron Kinnaird of Rossie from 1878)[36] married (1843) a niece of the Earl of Gainsborough, and was best man at Henry Roberts's marriage in 1847. Kinnaird's wife was Mary Jane Hoare (1816-88 – daughter of William Henry Hoare [1776-1819] and

CHAPTER I

Louisa Elizabeth Noel [d.1816]), who, from 1837 until her marriage, lived in the house of her uncle, Baptist Noel, and became a passionate Evangelical, especially in the cause of Protestantism in Italy (with which the Roberts family was also to be concerned), and, with her husband, became a 'driving force behind a formidable range of Evangelical initiatives'.[37] For the purposes of this essay, it is worth noting that, apart from his many Evangelical and philanthropic activities, Kinnaird was posted to St Petersburg (1835-7), where he served as private secretary to the British Ambassador, John George Lambton (1792-1840 – 1st Earl of Durham from 1833), and while there mixed with like-minded Protestants, a factor that was to be important in Roberts's life. Kinnaird, like Anthony Ashley Cooper (1801-85 – 7th Earl of Shaftesbury from 1851), 'took a keen interest in all matters concerning the well-being of the working classes',[38] and indeed did everything he could to better conditions on his Scottish estates.

Roberts carried out work at Peamore House, Alphington, near Exeter, Devon, for Samuel Trehawke Kekewich (1796-1873), M.P. for Exeter in 1826 and for South Devon from 1858. Between 1840 and 1841 he designed St Mary's Church, Hartley Wintney, Hampshire, in a Neo-Norman style, for George Calthorpe (1787-1851 – 3rd Baron Calthorpe from 1807), the drawings for which were exhibited at the Royal Academy in 1841.[39] Gullett was again the chief stonemason, and a memoir (1864) by his son (also Henry) records that the church spire was finished off with a stone cross at its apex.[40] Roberts also designed the Hartley Wintney parsonage (1839) in a reticent

1.7: 'The London Terminus of the Brighton and Dover Railroad' (*c.* 1841-4), from *Stationers' Almanack*, 1845, drawn by J. Marchant (*fl.* 1840s), engraved by Henry Adlard (*fl.*1828-49). (*Author's collection.*)

Classical style.[41] Once again, the connection was through philanthropy: Calthorpe was an Evangelical Churchman; he knew Baptist Noel, Kinnaird, and Ashley Cooper; he was associated with the London City Mission; and he was to become a Vice-Patron of the Society for Improving the Condition of the Labouring Classes (SICLC hereafter) with which many Evangelicals were involved, not least Roberts.

During these years Roberts had been consolidating his position: apart from membership of the Institute of British Architects[42] and regular exhibitions at the Royal Academy, he was elected (1840) to the Athenæum (his proposer was Samuel Boddington [1766-1843 – Dissenter, Whig, and Liveryman of the Fishmongers' Company] and his seconder was Edward Jacob [1795/6-1841 – barrister and legal writer]).[43] He also made an approach to the London and Croydon Railway Company (with which his father and brother, Frederick Roberts, were connected): in 1839 he was appointed Architect to this Company, in which capacity he designed several buildings, and when the Joint Committee of the Croydon, Brighton, and South Eastern Railway Companies decided to build a combined terminus at London Bridge, bringing in the London and Greenwich Company as well, Roberts was involved. The realised scheme, a handsome essay (**1.7**) in the Italianate style (1840-4, demolished 1851), was credited to Roberts, George Smith (1782-1869), John Urpeth Rastrick (1780-1856), and Frederick Thomas Turner (1812-77).[44] In 1840 also, Roberts designed a house at Bagshot, Surrey, for J.A. Giles.

In 1843 Roberts exhibited drawings of Norton Manor, Norton Fitzwarren, Somerset, an essay in a free Tudor-Gothic style. This was for Charles Noel Welman (1814-1907), and again the link between client and architect was through the Noel connection: Charles Noel, 1st Earl of Gainsborough, married (1809) Elizabeth Welman (d.1811), daughter of Thomas Welman of Poundisford Park, Somerset, and Welman took as his second wife (1813) the Hon. Charlotte Margaret Noel (d.1869). Charles Noel Welman was the son of Thomas and Charlotte Margaret Welman, and the latter was Baptist Noel's sister: Welman married (1835) Anne Eliza Bolton in Chipping Campden parish church, yet another connection with the Noel family. C.N. Welman was a pioneer of photography, and was the author of papers on the topic as well as of a volume 'by a Protestant Nonconformist' entitled *Sketches of the True Genius of Popery* published in London in 1852. When Roberts designed Norton Manor for him, Welman was firmly in the Evangelical camp, but following the Gorham affair he, like the Gainsboroughs, became a Roman Catholic, in his case in 1851.[45] Welman's daughter eventually married into the old Roman Catholic Stonor family.

Chapter 1

Philanthropic, ecclesiastical, and other works of an established architect

The SICLC was founded in 1844 under the patronage of Queen Victoria and presidency of Prince Albert. Roberts was a founder-member and was appointed Honorary Architect. From this period much of Roberts's output was concerned with the promotion of the Society's aims in tracts, books, booklets, or lectures, or in designs for model housing. The first built scheme was on a restricted site owned by Lord Calthorpe, near the former Spa of Bagnigge Wells[46] between Lower Road, Pentonville, and Gray's Inn Road, but the architectural press was not over-enthusiastic.[47] The next efforts were to improve lodging-houses for working men, and the Society purchased three houses in Charles Street, off Drury Lane, which Roberts converted into a hostel for 82 persons: then came the model lodging-house for 104

1.8: Prince Albert laying the foundation-stone of St Paul's Seamens' Church, Dock Street, on 11 May 1846 in the presence of the Bishop (from 1828) of London, Charles James Blomfield (1786-1857), other clerics, and John Labouchere (1799-1863 – banker, Evangelical, and philanthropist). The cleric with longish dark hair to the left of the tripod (second from left) is probably Baptist Noel, and Roberts is the figure standing to the Prince's left, with the leg of the tripod cutting across his chest. Engraving from the *Illustrated London News,* 16 May 1846, 321. (*Author's collection.*)

men in George Street, Bloomsbury, designed to improve health and comfort, whilst setting a good moral tone: Prince Albert performed the opening ceremony in 1848, and during the dreadful cholera epidemic of 1849 the imates of the lodging-house escaped unscathed.

By then Roberts occupied offices at 13 Suffolk Street, and his next project was for the East End. It was decided at a meeting[48] chaired by Thomas Hamilton (1780-1858 – 9th Earl of Haddington from 1828 and First Lord of the Admiralty 1841-6) to erect a new Church for Seamen in Dock Street near Roberts's Destitute Sailors' Asylum. It was determined to adopt the First Pointed style for the building, and Roberts was appointed architect: construction began in March 1846, and Prince Albert laid the foundation-stone on 11 May (**1.8**). St Paul's, seating 800, was finished in 1847 and cost £9,000: it originally had galleries (subsequently removed), and sittings were free. Unfortunately the combination of Roberts's Gothic, his Evangelical stance, and the vestigial chancel incurred critical wrath: the 'stale and insipid' design was 'extremely poor … a vulgar attempt' at First Pointed, 'commonplace … put together without harmony', and the weather-vane at the top of the spire representing a ship was denounced as 'singularly vulgar'. To have one's architecture described as having 'not the least idea in its composition'[49] cannot have been pleasant.

This did not deter the Revd John Welstead Sharp Powell (*c*.1808-81 – the first incumbent of St Peter's, Norbiton, Surrey, an Evangelical with Devonian connections who knew Baptist Noel) from commissioning Roberts to design the new parsonage, and he got a substantial house with mullioned and transomed windows in the Tudor Gothic style in 1846-7,[50] demolished in the late 1950s. Through Kennaway, who was the patron of All Saints' Church and a trustee of the school at Sidmouth, Devon, Roberts was also appointed architect of the Tudor-Gothic school and school-house (1846-8).[51] Then came the Romanesque National Scotch Church, Crown Court, Covent Garden, which Roberts enlarged in 1848 with two adjoining schools (rebuilt 1905-9 to designs by Eustace James Anthony Balfour [1854-1911 – brother of Arthur James Balfour (1848-1930), Prime Minister 1902-5] and his professional partner [from 1890], Hugh Thackeray Turner [1853-1937]):[52] Roberts's client was the minister, John Cumming (1807-81), whose anti-Papist stance gained him a following, though the failure of his thunderous prophecies to come true led to an inevitable decline in his reputation. George Eliot (1819-80) condemned Cumming's 'bigoted narrowness', 'unscrupulosity of statement', and 'lack of charity'.[53]

When Michael Solomon Alexander (1799-1845), born of a Jewish family in the Grand Duchy of Posen, was consecrated first Bishop of the United

Chapter 1

Church of England and Ireland and of the Protestant Church of Germany in Jerusalem in 1841, and left for the Holy Land on the unfortunately-named warship *Devastation*, it was the culmination of a scheme dreamed up by King Friedrich Wilhelm IV of Prussia (reigned 1840-58), Christian Charles Josias von Bunsen (1791-1860), and Prince Albert. Ashley Cooper linked the return of the Jews to Palestine and the establishment of the joint bishopric with the Second Coming, but the immediate effect of Alexander's appointment was the secession of John Henry Newman (1801-90) and other Anglicans who were received into the Roman Catholic Church, events which 'proved' to Evangelicals that Tractarianism, Ecclesiology, and Ritualism led to Rome. Lord Ashley's (as Shaftesbury was then) intensification of his religious views took place around 1835, and by 1840 he was involved with numerous Evangelical societies, including the Church Missionary Society and the London Society for Promoting Christianity among the Jews. Bunsen and Ashley were close friends, and Roberts was also on intimate terms with the Prussian diplomat, who was both a philanthropist and an Evangelical. Bishop Alexander had links with the Victoria Emigration Society, and the

1.9: Arcade in Wigtown Church (1851-3), with octagonal piers of similar type to the nave arcades in St Peter's, Yoxford, St John's, Saxmundham, and St Paul's, Dock Street, London. (*Author.*)

Roberts family also had close connections with Australia which lasted well into the twentieth century. Furthermore, the Robertses and Alexander's children were eventually related by marriage, and after the bishop's death his children and widow were cared for by a committee set up by Lord Ashley.[54]

After his father's demise in 1846, Roberts married (15 April 1847) Catherine de Swetschine (*c.* 1820-1905), born in Archangel,[55] the daughter of Demetrius de Swetschine, a Russian nobleman:[56] it was probably through Kinnaird that Roberts met his bride. The marriage took place in the parish church of Paddington: Baptist Noel officiated, Kinnaird (as noted above) was best man, and other signatories of the marriage certificate were Henry's brother, Charles, James Foster from the London City Mission, and John Coles Symes, partner in the firm of Teesdale, Symes, & Weston, solicitors, of 31 Fenchurch Street.[57] At the time of the marriage, therefore, Henry Roberts was one day short of his 44th birthday, and his wife was 27.[58] The newlyweds moved to 10 Connaught Square, and in 1848 Olivia Maria Pauline Roberts was born (she was still alive[59] at the time of the Census in 1851, but does not appear to have survived childhood). Catherine Roberts, like many other old Baltic families, was of the Evangelical Protestant rather than Orthodox persuasion, and her religious beliefs brought her into contact with English Evangelicals, especially through the London Missionary Society.

There followed several commissions. The first was a large northern extension in 1849 to the church of Holy Trinity, Walton Street, Aylesbury, Buckinghamshire, built 1843-5 to designs by David Brandon (1813-97). In the same year Roberts patented an invention: hollow bricks that provided cheap, light, strong, well-insulated building components. Then, in 1850-1 he designed an extension to Toft Hall, Cheshire, for Ralph Gerard Leycester (1817-51), with handsome Grecian fire-surrounds identical to those he had previously designed for Escot House. For his earlier client, Powell, he designed the National Schools at Norbiton, Surrey (1851), in a late Gothic style.[60] At Exton Hall, Rutland, he rebuilt the central portion (1851-2) for the 1st Earl of Gainsborough: the interior of this otherwise Tudorbethan building has some Classical features (including a handsome fire-surround), but other details are similar to those of Norton Manor, and, given the family connections and Roberts's friendship with Baptist Noel, his involvement causes no surprise. Besides, in the village of Cottesmore near Exton a pair of red-brick dwellings was built to Roberts's designs, and in Clipsham stands another stone-built pair.

Yet another Suffolk church acquired a new north aisle and other works by Roberts in 1851-2:[61] this was St John the Baptist, Saxmundham, where the nave-arcades are carried on octagonal piers similar to those at Yoxford.

Chapter 1

Roberts also appears to have been responsible for repairs, a new transept, and a vestry at the church of St Mary, Benhall, near Saxmundham, in 1841, for which Gullett was the stonemason: the Gullett family seem to have lived for a few months at Benhall from the time of the completion of the works at Hartley Wintney until they moved to Southwark in London for the works on the railway terminus.[62]

After this Roberts designed two churches from scratch. The first was at Wigtown, Dumfries and Galloway, for the Church of Scotland, and was built in 1851-3 under the aegis of Randolph Stewart (1800-73 – 9th Earl of Galloway from 1834): it is a dour building in the First Pointed style. Essentially a Presbyterian preaching-box, it has an aisle separated from the nave by a three-bay arcade with octagonal piers not unlike those at Yoxford, Saxmundham, and St Paul's Church for Seamen, Dock Street (**1.9**). Roberts had worked for Scots congregations at Manchester and Covent Garden, but there was another reason for his appointment: Galloway was acquainted with Kinnaird, and also took a close interest in the SICLC, having attended at least one Annual General Meeting where he met Roberts. Lord Ashley was also a friend of Galloway, and stayed with him on visits to Scotland.

There may be another reason why Roberts was appointed: William Burn (1789-1870) had carried out works in Dumfries and Galloway, including some for the Earl at Galloway House, Wigtownshire, in 1842-6, and Burn was a former pupil of Smirke. With Charles Robert Cockerell (1788-1863) and Roberts, he had presented the old master with a portrait-bust by Thomas Campbell (1790-1858) in 1845, and Campbell had made a statue of young Kinnaird as Ascanius in 1822, portraits of members of the Kinnaird family (various dates), and of Lady Ashley (1832). So there were several threads joining these personalities, and Burn may have put in a word in Roberts's favour.[63] The drawings by Roberts for the church have 10 Connaught Square as his address.[64]

The last complete church by Roberts was St Matthew's, Talbot Street, Nottingham (1853-4), another essay in First Pointed, demolished in the 1950s. The begetter of this project was the Revd Joshua William Brooks (1790-1882), Vicar of St Mary's, Nottingham, who subscribed money for promoting the erection of churches. Other supporters were Henry Robert Kingscote (1802-82 – London philanthropist and Evangelical), the Revd Charles Wasteneys Eyre (1802-62 – Evangelical with aristocratic connections), and George James Philip Smith (1805-86), of the Inner Temple.[65] Supervision of the construction was left to a local man, R. Jalland (*fl.*1837-68): St Matthew's was lambasted by the critics, who declared it 'had little merit or power', with an 'unsatisfactory … arrangement'.[66]

One final work connected with the Anglican Church was the new vicarage (or 'Parsonage House') of St Mary's, Brampton, Huntingdonshire (1853-4),[67] commissioned by the Revd Thomas J. Mackee (d.1870): again, the reasons for Roberts's appointment concerned his links with the aristocracy and landed gentry, in this case with George Montagu (1799-1855 – 6th Duke of Manchester from 1843, for whom Roberts had designed buildings at Kimbolton Castle, Huntingdonshire in 1850, including gate-lodges constructed of Patent Hollow Bricks [Roberts billed Manchester for these, but did not get paid for his services until 1855]) and Lady Olivia Bernard Sparrow (1774-1863 – of Brampton Park, for whom Roberts designed a model lodging-house for labourers in 1848 among other works).[68] Lady Sparrow's daughter, Millicent (1798-1848), married the Duke of Manchester. The 6th Duke was a Vice-President of the SICLC, and Lady Olivia was celebrated for her philanthropic concerns for itinerant labourers (especially Irish navvies, given her own Irish background[69] and that of her late husband, Brigadier-General Robert Bernard Sparrow [1773-1805]),[70] which would explain why she got Roberts to design the model lodging-house for her estates (**1.10**). So we have important connections between Roberts, the Sparrows, the Dukes of Manchester, and therefore with Huntingdonshire and Suffolk: it is therefore hardly surprising that Roberts's first-born child, Olivia Maria Pauline Roberts, should have been named after his Evangelical client.[71] There is a further Suffolk connection with Roberts through the Longs: in St John's Church, Saxmundham, are monuments to Charles Long (1705-78) by William Tyler (*c.* 1728-1801), to Beeston Long (1710-85) also by Tyler, to Charles Long (1748-1812) by Joseph Nollekens (1737-1823), and to yet another Charles Long (1760-1838 – 1st Baron Farnborough from 1826 – a leading figure in the world of the arts and in the foundation of the Institute of British Architects) by Sir Richard Westmacott (1775-1856). The Longs were long-established in Suffolk and in the City, and Maria Long (1800-32 – daughter of another Beeston Long [1757-1820]) married Henry Seymour Montagu, who was connected with many families of that surname, so it is a reasonable proposition that Roberts obtained his Suffolk and Huntingdon commissions through relations and his Evangelical and professional associates.

Model dwellings

So much for Roberts's general practice, but his work for the SICLC and for philanthropic housing was of immense importance. Some of his first efforts have been mentioned above, but when the SICLC formed a branch at Tunbridge Wells, Kent, in 1847, Roberts laid out (1848-50) a whole estate

Chapter 1

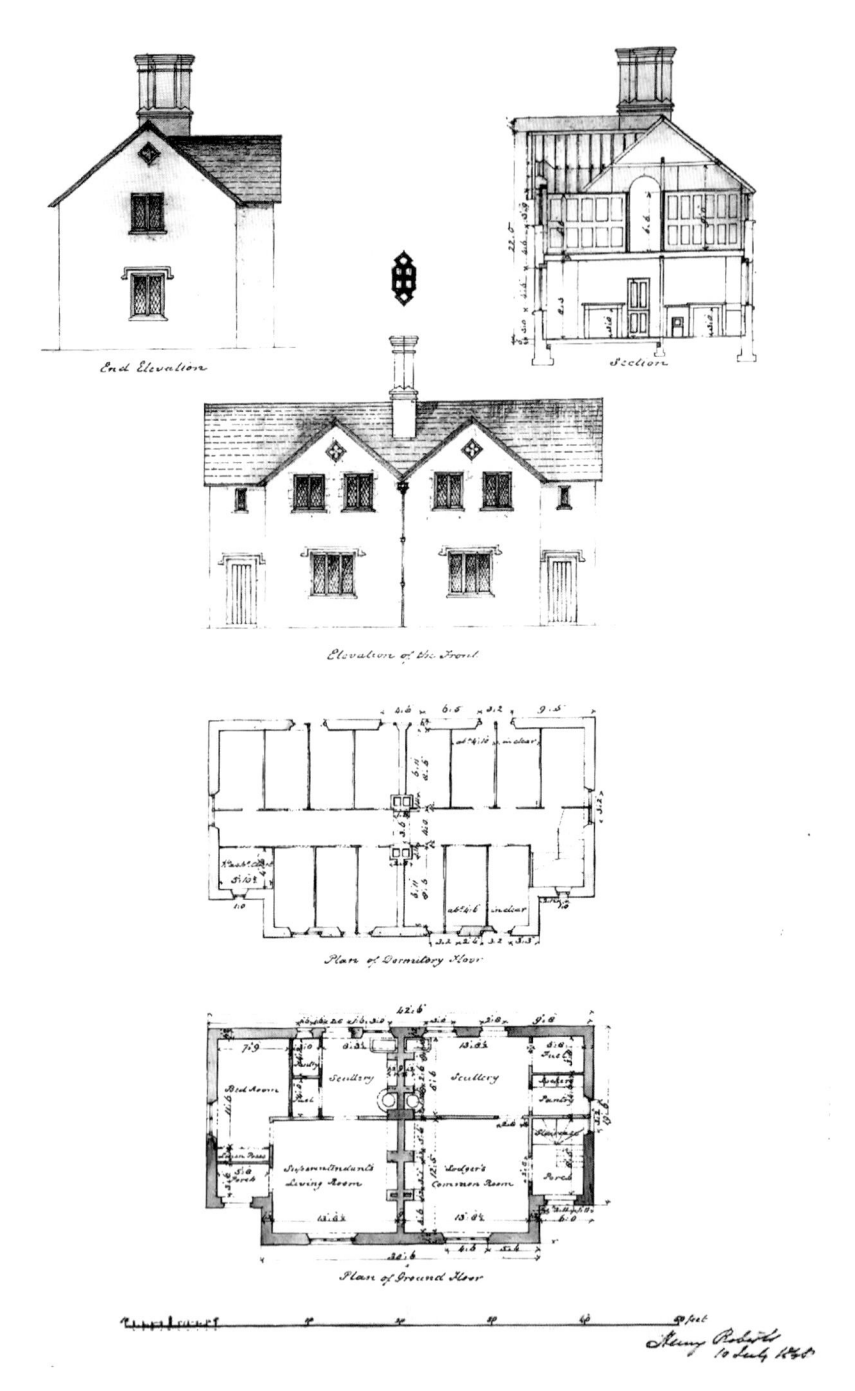

1.10: Drawing by Roberts (10 July 1848) among the Manchester Papers in Huntingdon Archives, Huntingdon, showing a lodging-house on Lady Olivia Bernard Sparrow's estates. (*Author's collection*.)

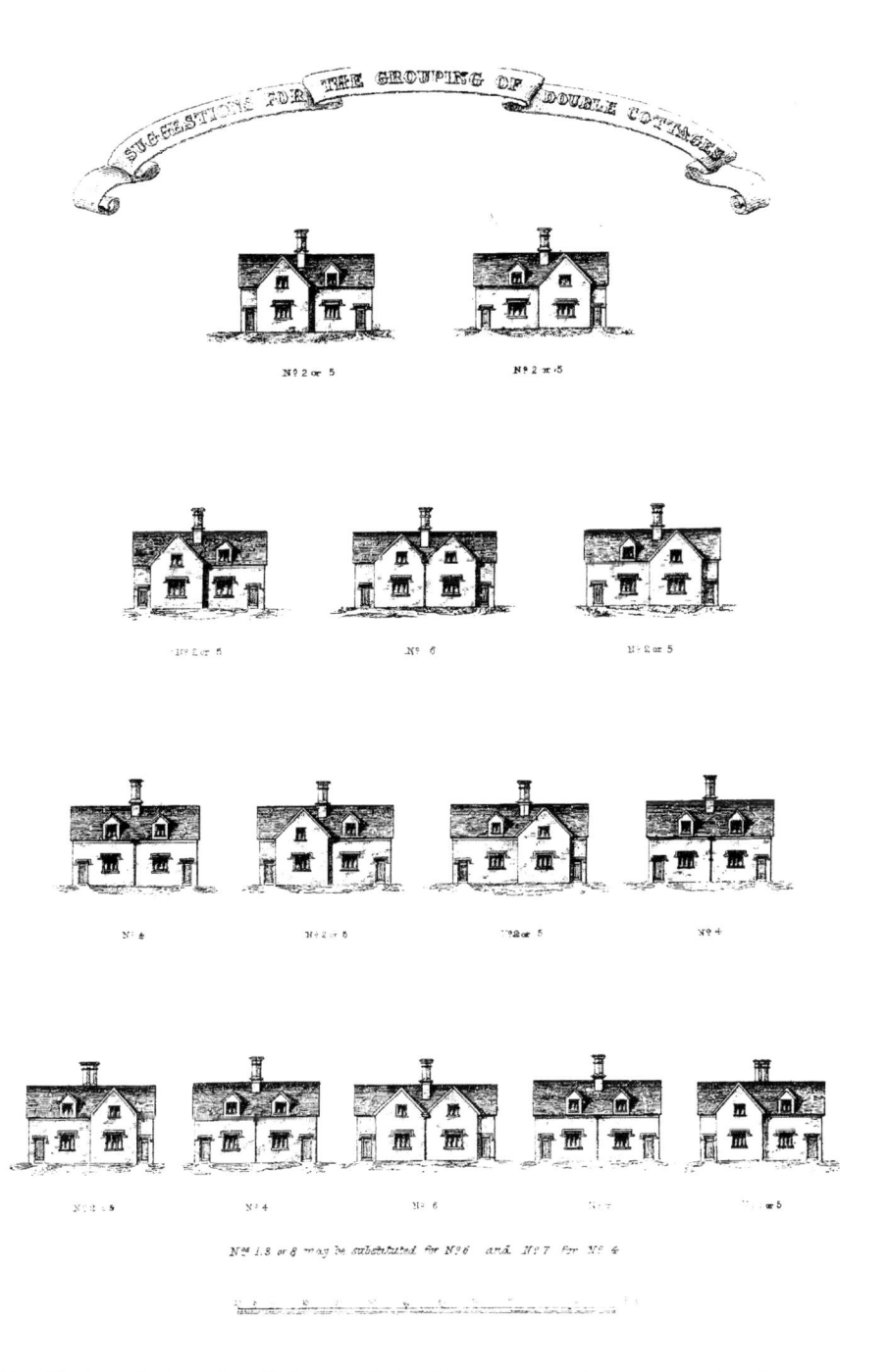

1.11: Typical designs by Roberts, all in his seventeenth-century-style, showing 'Suggestions for the Groupings of Double Cottages': these buildings could be arranged as terraces. (*Author's collection*.)

CHAPTER I

1.12: Watercolour of the exterior of the Model Houses for Families in Streatham Street, Bloomsbury, London, once in the possession of the SICLC. (*Author's photograph, by permission of The Peabody Trust.*)

of model dwellings at Newcomen Road, complete with lodging-house in Currie Road. Although these buildings have been insensitively altered, and the lodging house demolished, the houses were based on Roberts's varied designs for the SICLC and published as exemplars. There are literally thousands of houses in England built to Roberts's designs (and even a group at Culmore, County Londonderry, erected in 1864-5 on land owned by The Honourable The Irish Society, to drawings prepared by Richard Williamson [*fl.*1847-74] based on Roberts's work[72]): sometimes entire estates were built of houses derived from the original plans published under the ægis of the SICLC. Here was pattern-book architecture on the grand scale, and it is no exaggeration to say that Roberts's work may be found all over the country (**1.11**).

With the Model Houses for Families, Streatham Street, Bloomsbury (completed 1850),[73] erected on land leased to the SICLC by the Duke of Bedford, Roberts achieved a great work (**1.12**). Roberts believed that domestic privacy and independence for each family were essential, and he was also mindful of the appalling overcrowding that led to incest and other abuses. Roberts's design included self-contained apartments with integral lavatories, fireproof construction, good ventilation, access by open galleries facing a generous court (**1.13**), accommodation for a superintendent, and a basement containing workshops, wash-houses, bathing-houses, and storage space. These model dwellings were important for many reasons not least of which were the changes in the law they heralded. Roberts argued that his wide galleries were in fact elevated streets, so that each flat, with its independent access from the gallery (**1.14**), was a separate dwelling-house, thus each dwelling had windows that could not be assessed for tax: window tax was abolished in 1851 to be replaced by house tax.[74] Roberts said that this was probably the most important concession to sanitary amelioration, and it made the whole business of providing model housing in large blocks economically possible. Pressure by Roberts and his Evangelical allies in Parliament and in positions of influence also led to the repeal of duties on bricks in 1850,[75] which greatly reduced potential costs incurred by philanthropic housing societies.[76]

By 1848 Roberts had given up his Suffolk Street address and worked from 10 Connaught Square, although he also used the Athenæum for correspondence. He sometimes chaired committee meetings of the SICLC from 1847, although he never presided at a General Meeting. There was a

1.13: Watercolour of the court with galleries giving access to individual flats at the Streatham Street Model Houses. (*Author's photograph, by permission of The Peabody Trust.*)

Chapter I

THE MODEL HOUSES FOR FAMILIES IN STREATHAM-STREET, BLOOMSBURY,
TO ACCOMMODATE 48 FAMILIES, AND HAVING WORKSHOPS ON BASEMENT.

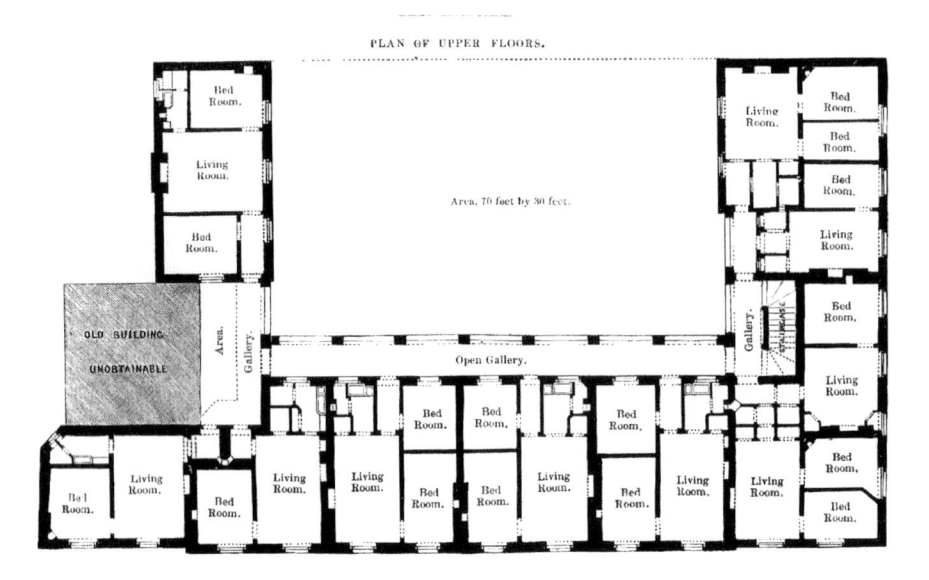

1.14: Plan of the Model Houses for Families in Streatham Street, Bloomsbury, showing the open gallery giving access to the self-contained flats (with internal w.c. facilities). (*Author's collection.*)

VIEW OF THE EAST SIDE OF THE THANKSGIVING MODEL BUILDINGS, PORTPOOL LANE, GRAY'S INN LANE.

1.15: Thanksgiving Model Buildings, Portpool Lane, Gray's Inn Lane. (*Author's collection.*)

HENRY ROBERTS (1803-76)

MODEL HOUSES FOR FOUR FAMILIES,

ERECTED BY COMMAND OF

HIS ROYAL HIGHNESS PRINCE ALBERT, K.G.,

AT THE EXPOSITION OF THE WORKS OF INDUSTRY OF ALL NATIONS, 1851,

And subsequently rebuilt in Kennington New Park, Surrey

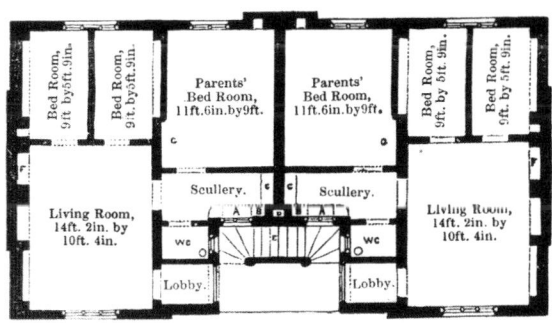

A   Sink, with Coal Box under
B   Plate Rack over entrance to Dust Shaft, D.
C   Meat Safe, ventilated through hollow bricks.
E   Staircase of Slate, with Dust Place under.
F   Cupboard warmed from back of Fireplace.
G   Linen Closet in this recess if required.

1.16: 'Model Houses for Four Families erected by Command of His Royal Highness Prince Albert, K.G., at the Exposition of the Works of Industry of All Nations, 1851'. Note the w.c. compartments inside each flat. (*Author's collection.*)

35

CHAPTER 1

close relationship between the Society and the London City Mission (many of the personalities were involved in both organisations): by the end of the 1840s it became clear to them that the demolition of numerous dwellings for modern 'improvements' was exacerbating overcrowding and pushing up the rents for accommodation, and that the various proposals for legislation relating to the Health of Towns would actually make matters worse. In 1851 Ashley (who became Shaftesbury that year) got two Acts (known as the 'Shaftesbury Acts') through Parliament: the Common Lodging Houses Act (which affected some 80,000 transient workers by insisting that all lodging-houses were subject to compulsory regulation and inspection by the police),[77] and the Labouring Classes Lodging Houses Act (which permitted the vestries to purchase land on which to build dwellings).[78]

The SICLC proceeded to acquire further premises for conversion by Roberts to lodging-houses, and property in Hatton Garden was purchased for that purpose. More important, perhaps, was Thanksgiving Buildings, Portpool Lane, Gray's Inn Road, so called because a large sum was gathered towards its construction in church collections on the Day of National Thanksgiving for deliverance from Asiatic cholera in 1849: Roberts designed a robust composition (**1.15**) with massive arched elements containing the staircases (Roberts was keen to have stairs well-ventilated, as he was aware of the tendency for them to be used as urinals and worse, a disagreeable phenomenon which has not diminished in the twenty-first century), and the building housed twenty families and 128 single women (there was a great need at the time for accommodation for poor, single needlewomen, who earned very low wages). An old building on the site was converted into a public wash-house, and visited annually 20,000 times.[79]

The most important scheme of the SICLC was, of course, the most celebrated of all its models: Roberts's design for the 'Model Houses for Families erected by H.R.H. Prince Albert' at the Great Exhibition of 1851. This earned the Society the highest award of the Exhibition: the Council Medal. The original idea of erecting these model houses derived from a desire to bring the work of the Society to as wide a public as possible. It was a brilliant design (**1.16**), for it consisted of four self-contained flats, each containing a lobby, a w.c. compartment, a living-room, a parents' bedroom, two smaller bedrooms, a scullery with sink and coal-box under it with storage, a plate rack, a ventilated meat safe, cupboards, linen closet, and dust-shaft connected to a 'dust-place' under the open stair. As there were no windows at the sides of each block, these could be repeated as terraces, and the floor-plan could also be extended upwards to four or even five storeys. Roberts's Patent Hollow Bricks were employed to improve

HENRY ROBERTS (1803-76)

VIEW OF THE MODEL HOUSES FOR FAMILIES, ERECTED IN HYDE PARK, AT THE EXHIBITION OF 1851.
BY COMMAND OF
His Royal Highness The Prince Albert, K.G.

Henry Roberts, Esq. F.S.A.

1.17: 'View of the Model Houses for Families, erected in Hyde Park, at the Exhibition of 1851 by Command of His Royal Highness The Prince Albert, K.G.', with the Crystal Palace on the right. Lithograph by Day & Son, with an acknowledgement to 'Henry Roberts, Esq. F.S.A.'. (*Author's collection.*)

insulation and waterproofing, deaden sound, and save a quarter of the cost of common bricks. Vaults of hollow bricks carried on cast-iron springers held together by tie-rods provided the structure of floors and roof, and concrete was employed to level off the tops of the vaults. The total cost of four such dwellings was £458 14s. 7d. which Prince Albert paid out of his own pocket, and the exhibit was erected on a vacant site belonging to the Cavalry Barracks, just across the road from the Crystal Palace (**1.17**).

Some 250,000 persons (many of them members of the labouring classes) visited the model houses, 7,400 on one day alone, and Roberts pointed out that this degree of usage was itself a severe test of the qualities of the materials and construction used in his design. Among those who inspected the buildings was Queen Victoria, who expressed her gratification. Letters of approbation were received from royal personages in Prussia and elewhere, addressed personally to Prince Albert, who graciously thanked Roberts for his 'exertions': the two men were clearly on friendly terms.[80] Roberts was also connected with the Great Exhibition in another capacity: he designed exhibits of the British and Foreign Bible Society, but there was at least some

Chapter 1

1.18: 'View of the Windsor Royal Society's Cottages for the Working Classes' showing an assortment of Roberts's designs. In the centre is a four-gabled block, in the middle of which is a variant of the Great Exhibition Model Houses linked to his standard cottages. (*Author's collection*.)

dissatisfaction, for Roberts seems to have ignored instructions regarding a bookcase, and a somewhat pained note records the fact.[81]

However, thanks to the SICLC's policy of publishing its schemes, the 'Model Lodge' was copied in many places throughout the country: an entire street of Roberts's designs was erected (1851-4) in the East End at Cowley Gardens through the good offices of W.E. Hilliard (d. 1884), a member of the SICLC; and the Revd William Quekett (1802-88), Vicar (1841-54) of Christ Church, Watney Street, a noted philanthropist, when appointed Rector of Warrington by the Crown in 1854, caused a variant of Roberts's design to be realised yet again at Church Street Cottages, Warrington (1856-7), though with a pitched roof and added bay-windows. Further adaptations of Roberts's designs were erected in other places. After the Great Exhibition closed, the Hyde Park houses were taken down and re-erected (though altered) in Kennington Park, South London.[82] Other examples based on the Great Exhibition Model Houses (or Lodge) were built at Hertford and at Abbot's Langley in Hertfordshire: the Hertford exemplar (with pitched roof variation) was erected on land owned by a member of the SICLC, Robert Dimsdale (1828-98), who was an M.P. 1866-92, and, curiously, a Baron of the Russian Empire, inheriting the title in 1872, so there was a connection with Roberts there as well. Also involved with the SICLC was Abel Smith (1788-1859), banker and M.P. for Hertfordshire 1835-47, who, as a local justice of the peace, 'maintained a strong interest in improving the social fabric of the locality'.[83] To Abel Smith can be credited the Abbot's Langley Model Dwellings.

However, by far the best example of a variety of designs by Roberts (including yet another, larger variation of the Great Exhibition exemplar) was erected at Windsor, Berkshire, by the Windsor Royal Society (formed under the Patronage of Queen Victoria and Prince Albert in 1852, registered under the Labourers' Dwellings Act of 1855).[84] Today, these attractive buildings are known as 'Prince Consort Cottages, Alexandra Road', combining Roberts's ingenious designs for the Great Exhibition Model Houses with cottages planned for rural areas and published by the SICLC (**1.18**).[85] One other work by Roberts should be mentioned here: St George's Buildings, Bourdon Street, Westminster (**1.19**), erected 1852-3 by John Newson (*fl.*1830-60 – who, significantly, hailed from Suffolk).[86] Newson, who had an interest in working-class housing, established himself as a builder and seems to have enjoyed a good relationship with the Westminster Estates (Lord Robert Grosvenor [1801-93] was on friendly terms with Prince Albert, and attended meetings of the SICLC). Newson also built various model dwellings on his own initiative, and Roberts recorded this fact.[87]

Decline and exile

Roberts had published numerous influential books, pamphlets, plans, specifications, and lectures (with some of his work translated into other European languages[88]), yet in the 1850s his relations with the SICLC soured. Doubtless the battering his church buildings had attracted did not help, and there was obviously a problem with the British and Foreign Bible Society, but the success of the Model Houses at the Exhibition, one might have thought, would have stood him in good stead, as he had a range of aristocratic friends and clients, knew the Prince, had contacts among the higher echelons of society in Prussia, France, and Russia, and was in touch with philanthropic housing organisations in many places. When Roberts was about to leave England to take up residence on the Continent 'for the sake of his health', he was presented in 1853 with a gift of plate from a group of 'Noblemen and Gentlemen' associated with philanthropic work rather than from the SICLC itself. The committee of the SICLC duly abolished the office of Honorary Architect, and Roberts was asked to resign from that position. So what had gone wrong?

Chapter 1

1.19: St George's Buildings, Bourdon Street, London, built by John Newson to designs by Henry Roberts, 1852-3. (*Author's collection.*)

There were the bad notices, of course, but they came mostly (and predictably) from Ecclesiologists who would follow the Tractarian line. Nevertheless, vitriolic denunciations of architecture would not have done the Society any favours. When Roberts, in 1856, was invited to become a Vice-President of the Society, he at first refused, but afterwards relented. From discussions held with surviving members of the family, it appears that, at some time between 1851 and 1853, Henry Roberts had had a liaison with 'a member of the lower orders'.[89] True to form, this was not regarded with favour among the Evangelicals of the SICLC, and suggests reasons why he received no honours for the important part he had played in the activities of the Society and in the success of the Great Exhibition. When the scandal broke it would also explain why the Society distanced itself from its Honorary Architect. He had one or two minor compensations, though: apart from the gift of plate, he was granted Achievement of Arms in 1853. Roberts himself wrote that his 'active participation in the management' of the SICLC ceased in 1853, when the effects of 'over-exertion in its cause' obliged him to go abroad.[90]

Roberts and his family visited Russia, France, Switzerland, and other European countries, but mostly lived in Florence, from which city he kept abreast of campaigns to improve conditions among the working classes, notably in Mulhouse, and he occasionally visited Britain to give lectures or see old friends. In Florence he met many intellectual members of the Italian aristocracy, and he contributed papers to learned societies until his death. His daughter, Olivia, does not seem to have survived childhood,[91] but two more daughters were born, one just before, and one just after he left England: Lydia Anastasie Davy (1851-77) in Russia in 1851 (it is unclear if Catherine went to Russia without her husband [perhaps in umbrage as a result of his dalliance] or if the affair took place in her absence); and Theodora Amélie (1856-1916) in Vevey, by Lake Geneva, Switzerland, significantly a predominantly Protestant town. Catherine Roberts seems to have been a formidable lady, given to single-mindedness: she smuggled Bibles and tracts into Italy under her voluminous skirts, and was convinced of the rightness of everything she did, which could have been somewhat tiresome.[92]

Lydia Roberts married 'Pietro de Schéhavtzoff', another Russian, related to the de Swetschines, and they had a daughter, Véra (1876-7): both Lydia and Véra were interred in the Cimitero degli Inglesi[93] in Florence, and when Henry Roberts died in 1876 at his handsome and substantial residence, the Villa Romana, Via Senese, he, too, was buried in that Protestant Cemetery.[94] A search in 1979 failed to reveal any grave-markers (though the interments *were* recorded in the *Registro Alfabetico*), but a perusal of the records of the newer Cimitero Evangelico degli Allori on the Via Senese near Roberts's home led to the discovery that Catherine Roberts was buried there in 1905, and in Section B.VII 68-71 were tombstones commemorating Henry, Catherine, and Theodora Amélie Roberts, as well as Lydia and Véra de Schéhavtzoff (**1.20**). Clearly, after the new cemetery for Protestant Strangers was opened in 1878, the bodies of Catherine's husband, daughter, and grand-

CHAPTER I

1.20: Graves nos B.VII 68-71 in the Cimitero Evangelico degli Allori, Florence: left is that of Henry Roberts; next is that of Lydia de Schéhavtzoff, *née* Roberts, and also in that grave is buried Véra de Schéhavtzoff; next is the grave of Catherine Roberts, *née* de Swetschine or Svétchine; and finally, right, is that of Theodora Amélie Roberts. (*Author.*)

daughter were exhumed so that the entire family could be reunited in death. Theodora Amélie's gravestone records that she was 'Founder and for 35 years Directress of the Medical Mission'. Evangelical attempts to convert the Papists in Italy were still going on well into the twentieth century.

Afterword

It has to be admitted that Roberts's Gothic was not inspired, and unlikely to enrapture Ecclesiologists. His Fishmongers' Hall, however, was a fine example of Smirkean Greek Revival, and compares well with other essays in that style. His domestic architecture is not really of even the second rank, although Escot House (again with fine internal details) is a robust and confident work, mixing Italianate and Grecian elements. With the Model Houses for Families in Streatham Street he achieved a monumentality and distinction unusual in such buildings, and with the 'Model Houses for Four Families Erected at Hyde Park at the Industrial Exhibition of 1851' Roberts created a brilliant design, remarkable for its time, that was widely copied, and even informed developments as late as the 1930s. His varied designs for labourers' cottages, combined together at Windsor, show his genius for pattern-book architecture, and there is no doubt of the importance of his contribution to architecture and to the reform of housing for the working classes. His writings, full of sound common sense, realism, compassion, and knowledge, can (and should) be read with profit today, and give fascinating insights into the approaches to problems at the time. In particular, his opposition to building societies should be trumpeted: he sensibly pointed out that easily-obtained mortgages would have the inevitable effect of *inflating* the *prices* of property, thus putting ownership of dwellings further beyond the reach of those who otherwise might eventually be able to buy. He also insisted that no more than a *fifth* of any family's weekly income should go on housing, because any more would adversely affect nutrition, recreation, dress, education, and the tone of society. Long study of the matter has convinced at least one student that he was absolutely right.

Abbreviations

B	*The Builder*
Eccl	*The Ecclesiologist*
ILN	*Illustrated London News*
ODNB	*Oxford Dictionary of National Biography*
RIBA	Royal Institute of British Architects
SICLC	Society for Improving the Condition of the Labouring Classes

Notes

1 This essay is based on research in England, Ireland, Scotland, the U.S.A., France, and Italy in 1978-81, published in J.S. Curl, *The Life and Work of Henry Roberts (1803-1876), Architect: The Evangelical Conscience and the Campaign for Model Housing and Healthy Nations*, Phillimore, 1983. Further research was carried out in Huntingdonshire, Cambridgeshire, and Suffolk in 2002, 2005, and 2010.
2 H. Colvin, *A Biographical Dictionary of British Architects 1600-1840*, Yale, 2008, 393.
3 *Transactions of The Society of Arts*, 42, 1824, 46-7.
4 G.G. Scott, *Personal and Professional Recollections*, Sampson Low et al., 1879, 73.
5 Royal Academy Schools Register, Royal Academy of Arts: information kindly provided by Constance-Anne Parker.
6 J.S. Curl (ed.), *Kensal Green Cemetery: The Origins & Development of the General Cemetery of All Souls, Kensal Green, London, 1824-2001*, Phillimore, 2001.
7 T.W.B. Aveling (1815-84), *Memorial of the Clayton Family*, Jackson & Co., 1867.
8 Confirmed by the Roberts family.
9 Aveling [n. 7].
10 *ODNB*, 35, Oxford U.P., 2004, 837-41.
11 Maclise's pencil and wash portrait (*c.* 1829) of Benjamin Disraeli at Hughenden Manor, Buckinghamshire, is similar in technique. *See* P. Murray (ed.), *Daniel Maclise*

Chapter 1

1806-1870: Romancing the Past, Gandon Edns, 2008, 88-9.
12 *See* Henry Roberts, *The Dwellings of the Labouring Classes*, SICLC, 1850, with many subsequent editions, especially that of 1867.
13 Suter designed buildings on The Fishmongers' Estates in County Londonderry. *See* J.S. Curl, *The Londonderry Plantation 1609-1914: The History, Architecture, and Planning of the Estates of the City of London and its Livery Companies in Ulster*, Phillimore, 1986, 232-77 and *passim*.
14 *See* J. Myles, *L. N. Cottingham 1787-1847: Architect of the Gothic Revival*, Lund Humphries, 1996, 157-60.
15 P. Metcalf, *The Halls of The Fishmongers' Company*, Phillimore, 1977, 125-56; Curl [n. 1], 62-71.
16 *Transactions RIBA*, 1857-8, 43.
17 Scott [n. 4], 73: probably an exaggeration.
18 Scott [n. 4], 73.
19 Ibid., 74.
20 Ibid., 73.
21 Ibid., 75.
22 *ODNB*, 22, Oxford U.P., 2004, 229-30. He was elected to the headship of the City of London School in 1836.
23 Minute Book of the Society of Antiquaries of London, 37, 1835-9. Roberts's other proposers were Smirke, Edward Dalton (*c.* 1800-76), and the herald and biographer, Sir Edmund Lodge (1756-1839).
24 *ODNB*, 40, Oxford U.P., 2004, 969.
25 For George Cornelius Gorham (1787-1853), *see* J.S. Curl, *Victorian Architecture: Diversity & Invention*, Spire Books, 2007, 133-4. *See* also *ODNB* [n. 22], 996-7.
26 *ODNB*, 40, Oxford U.P., 2004, 969-70. Other members of the Noel family became Roman Catholics in the early 1850s.
27 Roberts [n. 12] (1867 edn), 15.
28 The Consort of the 'Sailor-King', William IV (reigned 1830-7), Queen Adelaide (1792-1849), was involved in the patronage of homes for destitute sailors.
29 Reproduced in Curl [n. 1], plates 18a-23.
30 Francis Stephen Clayton was Roberts's solicitor, and Francis Hare Clayton (1869-1956) was Frederick Albert Roberts's (1848-1938 – Henry Roberts's nephew, son of Charles) solicitor. The Clayton and Roberts families were closely connected by marriage, conviction, belief, and business for at least three generations. *See* Curl [n. 1], 244, n. 7.
31 The precise relationship between S.T. and H. Roberts has not been determined.
32 Records of the Incorporated Church Building Society, Lambeth Palace Library.
33 Drawings in Devon County Records Office, Exeter, 961 M/E29.
34 Baptist Noel's brother, the Hon. and Revd Gerard Thomas Noel (1782-1851), married (1841) Susan (d. 1890), daughter of Sir John Kennaway, Bt, as his second wife, and *his* daughter by his first wife (Charlotte Sophia O'Brien of Dromoland [d. 1838]), Emma (d. 1843), married (1830) the Revd Charles Edward Kennaway (1800-75), Vicar of Chipping Campden, Gloucestershire, a place also closely associated with the Noels.
35 Information kindly provided by the late Judith O'Neill (1930-2000 – Gullett's

great-great-grand-daughter), to whom I am indebted.
36 Kinnaird's maternal grandfather was William Robert Fitzgerald (1749-1804), 2nd Duke of Leinster from 1773.
37 *ODNB*, 31, Oxford U.P., 2004, 738-40.
38 Ibid., 731-2.
39 1041 in the 1841 *Catalogue*, which specifically mentions the 'new tower and porch'. The large, showy statuettes (of angels and gargoyles) and the flying buttresses added to the broaches in *c.* 1860 were probably designed by Samuel Sanders Teulon (1812-73), who carried out major works for Frederick Calthorpe (1790-68 – 4th Baron from 1851) at that time.
40 Information kindly provided by the late Judith O'Neill: Gullett's memoir is a manuscript in the possession of the O'Neill family.
41 T. Brittain-Catlin, *The English Parsonage in the Early Nineteenth Century*, Spire Books, 2008, 237. *See* also Church of England Record Centre, Bermondsey, London, Box E.58, plans approved 30 May 1839 (I am grateful to Dr Brittain-Catlin for this reference).
42 It was not permitted to add 'Royal' until 1866.
43 Information from *The Athenæum*.
44 *The Civil Engineer*, 6, 1843, 403, 454; *Companion to the Almanac*, 1843, 248-9, and 1844, 239-41. The clerk of works (1841-4) for the terminus was Henry Gullett (information in a personal communication from the late Judith O'Neill).
45 W.J. Gordon, *'Rome's Recruits': A List of Protestants who have become Catholics since the Tractarian Movement*, The Whitehall Review, 1881.
46 J.S. Curl, *Spas, Wells, and Pleasure-Gardens of London*, Historical Publications, 2010.
47 These matters are discussed in detail in Curl [n. 1], *passim*.
48 At the meeting was Sir John Franklin (1786-1847), whose ill-fated expedition left London in May 1845.
49 *Eccl*, 6, 1846, 34-5; *B*, 4, 1846, 241; *ILN*, 8, 1846, 321. The building is illustrated in Curl [n. 1], plates 40a & b, 41a & b.
50 Surrey History Centre, Woking, Acc.1056/441. See Brittain-Catlin [n. 41], 239-40.
51 Devon Record Office, Exeter, 961 M/E 40.
52 *See* R. Stannard, 'The ecclesiastical work of Hugh Thackeray Turner' in G. Brandwood (ed.), *Seven Church Architects 1830-1930: Ecclesiology Today*, 41, 2010, 121-46. See also *The London Journal*, 17, 1992, 56.
53. *Westminster Review*, 64, 1855, 436-62.
54. J.F.A. de Le Roi, *Michael Solomon Alexander der erste Bischof in Jerusalem. Ein Beitrag zur orientalischen Frage*, C. Bertelsmann, 1897. Further information given by surviving members of the Roberts family to the author in 1979.
55 This from the burial records in Florence, which does not tally with the *Gubernia* of Tula mentioned below.
56 The 1851 census (PRO HO 107/1467/fol. 328 Kensington Parish) reveals that Catherine Roberts (aged 31) was the daughter of the Governor of Tula, but this is not true: a *Gubernia* was an Tsarist administrative region.
57 Coles Symes had connections with Poundisford Park, Somerset, and thus with the Welmans.
58 Marriage certificate: Registration District of Kensington, Paddington, and Fulham

Chapter I

in the Parish of Paddington. Roberts's rank was given as 'Esqr.' of St Martin-in-the-Fields, and Miss de Swetschine was of St James, Paddington. *See* also *The Times*, 16 Apr. 1847, notices of marriages.

59 She may have died in 1853, as Roberts was writing on mourning-stationery to Lord Galloway at that time.
60 Surrey History Centre, Woking, 264/51/1-5.
61 Records of the Incorporated Church Building Society in Lambeth Palace Library.
62 In 1852, doubtless encouraged by Roberts, the Gulletts emigrated to Australia, where they became prosperous.
63 The convoluted affairs at Wigtown are referenced in Curl [n. 1], 207, n. 135.
64 These were in a cupboard in the church in the late 1970s but may now be in Edinburgh.
65 Admitted 5 Feb. 1826. Roberts was on good terms with several lawyers.
66 *Eccl*, 15, 1854, 142-3.
67 Cambridge University Library: Ely Diocesan Records, Parsonage Papers, EDR/G3/39/77, 40/6, & MGA/70. Roberts's drawings for the Parsonage are dated 6 Apr. 1853, and are signed. The house, as conceived, was asymmetrical and extremely plain, without many concessions to aesthetic considerations. I am grateful to C.G. Chandler, Chairman of the Brampton Historical Society, for information.
68 She was the daughter of Arthur Acheson (d.1807), 1st Earl of Gosford from 1806.
69 Born Markethill, Co. Armagh.
70 Sparrow was connected with Tanderagee, Co. Armagh, and Worlingham, Suffolk: in the Church of All Saints in Worlingham is a monument (1821-2) by Sir Francis Leggatt Chantrey (1781-1841) inscribed with the General's name and with that of his son, Robert Acheson Bernard St John Sparrow (d. 1818): it cost £325 3s. See A. Yarrington *et al.* (eds), *An Edition of the Ledger of Sir Francis Chantrey, R.A., at the Royal Academy, 1809-1841*, Walpole Society, 56, 1991-2, 116.
71 Roberts appears to have designed some model cottages for Lady Olivia around Brampton Green. I am again grateful to C.G. Chandler for information.
72 J.S. Curl, *The Honourable The Irish Society and the Plantation of Ulster, 1608-2000: The City of London and the Colonisation of County Londonderry in the Province of Ulster in Ireland. A History and Critique*, Phillimore, 2000, 280-1.
73 *B*, 7, 1849, 325-7; 8, 1850, 49-50; 8, 1850, 250; Curl [n. 1], *passim*.
74 14 & 15 Vict., c. 36.
75. 13 & 14 Vict., c. 9.
76 For a detailed discussion of Streatham Street Model Dwellings, *see* Curl [n. 1], Ch. 4 and *passim*.
77 14 & 15 Vict., c. 28.
78 14 & 15 Vict., c. 34.
79 *B*, 8, 1850, 369.
80 Curl [n. 1], 105 and *passim*.
81 *Minutes of the Proceedings of Her Majesty's Commissioners for the Exhibition of 1851*, H.M.S.O., 1852, 373-5.
82 *B*, 9, 1851, 311-12.
83 *ODNB*, 51, Oxford U.P., 2004, 15.
84 18 & 19 Vict., c. 132.

85 *B*, 10, 1852, 468-9.
86 F.H.W. Sheppard (ed.), *Survey of London*, 39, Athlone Press, 1977, 138-9
87 Curl [n. 1], 120. Henry Roberts, *The Progress and Present Aspect of the Movement for Improving the Dwellings of the Labouring Classes,* Emily Faithfull, 1861, 10-11.
88 A comprehensive list of his publications is given in Curl [n. 1], 252-3.
89 Noted in 1979 at an interview.
90 For these matters, *see* Henry Roberts, *The Improvement of the Dwellings of the Labouring Classes through the Operation of Government Measures*, etc., Ridgway, 1859.
91 If Olivia Roberts died in 1853, it is possible that Roberts also went through some kind of depression.
92 Reminiscences of Frederick Albert Roberts, Henry Roberts's nephew, retailed by his great-niece to the author in 1979.
93 *Registro Alfabetico delle Persone Tumulate ne Cimitero di Pinti*, grave no.1382. The records state that she was 'Roberts *née* Schéhavtzoff', which is an error.
94 Ibid., grave no.1349.

2.1: Shops in Ranelagh Street and Cases Street, Liverpool, William Culshaw, 1843. (Author.)

2

William Culshaw (1807-74) and Henry Sumners (1825-95): rebuilding Victorian Liverpool

Joseph Sharples

Nineteenth-century Liverpool was the scene of a vast amount of building activity, the highlights of which are well-known: the great civic temple of St George's Hall, the incomparable dock system, several commercial buildings of metropolitan grandeur, and a handful of the best churches in the country. Architects of national standing were employed, and their buildings have tended to attract the attention of historians, yet the bulk of Liverpool's Victorian architecture was the work of locals who remain little-studied and largely unknown. Among the most prolific of these were William Culshaw and Henry Sumners.

It is fair to say at the outset that Culshaw and Sumners are probably less interesting for the quality of their buildings than as representatives of successful Victorian practice, whose activities also shed light on the development of a great Victorian city. Sumners certainly had talent, but Culshaw, as we shall see, was a designer of limited imagination. What makes both of them exceptionally interesting, however, is the survival of over 3,500

CHAPTER 2

drawings they produced between the mid-1830s and 1873.[1] Unfortunately, there are no accompanying financial records or correspondence, but the drawings themselves make Culshaw and Sumners unusually well-documented among their contemporaries, and give valuable insights not just into their architecture, but also into the range and scale of their business, their clients and the growth of Victorian Liverpool in which they played a significant part. Their story falls naturally into two parts: Culshaw's period of independent practice up to 1861, followed by twelve years of association with Sumners.

William Culshaw, surveyor and architect

William Culshaw was born in Ormskirk, a modest Lancashire market town twelve miles north of Liverpool.[2] One of his obituaries noted that he had not 'enjoyed the advantages of an architectural education', implying that he trained under his father, 'a small joiner and builder'.[3] The same source says that he left Ormskirk for Liverpool around 1834 to join Leather & Riding, a firm of architects and surveyors. Liverpool at this date had many attractions for an ambitious man wanting to make his way in the world of building. After a visit in 1837, George Godwin observed that 'the resident architects appear to have plenty of opportunities to display their taste and skill; indeed, the improvements which have been made there within the last ten years, and the extension of the town which has taken place during that time, are, perhaps, unprecedented. Vast ranges of warehouses now occupy ground formerly covered by the river, and many houses which were erected a few years ago as rural retreats, are now in the midst of a densely populated neighbourhood, and are surrounded by manufactories.'[4] The elegant plates in Samuel Austin's *Lancashire Illustrated*, published in 1831, record many new Liverpool buildings, and bear out Godwin's heady description of urban growth.

Into this lively scene Culshaw successfully launched himself. Soon after he joined Leather & Riding the junior partner died, and he took over as clerk of works on a building for the merchant and property-owner Launcelot Graham. The client was pleased, and the experience must have helped propel Culshaw towards an independent career. The earliest drawing in the archive that bears the signature 'Wm Culshaw Archt' is dated May 1836,[5] and by 1839 he was listed in Gore's Liverpool directory as 'William Culshaw, architect and surveyor'. Already in his late twenties when he came to Liverpool, he was nevertheless still financially dependent on his father. It is a measure of the opportunities available in the booming port, as much as his business ability, that by the time he died, forty years later, he occupied one of the larger houses in prestigious Rodney Street, and left property approaching £140,000 in value.[6]

According to his obituary in the *Daily Post*, '[a]lthough Mr. Culshaw combined with his principal business of surveyor and valuer the profession of architect, he did not profess to shine in that capacity, preferring rather that work in which he had a special aptitude'.[7] The *Mercury* went further, stating that he 'had little taste for architecture, and his practice, therefore, must be regarded as purely appurtenant to his employment as a surveyor.'[8] In round figures, surveys account for between 400 and 700 of the surviving drawings produced during Culshaw's career. But the archive shows that his office also turned out large numbers of designs for buildings, and it is this, the architectural side of the business, that concerns us here.[9]

The great bulk of the firm's output was in Liverpool and its immediate hinterland. There were occasional commissions as far away as Shropshire and Staffordshire – a house for John Wedgwood at Tunstall (1850), for instance, and additions to Maer Hall for William Davenport (1853) – but these always came from Liverpool businessmen or their families or associates.[10] Culshaw appears to have had no interest in developing a national practice by entering architectural competitions beyond Merseyside – drawings for a workhouse at Market Drayton, Shropshire, are an exception[11] – and in general he was kept fully occupied by the demands of Liverpool's prodigious nineteenth-century expansion. The work of his office reflected needs that had to be met in every British city at this date. There was housing, of course, from the extremely lowly to the decidedly superior, plus shops, hotels, pubs, churches, schools, charitable institutions and industrial buildings. And alongside these universal building types were others related to the particular requirements of maritime, mercantile Liverpool, notably office blocks and warehouses.

Office buildings, 1834-61

With a local economy based on trade and commerce, Liverpool needed an abundant supply of offices for rent. Purpose designed office blocks, built speculatively by private investors, began to appear near the Exchange in the 1830s, the first architecturally significant example being India Buildings of 1833-4, designed by Joseph Franklin for the cotton merchant George Holt.[12] More or less contemporary with India Buildings, though considerably smaller, was Rumford Court in nearby Rumford Place.[13] This was almost certainly the building on which Culshaw acted as clerk of works for Launcelot Graham, and immediately it became the location of Culshaw's own office, remaining so for the rest of his career.[14] His early association with this building proved a portent: his business thrived on the

Chapter 2

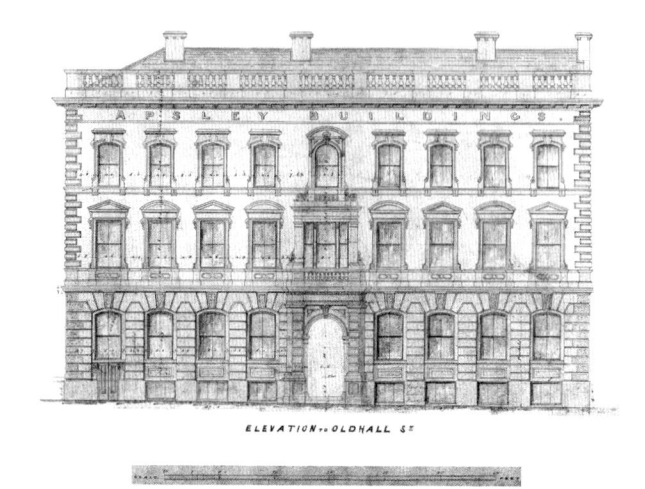

2.2: Elevation of Apsley Buildings, Old Hall Street, elevation, Liverpool, William Culshaw, 1854. (*Lancashire Record Office/reproduced by kind permission of Edmund Kirby.*)

office-building frenzy that gripped Liverpool from the 1840s to the 1860s, and he designed (or in some cases extended or significantly altered) some twenty such buildings before his partnership with Henry Sumners, and as many again afterwards.

There were variations, but Culshaw's basic formula for these office blocks remained the same: three principal storeys of self-contained suites, each consisting of an outer and an inner office plus a fireproof book safe, grouped round a light well and accessed from a common stair.[15] The attic might be used for sample rooms, the basement as a shop or restaurant, with warehouse vaults below. His style for these and other commercial buildings was invariably Classical. A few early ones – for example three shops at the corner of Ranelagh Street and Cases Street (1843) (**2.1**) – followed the pattern established in the 1820s by John Foster junior, the Corporation Surveyor, for rebuilding the central business streets of the town: the façades stuccoed, the windows dignified by simple architraves, pediments or consoled cornices, the corners treated as quadrants to improve the flow of traffic.[16] Later office blocks, such as Walmer Buildings (1853; dem.) in Water Street and Apsley Buildings (1854; dem.) (**2.2**) in Old Hall Street, adopted the palazzo model established by A. & G. Williams in their pioneering Brunswick Buildings (1842; dem.), with rusticated basements and quoins.[17] They appear to have been of brick with stone or stucco dressings. Later still, in the first phase of Knowsley Buildings (1860; dem.) and neighbouring Grosvenor Buildings (1861; dem.) in Tithebarn Street, Culshaw borrowed shamelessly from C.R. Cockerell's nearby Liverpool and London Insurance Co. in Dale Street (1856-8), no doubt in a bid to appear fashionable.[18]

In one respect, however, Culshaw was not merely a copyist. A good, even supply of daylight for examining cotton samples and other merchandise was vital in Liverpool office buildings, and Culshaw found a novel way of achieving it: rows of sash windows, separated only by slender cast-iron uprights, under continuous cast-iron lintels. This practice was to become widespread, and Culshaw may not have been the first to adopt it, but an office building he designed for Alfred and Henry Graham in Chapel Street (1846; dem.) (**2.3**) is the earliest documented example that has so far come to light in Liverpool.[19] He confined these long runs of windows to light wells and

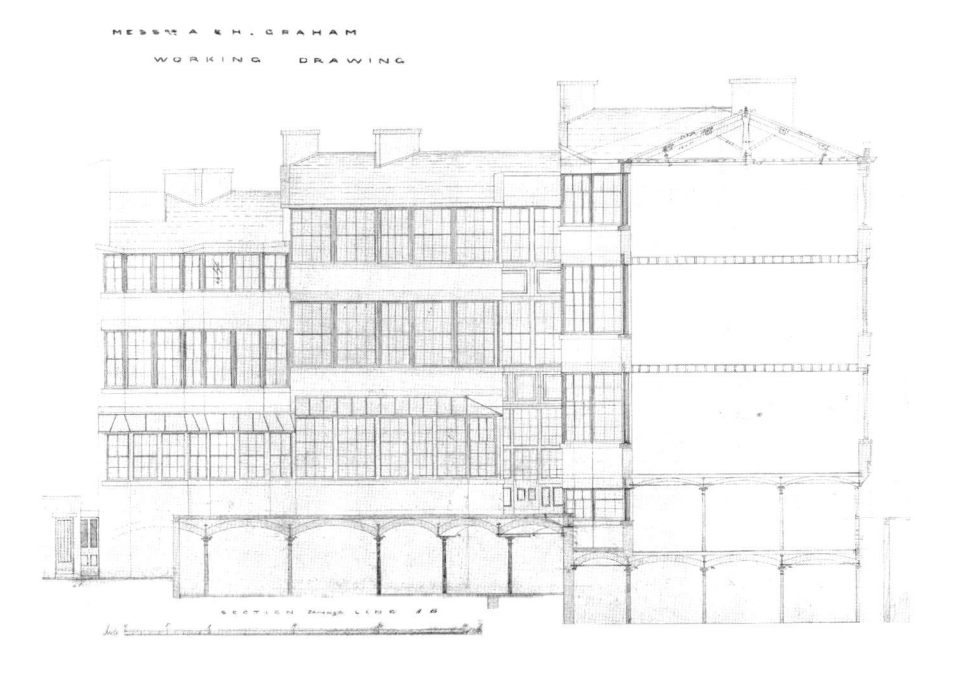

2.3: Courtyard elevation of offices for A. & H. Graham, Chapel Street, Liverpool, William Culshaw, 1846. (*Lancashire Record Office/Edmund Kirby.*)

CHAPTER 2

2.4: Elevation of Waterhouse's Building, Old Hall Street, William Culshaw, Liverpool, 1842. (*Lancashire Record Office/Edmund Kirby*.)

secondary elevations, but in one of his earliest office blocks, Waterhouse's Building (1842; dem.) (**2.4**) – a pedimented, temple-like block at the corner of Old Hall Street and Chapel Street, with giant Corinthian pilasters, clearly modeled on the nearby North and South Wales Bank of 1838-40 by Edward Corbett – he filled the spaces between the pilasters with exceptionally large windows.[20] The resulting well-lit offices attracted the attention of the *Civil Engineer & Architect's Journal*, where the building was described at length – possibly the only time that Culshaw achieved more than a passing mention in the professional press.[21]

Houses and other building types, 1834-61

The merchants who worked in these offices also needed houses. Culshaw began his Liverpool career just as the elite terraced streets of Mosslake Fields (Liverpool's early nineteenth-century 'new town', built to a grid plan on high ground east of the old centre) were yielding in status to suburban

William Culshaw (1807-74) and Henry Sumners (1825-95)

2.5: 70 Upper Parliament Street, Liverpool, William Culshaw, 1841. (*Author.*)

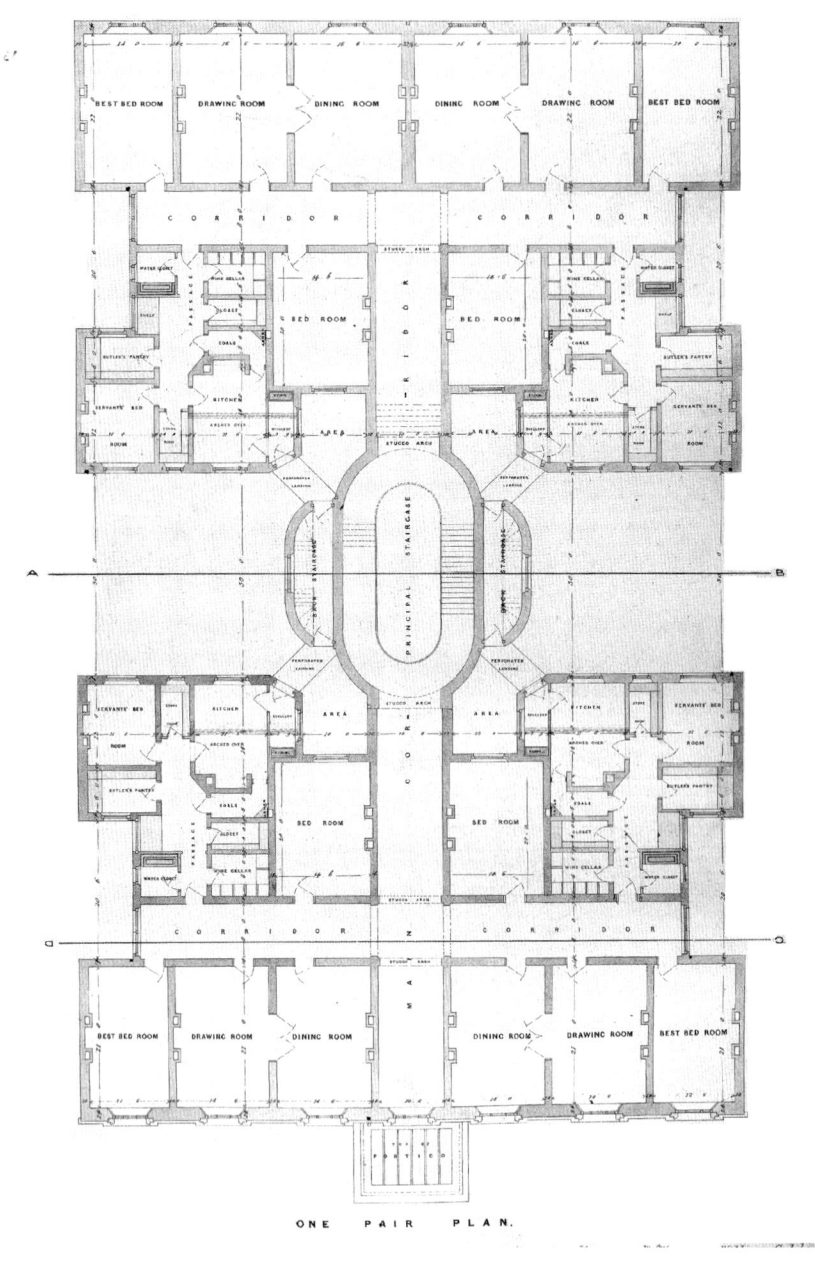

2.6: Plan of proposed apartment block for John Gladstone, Mount Pleasant, Liverpool, William Culshaw, 1846. (*Lancashire Record Office/Edmund Kirby.*)

William Culshaw (1807-74) and Henry Sumners (1825-95)

2.7. Elevation of 16 and 18 Croxteth Road, Liverpool, William Culshaw, 1843. (*Lancashire Record Office; reproduced by permission of Edmund Kirby.*)

villas. Nevertheless, he designed two large terraced houses at 68 and 70 Upper Parliament Street (1841) (**2.5**) for the shipbuilder Thomas Royden, and another at 29 Falkner Square (1845) that cost the merchant Richard Rowlinson £2,600.[22] He also made an interesting set of drawings for a block of up-market two-bedroom apartments in Mount Pleasant (1846) (**2.6**), which apparently remained unbuilt.[23] Commissioned by John Gladstone, they were presumably aimed at younger members of the mercantile community, unencumbered by families. As a building type, middle-class flats were quite alien to Liverpool, and this design may reflect the Scottish client's familiarity with tenement-living in his native Leith and Edinburgh.

But the bulk of Culshaw's domestic work was on Liverpool's leafy outskirts, and consisted of detached or semi-detached villas. Culshaw designed over 50 of these, and made extensions or alterations to almost as many more. An early example is a symmetrical pair of Italianate semis, now 16 and 18 Croxteth Road (1843), with a continuous veranda overlooking Prince's Park[24] (**2.7**). These seem to have been designed for specific owner-occupiers – the plans indicate a 'nursery' for one client, Mr Bennett, where the unmarried Misses Waterhouse next door have a 'breakfast room' – but others were built speculatively, with a single client commissioning two or more houses. Many were at Aigburth or Mossley Hill, two or three miles south of Liverpool, where large estates were being parceled out into

CHAPTER 2

smaller building plots at this time.[25] Other popular locations were across the Mersey at Liscard or New Brighton, made increasingly accessible since the introduction of steamers on the river from 1815; still others at Seaforth or Crosby, in seafront situations linked to Liverpool by canal packets, omnibuses and, from 1850, the railway. The sheer number of Culshaw's designs for such projects reflects the rapid transformation of the suburban scene that took place at this time, a transformation noted by the American consul Nathaniel Hawthorne in August 1855, when he described parts of the Wirral as 'speckled over with … semi-detached villas, built to let to well-to-do tradesmen, besides separate villas … for a somewhat higher class.'[26] Indeed, Culshaw designed three pairs of semis for the select Wirral enclave of Rock Park, where Hawthorne himself rented a house.[27]

Like his commercial buildings, the style of Culshaw's private houses was generally a sober Italianate. Stuccoed, or of brick with stucco dressings, their chief ornaments were window architraves with ears and keystones, and perhaps a modillion eaves cornice. One elegant villa at Mossley Hill (1842; dem.) had refined Greek details, but this was exceptional.[28] A few were on a grander scale: Stanton Hall (1855; dem.), a villa for Thomas Arthur Hope at Spittal on the Wirral, had eight bedrooms, and Edward Kemp made a drawing for laying out its extensive grounds.[29] More imposing still was Holly Lodge (1860), West Derby, where Culshaw added an Osborne-style wing with a belvedere tower to a pre-existing early nineteenth-century villa for the merchant F.C. Braun.[30] The tower was originally to have been higher, but was truncated, presumably an economy requested by the client.

Occasionally Culshaw used Gothic or Tudor motifs, but in an entirely superficial way, even presenting alternative Italianate and Tudor drawings for the same scheme, in which only the window shapes differed.[31] He also produced a handful of fairly minor Gothic churches and educational buildings. These included the late-Decorated schools attached to Christ Church, Everton (1850; dem.), for a member of the Horsfall family, and, on a smaller scale, those built by William Davenport at the village of Maer, Staffordshire (1857).[32] None of these, however, shows much engagement with the expanding knowledge of medieval buildings that was such a strong influence on other architects at the time.

As for shops, hotels and pubs, for the showier ones Culshaw tended to repeat the Classical formula of his office blocks, albeit on a reduced scale. Among surviving examples are the first phase of the dockside Baltic Fleet public house (1853) in Wapping, and a terrace of shops at 14–22 Hardman Street (1859); a more florid example was Martin's Union Hotel (1849; dem.), at the corner of Clayton Square and Parker Street.[33] His simpler

2.8: Warehouse at 66 Bridgewater Street, Liverpool, Liverpool, William Culshaw, 1857. (*Author.*)

CHAPTER 2

buildings of this type, however, were pure Georgian survival, and might to all appearances have been built 50 years earlier. The same is true of an 1843 design for back-to-back court housing in Blucher Place, Toxteth, which provides uniquely detailed evidence for a notorious building type once ubiquitous in Liverpool.[34] It is surprising to find an architect involved at all in so utilitarian a project, but it may be that the services of a professional were thought necessary because of the 1842 Liverpool Building Act, which laid down new rules concerning floor areas, ceiling heights and the dimensions of windows for this type of housing. In any case, the plans were rejected by Liverpool Corporation's Health of the Town Committee because, at only four feet wide, the entry to the court failed to satisfy the requirements of the Act.[35]

As typical of Victorian Liverpool as insanitary back-to-back houses were the multi-storey warehouses that lined the Dock Road and its tributaries. Between 1842 and 1861, Culshaw worked on sixteen schemes of this kind, ranging from the remodeling of individual warehouses to the design of a block of eight new ones between Harrington Street and Sefton Street (1845; dem.).[36] Most have been demolished, but a surviving example is 66 Bridgewater Street (1857) (**2.8**), the ground floor of which served as Messrs Stuart & Douglas's cooperage.[37] Unlike the well-known fireproof warehouses erected by Jesse Hartley on his dock quays, Culshaw's were of conventional design and construction: gabled to the street, with vertical rows of taking-in doors, and an internal structure of timber floors on cast-iron columns. Where fireproof brick vaulting was used, it was generally confined to basements where flammable goods were stored.

Henry Sumners

By the start of the eclectic 1860s, Culshaw's work must have looked old-fashioned and unimaginative. This was certainly the view of Thomas Mellard Reade (1832-1909), a local architect who in 1865-6 wrote a series of stinging articles about Liverpool architecture in the satirical journal *Porcupine*. Reade lambasted the dull, repetitive Classicism of the many new office buildings round the Exchange, decrying the employment of an older generation of surveyor-architects, and singling out examples of Culshaw's work for particular criticism (though without mentioning him by name). He expressed a Puginian contempt for Culshaw's use of tawdry stucco ornament: the Hardman Street shops were included in a general denunciation of 'be-moulded, be-panelled, bedizened cement fronts and diseased acanthus decorations', while the cornice of Waterhouse's Building became 'that huge compo monstrosity under whose shadow we never pass without a shudder'.[38]

William Culshaw (1807-74) and Henry Sumners (1825-95)

2.9: Henry Sumners, proposal for St George's Place, Liverpool, *Liverpool Mercury*, 19 September 1854. (*Liverpool Record Office, Liverpool Libraries, local illustration 735.*)

It was presumably in response to competition from more able practitioners of the palazzo style such as J.A. Picton (1805-89), and the prospect of up-and-coming rivals, that Culshaw brought Henry Sumners into the practice in 1861. A generation younger, Sumners had had a very different professional formation.[39] Born in Liverpool, the son of a boot maker with a shop in fashionable Bold Street, he was apprenticed to the young Birkenhead architect Charles Reed (d. 1859), and in 1847 won a competition for the layout of the residential estate of Cressington Park, Aigburth.[40] He worked for a period in London 'with Mr. Barry and other architects', then undertook a 'pedestrian tour' through France and Italy from 1848 to 1849, journeying as far as Rome before returning to his native town by the end of 1852.

Not much is known of his work in Liverpool before he joined Culshaw's office, but two projects stand out. The first was a speculative scheme to create a monumental setting for the newly completed St George's Hall. Sumners proposed an exuberantly domed salt-water swimming baths as a counterpoint to Elmes's masterpiece, separated from it by an elevated piazza.[41] The design was published as a supplement to the *Liverpool Mercury* (**2.9**), and although it came to nothing, its metropolitan scale must have marked Sumners out as a young man of vision. The second was a pair of 'marine residences' on the seafront at Waterloo, for a Liverpool physician,

2.10: Houses for Dr Drysdale at Waterloo, Henry Sumners, 1861. (*Building News*, 31 May 1861.)

Dr Drysdale. In polychrome brick and stone, with quirky details to the bay windows, the houses were a thoroughly modern piece of High Victorian Gothic, a world away from Culshaw's flat, Tudor efforts. They were published in the *Building News* in 1861 (**2.10**), evidence of professional recognition in the very year that Sumners entered Culshaw's employment.[42] He began as manager of the architectural side of the business, before being taken into partnership in 1866, an arrangement that lasted until early in 1873.

Offices and commercial buildings, 1861–73

Sumners' arrival marked a watershed in the firm's development. The character of its work was transformed, and although the drawings continued to be signed by Culshaw until 1866, they are clearly the work of his new associate. Reade recognised the change when he compared Culshaw's Savings Bank in Bold Street (1861) (**2.11**) with the National Bank and Liverpool Law Association buildings in Cook Street (1863) (**2.12**), and noted 'some decided influx of talent in the intervening years.'[43] In place of

2.11: Former Savings Bank, Bold Street, Liverpool, William Culshaw, 1861. (*Neil Jackson.*)

the tired Classicism of the former, with its weak borrowings from Cockerell, the Cook Street building used a variety of Renaissance motifs in a richer and altogether livelier way.

In an earlier, unexecuted design for the Cook Street building Sumners incorporated Gothic elements too, and he developed this eclecticism further at Batavia Buildings (1862; dem.) in Hackins Hey and Berey's Buildings (1864) (**2.13**) in George Street.[44] These may have been among the recent

Chapter 2

2.12: Former National Bank and Liverpool Law Association buildings, Cook Street, Liverpool, 1863, designed by Henry Sumners but produced in William Culshaw's name, 1863. (*Author.*)

2.13: Berey's Building, George Street, Liverpool, 1864, designed by Henry Sumners but produced in William Culshaw's name, 1864. (*Author.*)

Chapter 2

2.14: Elevation of Peters Buildings, Rumford Street, Liverpool, 1864, designed by Henry Sumners but produced in William Culshaw's name. (*Lancashire Record Office/ Edmund Kirby.*)

Liverpool office buildings that an anonymous correspondent of the *Building News* praised for their signs of 'free and independent thought', showing 'a liberal and enlightened treatment of architectural style; and … an aim at a proper originality of design.'[45] The same journal certainly admired the eclecticism of Sumners' Exchange Court in Exchange Street East (1864; dem.), which, 'though presenting features borrowed from very different styles, giving us reminiscences of Elizabethan as well as of Greek and Italian detail, is most happily and artistically blended into one whole, and presents more of originality combined with grace than can be found in most buildings in Liverpool.'[46]

As for fenestration, while Culshaw had confined his long runs of linked sash windows to light wells and back streets, generally using windows of conventional proportions for principal elevations, Sumners made a conspicuous feature of large areas of glazing. Triplets of windows under continuous cast-iron lintels dominated the main façade of Batavia Buildings, while in the second phase of Knowsley Buildings (1863-4; dem.) the bipartite windows with central cast-iron mullions were even larger. In Peters Buildings, Rumford Street (1864; largely dem.) (**2.14**), the masonry was pared back to leave only the slenderest residual strips between the windows.⁴⁷ Stylistically similar to these office blocks, but more massive and imposing, were such maritime-related industrial buildings as the Canning Foundry, Cornhill (1864; dem.), for the engineer and brass-founder John Hays Wilson, and the Midland Railway goods warehouse, Victoria Street (1872) (**2.15**).⁴⁸ The latter – a depot for the storage of railway freight – follows the curve of the street with a blind arcade of huge round arches in polychrome brick and stone, at once powerfully functional and richly ornamental. Charles Reilly thought it 'one of the best buildings in the town'.⁴⁹

Houses, churches and institutional buildings, 1861–73

Among Sumners' surviving houses, one of the grandest is 19 Abercromby Square (1862), for the American-born banker and Confederate fundraiser Charles Kuhn Prioleau (most unusually for the date, Prioleau chose to build in Mosslake Fields rather than the remoter suburbs).⁵⁰ Although the house had to conform broadly with pre-existing neighbours, designed in 1819 by John Foster senior, Prioleau was allowed the distinction of a higher parapet.⁵¹ Inside is a sky-lit hall rising through two floors, with circular balconies on each landing, and a lavish painted ceiling in the dining room. Of suburban houses, Sumners' most ambitious was the red sandstone Quarry Bank (1866)

2.15: Midland Railway Goods warehouse, Victoria Street, Liverpool, Culshaw & Sumners, 1872, designed by Henry Sumners. (*English Heritage: NMR, AA40903.*)

2.16: Quarry Bank, Allerton, Culshaw & Sumners, 1866, designed by Henry Sumners, 1866. (*Author.*)

2.17: Christ Church, Linnet Lane, Liverpool, Culshaw & Sumners, 1867, designed by Sumners. (*Author.*)

(**2.16**) at Allerton, a muscular Gothic mansion complete with gatehouse and stables, built for the timber merchant James Bland.[52]

Churches provided an important outlet for Sumners' Gothic inventiveness. Most were modest in scale, built on confined sites in poor areas, and reflected Liverpool's Low-Church leanings in their rejection of Ecclesiology. All,

CHAPTER 2

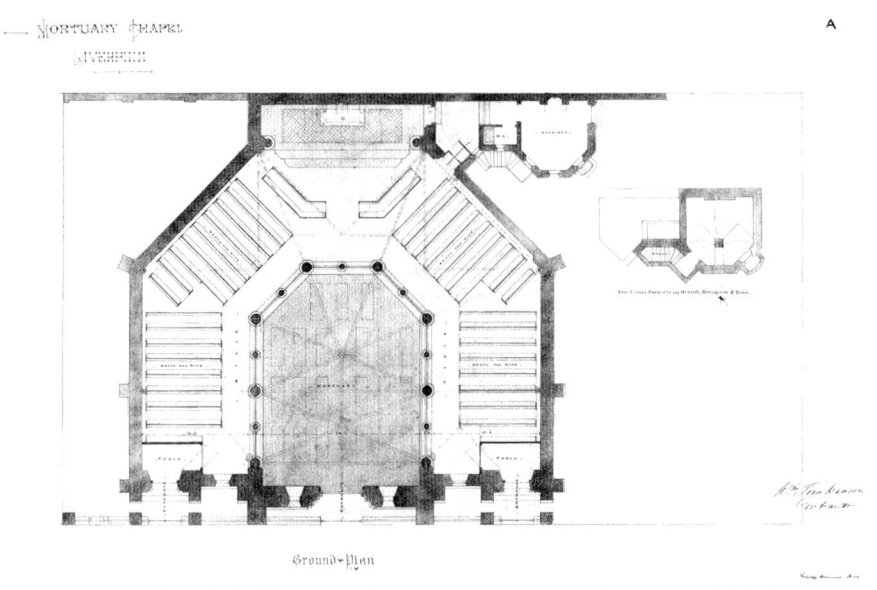

2.18: Mortuary Chapel, Collingwood Street, Everton, Henry Sumners, 1866. (*Lancashire Record Office/Edmund Kirby*.)

however, were enlivened by roguish details. An unusually imposing example was St Stephen, Byrom Street (1867–8; dem.), its nave raised above a school room and soup kitchen, giving it the tall, narrow proportions of a church such as E.W. Pugin might have designed.[53] At Christ Church, Linnet Lane (1867), in the affluent villa territory between Prince's Park and the future Sefton Park, a more spacious site gave prominence to the imaginatively detailed spire (**2.17**), and allowed for entrances in two parallel streets and a display of gables over the aisle windows.[54] Christ Church was paid for by George Henry Horsfall, member of a great Liverpool church-building family, and its planning embodies his Evangelical views.

But easily the most remarkable of Sumners' churches was the Mortuary Chapel, Collingwood Street (1866; dem.), in the heart of Everton's densely packed terraces.[55] This singular building offered a sanitary alternative to the practice, widespread among the area's poor Irish Catholics, of retaining the bodies of the dead in their overcrowded homes until burial. It had a semi-octagonal plan (**2.18**), the central 'nave' being reserved for the reception of up to 21 coffins, separated from the aisle-cum-ambulatory by an arcade (**2.19**). The arches were filled with plate glass, through which relatives could see the deceased while remaining safely insulated from them. Pevsner described

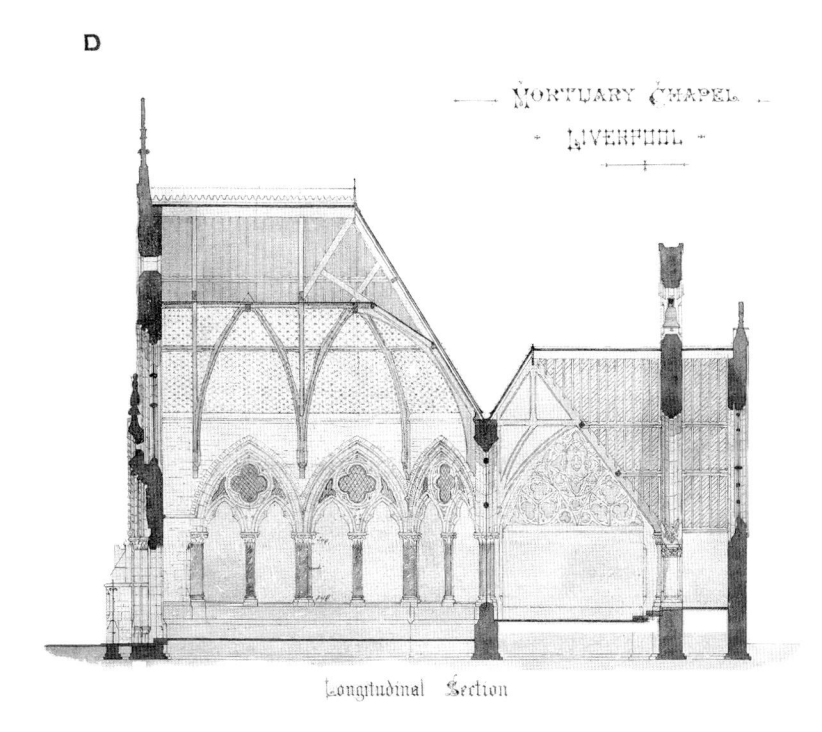

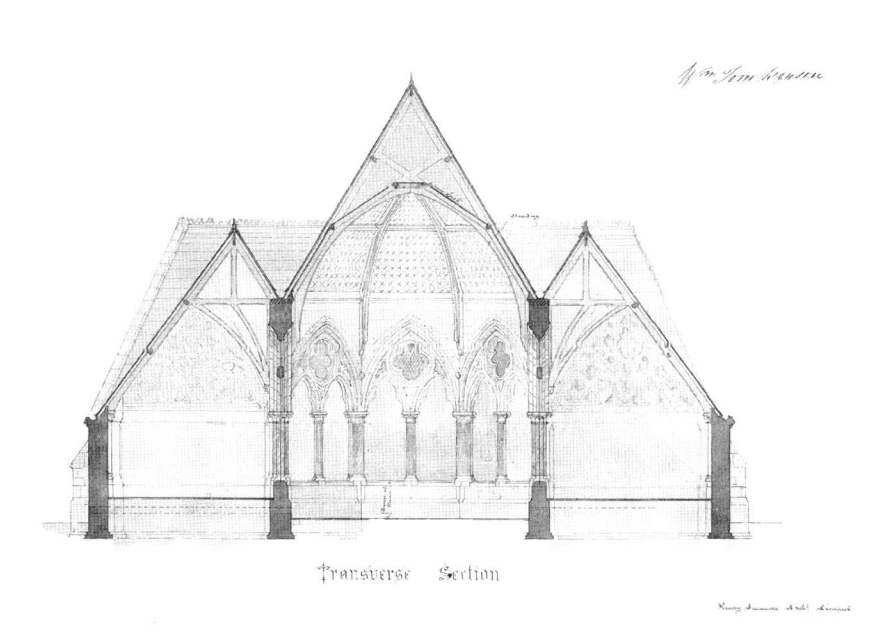

2.19. Mortuary Chapel, Everton, 1866. (*Lancashire Record Office/Edmund Kirby.*)

Chapter 2

2.20: West Derby Union Workhouse, Walton, designed by Henry Sumners but produced in William Culshaw's name 1863. (*Author*.)

the church's 'wild, low façade', dominated by a large, almost triangular window of flowing Decorated tracery, and characterised the whole building as 'demonstratively unbeautiful' while clearly being fascinated by it.[56]

Other buildings designed to serve the needs of a poor and disadvantaged urban population included ragged schools in Everton (1863–8; dem.) and College Lane (1865; dem.); a home for discharged prisoners at Kirkdale (1870; dem.); a residential Industrial Institution in Dingle Lane (1869; dem.); and the Royal Southern Hospital in Caryl Street (1867; dem.).[57] But Sumners' most significant project of this type was the West Derby Union workhouse at Walton (1863; partly dem.).[58] Early on, Culshaw had established workhouses as an important area for the practice: he did the Prescot Union workhouse at Whiston in 1842, and was employed alongside Scott & Moffat in 1843 to suggest modifications to the Liverpool workhouse in Mount Pleasant.[59] There followed new buildings for the Poor Law Unions of Ormskirk (1851) and Runcorn (1855), and for the West Derby Union at Toxteth Park (1858). Sumners later made additions to the Toxteth Park site, but he designed the whole of the Walton workhouse from scratch. A huge complex, with subsidiary elements ranging from a boys' school and plunge bath to a cemetery, it included laundry, stables, coach-houses, piggeries, joiners' and blacksmith's shop, stone-yard, female infirmary and a terrace of cottages for 'aged married couples'. Only the 23-bay main range survives, with a polychrome clock tower that remains a suburban landmark in north Liverpool (**2.20**).

Clients

As well as providing a visual record of numerous demolished or altered buildings, many of Culshaw's and Sumners' drawings are inscribed with the client's name, making them a rich source of information about architectural patronage in Victorian Liverpool. It goes without saying that many commissions came from the mercantile elite, and patterns can be discerned which suggest the important role played by informal networks in obtaining work. Businessmen with offices close to the practice in Rumford Place (such as C.K. Prioleau and F.C. Braun) turned to them with their domestic commissions. Some clients were linked to each other by blood or marriage: Sir John Bent, for instance, whose house in Rake Lane Culshaw extended, was the son-in-law of John Davenport of Staffordshire; and his daughter married Robert Frank, whose house at Aigburth Culshaw also enlarged. And some clients who were relatives were professional associates too: the brothers-in-law Edward Hatton and Thomas Worthington Cookson were also business partners, and as well as their premises in Canning Place the practice designed their matching houses on the waterfront at Seaforth.

Certain families, notably the Grahams and the Horsfalls, employed Culshaw & Sumners loyally over many years. And the fact that mercantile patrons like these also served on a range of charitable committees and in various company boardrooms is likely to have brought further work: G.H. Horsfall, for example, was not only president of the Southern Hospital and chairman of the Poor Law Guardians for Toxteth Park, but also a director of the Royal Insurance Company, another organisation that employed the firm extensively.

Described in his *Mercury* obituary as 'a zealous politician of the ultra Tory type', it would be surprising if Culshaw did not obtain work from clients who shared his party allegiance, and yet alongside Tories such as James Bland and Thomas Berry Horsfall the practice also worked for prominent Liberals such as Philip Henry Rathbone and John Hays Wilson. In the end, political, familial or business ties probably counted for less than clients' direct knowledge of their work, with many no doubt making the safe choice of a firm whose buildings were familiar from neighbourhood examples. The clustering which is a striking feature of their output tends to support this view: a series of extensions to neighbouring West Derby villas, a clutch of Bold Street shops, several commercial buildings bordering Canning Place, and, most obviously, the numerous office blocks round the Exchange.

The partnership dissolved

The firm of Culshaw & Sumners was dissolved in March 1873, when William Culshaw entered into a new partnership with his eldest son, Alfred (1849/50-1926).[60] The terms of the split do not appear to have been generous to Sumners: the practice had been appointed architects for the new Town Hall at St Helens in April 1872, and when Sumners took over the project he reportedly had to pay his former partner £350 for the plans.[61] It is difficult to follow his subsequent career in detail, but he was evidently successful, serving as president of the Liverpool Architectural Society in 1878, and designing such prominent and idiosyncratic buildings as St Cyprian's, Durning Road (1879-81), and St Luke's Art Workshops, Myrtle Street (1880).[62] William Culshaw, meanwhile, died within two years of separating from Sumners, though the practice he founded continued under his son until 1916.[63]

The work of Culshaw and Sumners reflects the immense quantity and variety of building generated by the economic powerhouse of Victorian Liverpool. Much of it – the offices, warehouses and manufacturing premises – flowed directly from the port's role as an international centre of maritime trade. The rest – elite suburban housing, specialist shops and hotels, schools and charitable institutions – mirrors the wider pattern of nineteenth-century urbanisation and the growing complexity of Victorian society. The sheer number of large new buildings undertaken by this one practice is striking, but at the same time, much of their work consisted of the alterations, extensions and conversions that are the bread and butter of all architects. Such jobs may not be 'architecture' as generally understood by architectural historians, but like the more prestigious office blocks, churches and villas, they show how the built environment of the Victorian city was in a state of continual flux and evolution. J.A. Picton was one of a number of contemporary observers of Victorian Liverpool who wrote of the complete transformation of its fabric during this 'most prosperous and progressive' period in its history.[64] The drawings of Culshaw and Sumners are a unique record of this wholesale rebuilding, and they offer a wealth of detailed information not just about the architects' approach to design, but about the setting of urban life in the nineteenth century.

This chapter is an outcome of the research project 'Culshaw & Sumners: a mid Victorian architectural practice in Liverpool, and its impact on the city's built environment', funded by the Arts & Humanities Research Council and carried out under Professor Neil Jackson at the University of Liverpool, 2008-9. The author would like to thank Professor Jackson; the project archivist, Sarah Pymer; and the staff of the Lancashire Record Office and the Liverpool Record Office.

Abbreviations
BN *Building News*
LM *Liverpool Mercury*
LRO Lancashire Record Office, Preston

Notes
1   LRO, DDX 162. The collection contains 6,017 items, mostly drawings. Of these, approximately 3,500 appear to have been produced during William Culshaw's period of independent practice or during his partnership with Henry Sumners. The remainder were produced by William's son Alfred between 1873 and 1915, or by other architects at a wide range of dates, or are unsigned. A few buildings known to have been designed by William Culshaw and Henry Sumners are not

represented, but there are no large gaps in the chronological sequence of surviving drawings, so the collection is probably substantially complete.

2   The baptismal register of Ormskirk parish church records the christening of William, son of Henry and Jane Culshaw, on 4 Feb. 1807. This almost certainly refers to the future architect.
3   *LM*, 24 Sep. 1874.
4   *Architectural Magazine*, 4, 1837, 484 ff.
5   LRO, DDX 162/6/62.
6   Calendar of Probate.
7   *Liverpool Daily Post*, 23 Sep. 1874.
8   *LM*, 24 Sep. 1874.
9   The volume of work undertaken indicates that he must have had assistants, though little information about them has so far come to light. One was Joseph Fisher (1832-77), employed from 1852 to 1857; another was the grandson of his first client, Launcelot Graham.
10 House for John Wedgwood: LRO, DDX 162/36/24-DDX 162/36/28; Maer Hall: included in LRO, DDX 162/06/47-DDX 162/06/71.
11 LRO, DDX 162/40/01-DDX 162/40/05.
12 *A Brief Memoir of George Holt, Esquire, of Liverpool*, privately printed, Liverpool, 1861, 70-2.
13 It was built between 1832, when the buildings previously on the site were surveyed by Foster & Stewart (LRO, DDX 162/44/47), and 1836, when it was shown on John Gage's *Trigonometrical Plan of the Town and Port of Liverpool*. LRO, DDX 162/64/12 is an undated elevation for this building, inscribed on the back, 'Mr. Graham's elevation'.
14 Culshaw's address is given as 4 Rumford Pace on a drawing dated May 1836, LRO, DDX 162/6/62.
15 For Liverpool office buildings, *see* J. Sharples & J. Stonard, *Built on Commerce: Liverpool's Central Business District*, English Heritage, 2008.
16 LRO, DDX 162/66/01-DDX 162/66/15. For Foster, *see* H. Hollinghurst, *John Foster and Sons, Kings of Georgian Liverpool*, Liverpool History Society, 2009.
17 Apsley Buildings: LRO, DDX 162/14/39-DDX 162/14/41, DDX 162/14/49; Walmer Buildings: LRO, DDX 162/75/05-DDX 162/75/13.
18 LRO, DDX 162/52/31- DDX 162/52/32, DDX 162/52/34, DDX 162/52/37, DDX 162/52/22-DDX 162/52/27, DDX 162/52/29.
19 LRO, DDX 162/44/40, DDX 162/44/45- DDX 162/44/46, DDX 162/44/ 48-DDX 162/44/49, DDX 162/44/55.
20 LRO, DDX 162/14/31-DDX 162/14/38, DDX 162/14/42-DDX 162/14/48.
21 *Civil Engineer & Architect's Journal*, 1842, 278.
22 70 Upper Parliament Street: LRO, DDX 162/116/01-DDX 162/116/22; 29 Falkner Square: LRO, DDX 162/23/38-DDX 162/23/53. The cost of 29 Falkner Square is cited in a report of a court case concerning subsidence allegedly caused by construction of the neighbouring house in *LM*, 22 Aug. 1851.
23 LRO, DDX 162/58/05-DDX 162/58/15.
24 LRO, DDX 162/84/29-DDX 162/84/39, DDX 162/38/65-DDX 162/38/75.
25 For example the Holmfield estate, advertised for sale in lots for villa building in

    LM, 23 May 1834.
26 *The English Notebooks by Nathaniel Hawthorne*, ed. Randall Stewart, Oxford U.P., 1941, 190.
27 The drawings for one pair (LRO, DDX 162/84/30, DDX 162/84/31, DDX 162/84/33) are dated 1843 and inscribed with the client's name, Mr Manifold. They can be identified with 8 and 9 Rock Park. The drawings for the others (LRO, DDX 162/15/30-DDX 162/15/41), possibly of 1846 or 1847 and inscribed 'Mr Cato', do not appear to be related to any of the surviving houses.
28 LRO, DDX 162/33/43-DDX 162/33/58.
29 LRO, DDX 162/22/05-DDX 162/22/32.
30 LRO, DDX 162/10/23-DDX 162/10/30.
31 LRO, DDX 162/35/55-DDX 162/35/60. The drawings for a site at Aigburth are dated 1847. The client was T.F. Bennett.
32 Christ Church Schools: LRO, DDX 162/100/21-DDX 162/100/26; School at Maer: LRO, DDX 162/55/34.
33 Baltic Fleet: LRO, DDX 162/25/57-DDX 162/25/58; 14-22 Hardman St: LRO, DDX 162/39/01-DDX 162/39/13; Martin's Hotel: LRO, DDX 162/19/15-DDX 162/19/19.
34 LRO, DDX 162/62/29-DDX 162/62/32.
35 Liverpool RO, Health of the Town Committee minutes, 352 MIN/HEA I 1/1(i), 17 July 1843.
36 LRO, DDX 162/99/23-DDX 162/99/25.
37 LRO, DDX 162/56/14, DDX 162/56/16, DDX 162/56/19.
38 *Porcupine*, 17 Feb. 1866, 452; 6 Jan. 1866, 380.
39 The best biographical account is in a report of his funeral, *LM*, 27 May 1895.
40 R. Pollard & N. Pevsner, *Lancashire: Liverpool and the South West*, Yale U.P., 2006, 385.
41 *LM*, 19 Sep. 1854.
42 *BN*, 31 May 1861, 457.
43 Savings Bank: LRO, DDX 162/52/62-DDX 162/52/72; National Bank and Liverpool Law Association buildings: LRO, DDX 162/80/19-DDX 162/80/37; *Porcupine*, 20 Jan. 1866, 404.
44 Batavia Buildings: LRO, DDX 162/25/30-DDX 162/25/45; Berey's Buildings: LRO, DDX 162/88/95-DDX 162/88/102, DDX 162/88/104-DDX 162/88/107.
45 *BN*, 12 May 1865, 333-4.
46 LRO, DDX 162/52/3-DDX 162/52/13; *BN*, 7 Feb. 1868, 90.
47 Knowsley Buildings: included in LRO, DDX 162/52/22-DDX 162/52/46; Peters Buildings: LRO, DDX 162/83/10, DDX 162/83/11, DDX 162/83/15, DDX 162/83/17, DDX 162/83/22, DDX 162/83/26-DDX 162/83/33.
48 Canning Foundry: LRO, DDX 162/30/01-DDX 162/30/15, DDX 162/47/51; Midland Goods Warehouse: LRO, DDX 162/06/32-DDX 162/06/46.
49 C.H. Reilly, *Some Liverpool Streets and Buildings in 1921*, Liverpool Daily Post & Mercury, 1921, 48.
50 LRO, DDX 162/89/16-DDX 162/89/30. Three years later Sumners designed a weekend cottage for Prioleau in the village of Halewood: LRO, DDX 162/89/22, DDX 162/89/23.
51 A.R. Allan, *The Building of Abercromby Square*, Liverpool U.P., 1986, 14.

52 LRO, DDX 162/26/77-DDX 162/26/92, DDX 162/41/01, DDX 162/66/33, DDX 162/119/01.
53 LRO, DDX 162/29/02-DDX 162/29/10, DDX 162/29/27, DDX 162/29/29-DDX 162/29/31.
54 LRO, DDX 162/03/09-DDX 162/03/18.
55 LRO, DDX 162/60/19-DDX 162/60/23. A full description is in *LM*, 12 Dec. 1866.
56 N. Pevsner, *The Buildings of England: South Lancashire*, Penguin, 1969, 147, 220.
57 The drawings for the Southern Hospital are not in the LRO, but Culshaw & Sumners are identified as the architects in *LM*, 24 Oct. 1867.
58 LRO, DDX 162/32/16-DDX 162/32/18, DDX 162/53/38-DDX 162/53/55, DDX 162/91/05-DDX 162/91/37, DDX 162/101/01-DDX 162/101/13.
59 Liverpool Record Office, minutes of a special meeting of the Workhouse Committee of the Liverpool Select Vestry, 353 SEL 10/1, 23 Feb. 1843.
60 *Daily Post*, 23 Sep. 1874, 5. Gore's Liverpool *Directory* for 1874 lists the practice as 'William Culshaw & Son' for the first time.
61 *St Helens Standard*, 27 Apr. 1872; 29 Mar. 1873; 9 Aug. 1873.
62 *LM*, 28 Nov. 1878; Pollard & Pevsner [n. 40], 2006, 378, 410.
63 In Gore's Liverpool directories for 1876 and 1877 the practice is listed as 'William Culshaw & Sons', Alfred apparently having been joined by his brother William H. Culshaw after their father's death. In 1878 it reverts to 'William Culshaw & Son', remaining so until it appears in the directory for the last time in 1916.
64 J.A. Picton, *Memorials of Liverpool*, Longmans, Green, 1903, vol. 2, 479-84.

3

The rewards for diligence and prudence: the exemplary career of William Hill (1827-1889)

Christopher Webster

William Hill's career reached a stunning climax with his *invitation* – no competition was involved – to erect Portsmouth Town Hall[1] in 1886, one of the iconic public buildings of the century; it was a fitting reward for a long and distinguished career which had been based in Leeds. Yet Hill is unlikely ever to reach the pantheon of the great nineteenth-century architects and it would be easy to dismiss him as just one more mid-Victorian provincial practitioner: competent and astute, but ultimately unremarkable. However, looked at from other perspectives, Hill's practice reveals much of interest in a period of seminal importance for the establishment of the architectural profession, one – so far as the provinces were concerned – barely half a century old and still in the process of defining its role to the public, as well as to those claiming membership of the 'profession'. Indeed, it would be hard to find *any* architect who better exemplified some of the crucial issues that a study of this period raises: the professional benefits to be gained from exploiting one's own Nonconformist allegiances as a means of securing country wide commissions within a specific denomination at a time of massive expansion of chapel provision; and the rewards that could be accrued from entering competitions advertised in the national building press for relatively small-scale building projects way beyond one's regional

CHAPTER 3

base. Hill was no genius, but a study of his career suggests that ambition and hard work, especially when coupled with reliability, financial prudence and a well-run office – qualities sadly lacking in many architects at this time – could be just as useful as artistic virtuosity in a climb towards the top of the professional ladder.

Hill was born 'in Halifax'[2] on 18 June 1827 but was baptised at St Peter's, the parish church of Bradford, on 29 July. His entry in the baptism register gives the family address as 'Brighouse', 4 miles south-west of the centre of Halifax, but still within the parish, although the 1861 Census records his birthplace as 'Salterhebble', rather closer to the centre. His parents were John and Ann Hill, both born in 1791. John is recorded as a 'delver' on the baptism form, a term usually used for the humble occupation of digging foundations, but it could also be used to describe the man who owned the company and we should not assume John Hill was a labourer.[3] Indeed, by the time of the 1851 Census – the first to record trades and professions – he is described as a 'stone merchant', as is Hill's older brother; by that date the Hills were prosperous, living at Heaton High Park on Bradford's north-east side, one of the town's most exclusive addresses.

We have few clues about the parents' religious affiliations except that we know Hill was educated at the West Riding Proprietary School in Wakefield,[4] opened in 1834 in a fine Tudor building designed by Richard Lane of Manchester, now Queen Elizabeth Grammar School. The Proprietary School was a popular establishment for middle-class Nonconformists seeking an education for their sons that was both modern – i.e. not dominated by the study of the classics – and free of the Anglican bias of the grammar schools. Fees introduced a degree of exclusivity. It was not specifically a boarding establishment, although some scholars from outside Wakefield are known to have taken lodgings in the town and Hill might well have been one of them[5] as daily travel from Calverley, between Bradford and Leeds, where the family lived in 1841, would have been impossible.[6]

In his mid-teens, around 1843, he went as a pupil to the Leeds practice of Perkin and Backhouse,[7] the first young man to be articled to them.[8] His training there coincided with a brief period – between Chantrell's retirement and Brodrick's arrival – when this was the town's most successful firm and when several big projects were undertaken. Hill was one of a number of their pupils who went on to have successful careers and it can be concluded that the training offered was thorough. Mid-1840s commissions included the Borough Gaol (1843-7), the Moral and Industrial Training Schools (1845-8) and the House of Recovery (1846) – all very substantial buildings in Leeds – as well as a series of schools, churches and houses elsewhere. We can assume that Hill was familiar with exceptionally large-scale projects as well as all the stylistic alternatives of the middle of the century.

In June 1850, aged just 22, he announced the opening of his own office with 'A Card' in the *Leeds Intelligencer*,[9] based at 59 Albion Street. That he could afford to do this confirms the likelihood of familial support. On 19 February 1852, he married Eliza Longfield (1825-84), the daughter of Joseph (sometimes referred to as Josh or Joshua) (1796/7-1852). Joseph was a prominent Leeds Nonconformist and successful 'tinner' who, by 1851 employed '3 men and 2 apprentices' and lived at 95, Portland Crescent, on Leeds' fashionable north side. Following their marriage, Hill and his bride appear to have moved into the Portland Place house.[10] Joseph died only a few months after the wedding and although Eliza had two brothers, she might well have enjoyed a useful inheritance.

Hill's first recorded commission came in November 1850: '9 dwelling houses in the vicinity of Leeds'.[11] These would have formed a row of modest terraced houses, but the commission is not without interest, despite its utilitarian nature. Dwellings of this type were built in huge numbers in Leeds throughout the nineteenth century to accommodate the influx of families seeking work in this thriving industrial centre. However, traditionally it had been an area of construction provided by builders, not architects, and later in the century such work was undertaken by men who might call themselves 'architect', but were very much the profession's second division. Nevertheless, around the middle of the century it appears to have been the bread and butter of several of the town's best architects, including Thomas Ambler, Thomas Shaw and Perkin & Backhouse (although not Brodrick), artistically unrewarding, probably, but a useful source of income as well as contacts. For the next five years, Hill's known work was dominated by such jobs. However, his career was soon to take an upward trajectory.

In so far as one can make generalisations about Victorian provincial architects, one is widely sustainable: they rarely strayed far from their home town;[12] Hill is thus a rare exception. Indeed, commissions took him the length and breadth of the country. Two factors help explain this. The first is that his career was perfectly timed to exploit the practice of those intending to build appointing an architect following a competition advertised in *The Builder* (founded in 1843), or one of the other nationally distributed professional journals that started around this time. This was an especially popular tactic among committees erecting public buildings. But while this explains how Hill came to know of proposals for (say) the Corn Exchange in distant Devizes, it does not explain why so few other provincial architects seem to have pursued this means of securing work in the way that Hill

Chapter 3

did.¹³ Indeed, Cunningham sees Hill's commitment to competitions as exceptional and includes him in his list of 'inveterate competers'.¹⁴ Certainly Hill was unusually ambitious, but it also suggests most provincial architects were content with the local opportunities.

Chapels

The second explanation for Hill's remarkably extensive area of operation is that he was a committed member of one of the Nonconformist groups, in his case, the Methodist New Connexion (hereafter MNC).¹⁵ The reigns of Victoria and Edward are marked by increasing prosperity for Nonconformists and a desire to erect landmark buildings as public statements of their faith, often re-buildings of earlier, modest structures. However, the period is also marked by regular schisms in which congregations were divided and new groupings were created. Both contributed to prolific chapel building as the denominations vied with each other for converts as well as prestige. Within this frenzy of chapel building, another factor is pertinent here: the denominations liked to appoint an architect from within their own ranks. It was not quite a hard and fast rule, but the principle certainly gave endless employment to certain architects: based in Leicester, James Tait¹⁶ worked extensively for the Congregationalists; Thomas and Charles Barker Howdill (father and son) in Leeds travelled the country building chapels for the

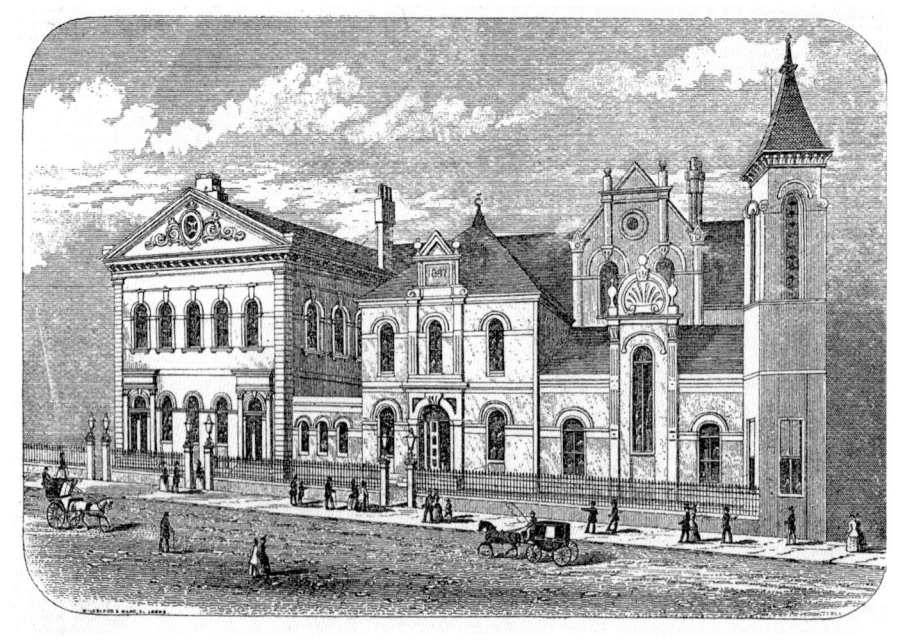

3.1: Leeds, Woodhouse Lane MNC, chapel (on the left), 1853-8; school (right) added by Hill in 1887. (*Packer [note 15], 7.*)

WILLIAM HILL (1827-1889)

3.2: Halifax, Salem MNC, 1871-4. (*Packer [note 15], 48.*)

Primitive Methodists; Bowman and Crowther of Manchester built several chapels for the Unitarians;[17] A.H. Goodall of Nottingham, a son of the manse, also designed a number of MNC chapels,[18] but for sheer quantity in any denomination, Hill had few rivals.

His first diversion from the world of workers' cottages came in 1853 with his appointment to build a new chapel in Woodhouse Lane, Leeds, for the MNC, at which Hill would later worship (**3.1**). The result was a substantial, Classical, temple-form chapel with an embellished gable end forming the principal elevation. It was a type that had been popularised by James Simpson[19] – a Leeds architect and prolific builder for the Wesleyans – from 1835 and exploited extensively by others subsequently so that by 1853, it was almost the norm. Nevertheless, Hill's first chapel was an accomplished performance, broadly conservative, but with currently fashionable Classical flourishes. It opened in 1858, and further work for the Connexion soon followed: St Paul's MNC, Leicester (*c.* 1860-1); Dewsbury Road, MNC, Leeds (1861-3); Salem MNC, Dewsbury (1863-4); Andover Street MNC, Sheffield (*c.* 1865); Stockport MNC (*c.* 1867-8); Halifax, Salem MNC (1871-

Chapter 3

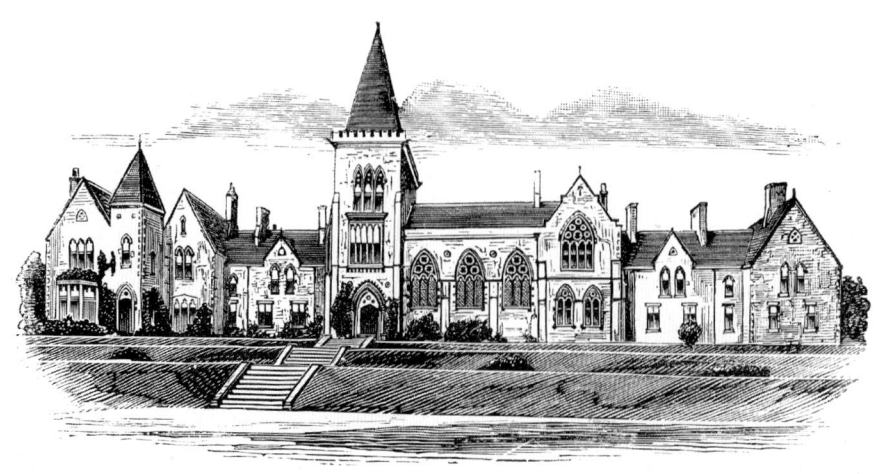

FANMOOR COLLEGE, SHEFFIELD.

3.3: Sheffield, Ranmore College, 1862-4. (*Packer [note 15], 141.*)

4) (**3.2**); Ladywood MNC, Birmingham (1873-4); Bethel MNC, Durham (remodelling, 1883); Bethesda MNC, Hanley (alterations, 1887), and there were many others.

Perhaps the jewel in Hill's MNC crown was his appointment to build the Connexion's most important institution apart from its chapels: its ministerial training establishment Ranmoor College in Sheffield (1862-4) (**3.3**). It comprised a picturesque arrangement of units, dressed in 'Collegiate Gothic of the fourteenth century [which had] an imposing and beautiful aspect',[20] although Pevsner thought it 'rather a deplorable design'![21] Here the financial support and influence of the Firth family of steel manufactures, leading members of the Connexion in Sheffield, was important and soon after, in 1869, Hill was appointed the architect for the town's Firth Almshouses. A number of other influential New Connexion families gave Hill private commissions, including the Hepworth tailoring family of Leeds.

The MNC was certainly central to Hill's early success, but quite how did he ingratiate himself so effectively with the denomination? He was recorded as 'a member of the congregation' at Woodhouse Lane,[22] but was he committed to the MNC *before* he received that commission, or only afterwards? We know nothing of his earlier allegiances – there is merely a hint of Nonconformity via his schooling – and his father-in-law was recorded as a trustee of Ebenezer Primitive Methodist Chapel, Quarry Hill, Leeds, in 1837.[23] However, it is known that a number of 'upwardly mobile' members of Primitive Methodist congregations – well known for their working class membership – graduated to the MNC and Joseph Longfield might well have been one of them by the time of his daughter's marriage. Yet it is just possible that Hill's MNC involvement was professional expediency, rather than religious conviction.

Whatever the answer, so well regarded was he in Nonconformist circles that he secured much work from other denominations: the Wesleyan Methodists appointed him for Fulwood, Sheffield (*c.* 1865); Wesley, West Hartlepool (1871-3), and for several in or around Leeds; the Congregationalists gave him a number of jobs including Heckmondwyke, West Yorkshire (*c.* 1858) and Beeston Hill, Leeds (1864-5). He also did work for the Unitarians, Baptists, United Methodist Free Churches and even occasionally the Anglicans. His obituary calculated that he had produced 'upwards of 100 chapels and schools', that is schools associated with chapels.

So far as style is concerned, Hill would provide his chapel builders with whatever they wanted. The Classical ones were conservative, but big and impressive; Mount Tabor MNC, Stockport (1865-8) (**3.4**) and the similar Wesley in West Hartlepool (1871-3), with budgets sufficiently large for a tetrastyle portico, are particularly commanding. His Mannville MNC in

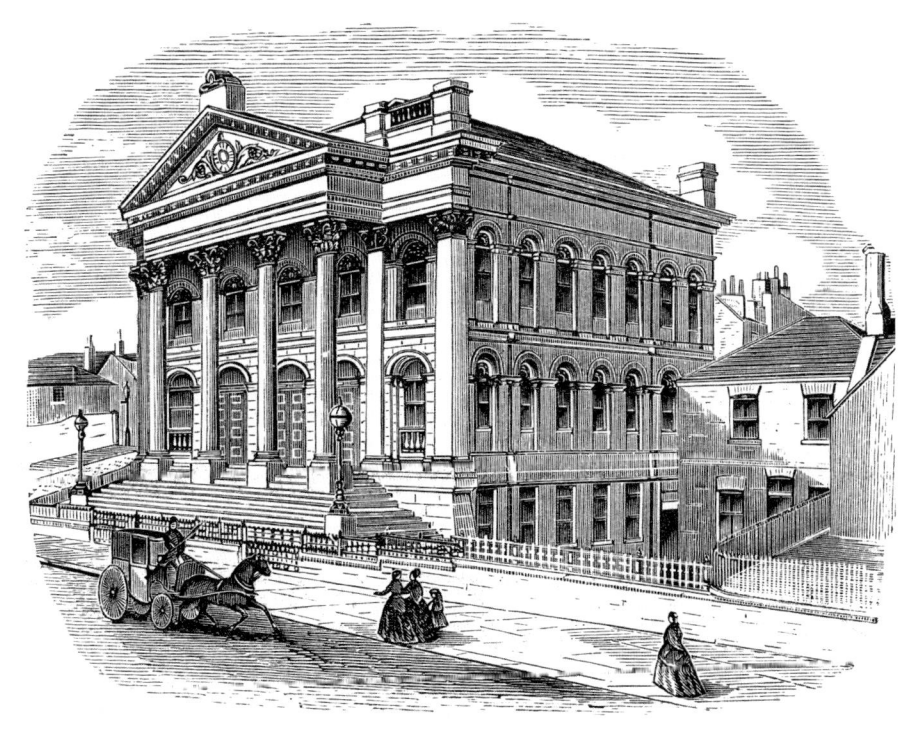

MOUNT TABOR, STOCKPORT

3.4: Stockport, Mount Tabor, MNC, 1865-8. (*Packer [note 15], 57.*)

Chapter 3

3.5: Bradford, Mannville MNC, 1875. The buildings on the left are later. (*Author.*)

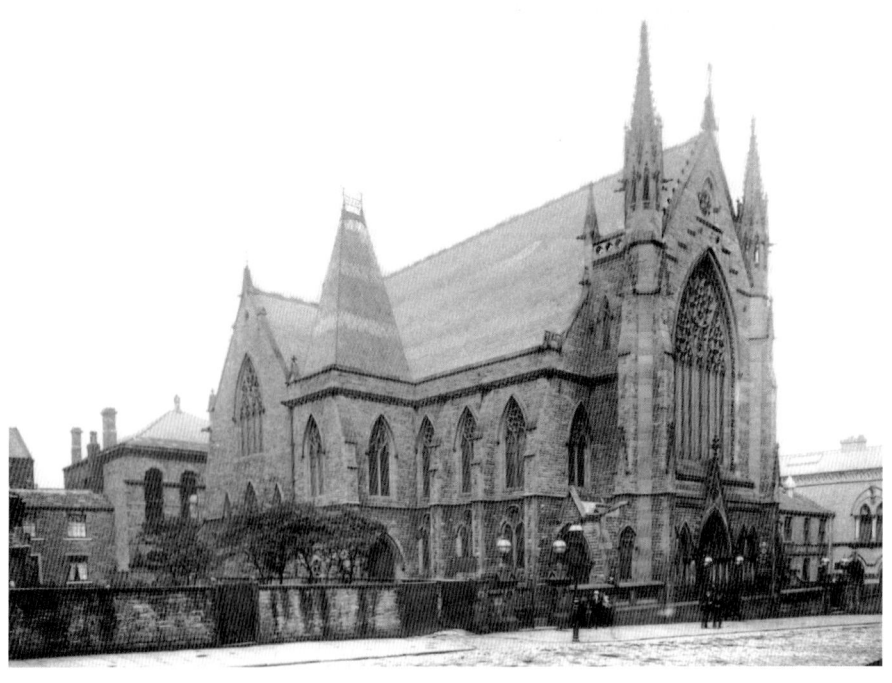

3.6: Huddersfield, High Street MNC, 1864-7. (*Kirklees Images.*)

William Hill (1827-1889)

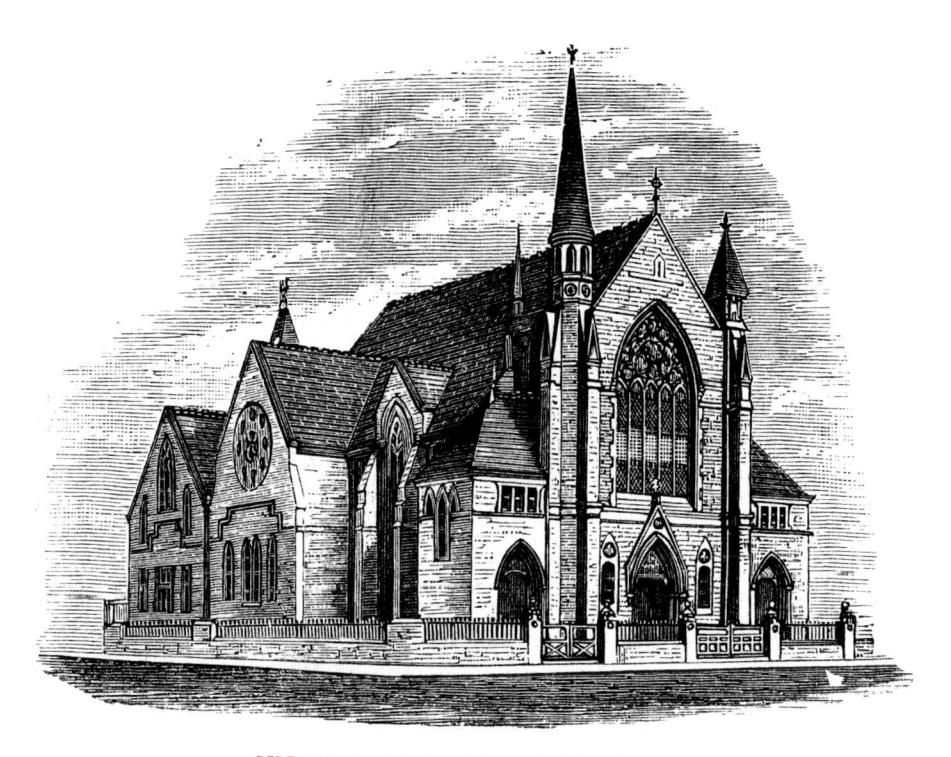

CHRIST CHURCH, BARROW-IN-FURNESS.

3.7: Barrow in Furness, Cumbria, Christ Church MNC, 1873-5. (*Packer [note 15], 244.*)

Bradford (1873), with its lighter Classical repertoire, is rather elegant (**3.5**). But it is in his Gothic ones that he really shone, developing his own brand of 'Nonconformist Gothic' in which he displayed at least as impressive a knowledge of medieval forms as most of the contemporary Anglican architects, yet the buildings were unmistakably chapels. High Street MNC, Huddersfield (1864-7) (**3.6**) and the related design for Christ Church MNC, Barrow in Furness (1873-5) (**3.7**) illustrate the point. The principal window of Huddersfield is especially memorable.

These Gothic chapels were not cheap. The one in Barrow cost £8,500 just for the building – the land was given by the Duke of Devonshire on condition that a dignified structure was erected, although the duke was not a member of the Connexion.[24] Huddersfield's cost £10,000, including the site.[25] However, the plain Classical example in Beeston, Leeds, cost only 'about £2,000'[26] for almost as many seats. Beeston, like many of Hill's chapels, was a three-storey arrangement: schoolrooms in a semi-basement with chapel and balcony above.

CHAPTER 3

The smaller public buildings

Alongside his prolific output of chapels, Hill also devoted his energies to entering competitions all over the country for what might be termed minor public buildings. Harper[27] lists sixteen, but more recent research[28] has revealed many others. In these he was remarkably successful. His three 1850s corn exchanges form an interesting group: Devizes, Wiltshire (1856-7) (**3.8**); Banbury, Oxfordshire (1857) (**3.9**) and Hertford, Hertfordshire (1857) (**3.10**). As well as sharing a function, the three are broadly similar in size; being designed almost concurrently and with each located so far from the others, one might have expected a busy architect like Hill to have repeated the design, or at least broad elements of it. However, they are commendably varied within the confines of fashionable mid-century Classicism. Devizes has three-quarter Corinthian columns and an elaborate parapet with vases to articulate the five bays of its narrow street façade, topped by a statue of Ceres – the Roman goddess of agriculture – on a huge tapering pedestal. Banbury is the grandest. Three-quarter Corinthian columns again, but this time coupled, and with a pediment. There is another swaggering balustrade

3.8: Devizes, Wiltshire, Corn Exchange, 1856-7. (*Wiltshire & Swindon History Centre.*)

William Hill (1827-1889)

3.9: Banbury, Oxfordshire, Corn Exchange, 1857. (*Author.*)

and another figure of Ceres on a similar pedestal. Hertford is fundamentally different: two-storey, three bay façade with pilasters, huge, richly ornamented pediment and a sophisticated treatment of the tripartite windows linking the two floors. Following these three corn exchange victories, he might have believed he was well placed when, in 1860, his home town decided it was time for a new one. However, he could only manage second place,[29] runner up to Cuthbert Brodrick's memorable, oval, domed design, a world away from Hill's trio of built exchanges.

Hill also actively pursued commissions for new cemeteries, including Salford (*c.* 1856),[30] Chichester (*c.* 1857),[31] of which more later, and Farnley, Leeds (*c.* 1859-60).[32] In addition, he entered competitions – not always successfully – for workhouses (Leeds, 1855),[33] town halls (Preston, 1855; Bolton, 1863-73; Alton, 1879),[34] poor law offices (Leeds, 1859-60),[35] mechanics institutes (Lincoln, 1861; Bolton, 1866; Barnsley, 1876-8 and

Chapter 3

3.10: Hertford, Corn Exchange, William Hill, 1858-9. (*Hertfordshire Archives & Local Studies*.)

Yeadon, West Yorkshire, 1879-80),[36] markets (Rotherham, West Yorkshire, n.d.)[37] and dispensaries (Leeds, 1865).[38]

Amongst the smallest, but at the same time most picturesque, of his public buildings is the Flood Monumental Almshouses in Holmfirth, West

3.11: Holmfirth, West Yorkshire, Flood Memorial Almshouses, 1856. (*Getty Images*.)

Yorkshire (1856),[39] a complex of five cottages built as a memorial to those who lost their lives in the catastrophic flood that had torn through the village in 1852, killing 80 (**3.11**). Although the budget was a mere £700, Hill produced a fine design, exploiting '14th century Gothic', bravely innovative in its asymmetry for a building type invariably symmetrical at this date. He beat thirteen others for the first prize.[40] He used a similar set of compositional devices for the much larger Ranmore College in Sheffield.

Equally brave was a style Hill developed for some of his later small-scale Classical public buildings, for instance the Dispensary for Leeds (1865-7) (**3.12**) and the Mechanics' Institute for Barnsley (1878) (**3.13**). A simplified version of the Dispensary repertoire was used effectively for commercial buildings in Leeds a few years later (**3.14, 3.15**). At Barnsley, he worked in an idiom that defies easy labelling – even *The Builder* was careful to avoid stylistic classification – a species of High Victorian Classicism, with hints of Second Empire, but perhaps closer to Robert Macleod's classification

CHAPTER 3

3.12: Leeds, former 'Old' Dispensary, Vicar Lane, 1865-7. The entrance front was originally symmetrical, but the left hand side was truncated to accommodate road-widening. (*Ruth Baumberg*.)

of 'rampant eclecticism'.[41] The local paper stuck its neck out with the announcement that it would have 'a tower of fancy design'.[42] Undisciplined, certainly, but not entirely without charm. From a planning point of view, it was something of a triumph. Within an awkward, narrow site, with a significant bend in it, Hill managed a building that combined a series of shops, offices, mechanics' institute, public hall, library, classrooms and school of art. The Mechanics' Institute for Yeadon of only a year later could hardly be more different: still symmetrical, still with a tower, but verging on Ruskinian Gothic in the Godwin manner (**3.16**).

Hill must have pleased his paymasters as there are several instances of private commissions following quickly behind these competition victories. For instance, within months of Banbury's Corn Exchange opening, Hill was seeking tenders for 'Three Houses in Bath Terrace' and a 'Pair of Semi-Detached Villas, Broughton Road' in the town.[43] And while the Holmfirth almshouses were being constructed, he sought tenders for 'A Villa Residence' in the village.[44] On a larger scale, in 1862 Hill sought tenders for 'A Mansion'

William Hill (1827-1889)

3.13: Barnsley, Mechanics' Institute, 1878. (The Builder, *36, 1878, 242.*)

at Hurst, Ashton-under-Lyne, Greater Manchester, possibly Hurst Hall for John Whittaker, a wealthy mill owner and prominent MNC member.

Hill's professional successes are marked in his residential addresses. He was still in Portland Place for the 1861 Census, living in the Longfields' former home; later in that decade he was at the even more fashionable De Grey Road (demolished for the university's Parkinson Building), and in 1874, the family moved to Adel, one of the town's most exclusive suburbs, where he had two live-in servants (**3.17**).

The town halls

However, it is for two great town halls that Hill is best remembered, both well away from Leeds, but with an obvious link to the town as we shall see. His first town hall appointment was announced in 1854, for a new building in Preston, although the project came to nothing[45] and in 1867 G.G. Scott

CHAPTER 3

3.14: Leeds, warehouses, Aire Street, 1868-9. (*Ruth Baumberg.*)

was employed to erect one. Nearby in Bolton, the council also desired a fine town hall and in 1863, sent a committee to visit 'various boroughs to inspect and derive lessons from similar erections; and the structure which appeared to have produced the most favourable impression upon the minds of members ... was Leeds.'[46] Brodrick was invited to supply a design and work in collaboration with a local man – sharing the fee – but he declined. A competition was thus organised which generated interest 'from 200 architects' and entries from thirty-nine[47] including Brodrick and Hill. The latter, knowing what the good folk of Bolton admired most, set out to give them just what they wanted: a slightly scaled down version of Leeds.[48] Brodrick's entry was more original, but only achieved third place, while Hill emerged as the victor, no doubt much to Brodrick's chagrin. Professor Tomas Leverton Donaldson, then president of the RIBA, was the assessor.

The *Blackburn Standard* reported the outcome.[49] Hill was awarded £120 for his design which had no tower, presumably to reduce the cost to his estimated £47,000, but even without one, 'like St George's Hall, Liverpool, [it will] have a really noble and imposing appearance.' However, Donaldson believed a 'lofty clock tower [was] an essential part of the design'[50] and Hill

3.15: Leeds, commercial premises for Watson Brothers, Aire Street, 1872. (*Ruth Baumberg.*)

Chapter 3

3.16: Yeadon, West Yorkshire, Mechanics' Institute, now Town Hall, 1879-80. (*Clive Woods*.)

3.17: Adel, nr Leeds, *The Heath*, 1874. (*Ruth Baumberg.*)

3.18: Bolton, Town Hall, 1863-73. (The Builder, *31, 1873, 446-7.*)

was urged to add one. Although he claimed his initial design was 'based upon Grecian models',[51] its similarity to that in Leeds must have been obvious to all, and the addition of a tower made it even more so (**3.18**). In fairness to Hill, while the exterior's debts to Brodrick are clear, the plan is radically different (**3.19**).

It was completed in the summer of 1873.[52] Throughout, Hill had been assisted by the Bolton architect George Woodhouse, but it seems the design was entirely Hill's; Woodhouse merely looked after day-to-day supervision. Cunningham gives the final cost as a staggering £167,000;[53] using his figures, it appears by far the most expensive town hall ever erected at that date, although Manchester's would soon surpass it. Despite its final price, the citizens of Bolton were thrilled with their municipal palace.

The Builder offered lukewarm praise for the exterior: 'the usual "school" type of Roman design' although it acknowledged 'the plan is in most respects praiseworthy'.[54] *Building News* was more enthusiastic: 'from all points of view, the exterior is a good Italian composition … a worthy companion to its sister buildings [in Leeds and Liverpool] … while it is the more important of the triad in the extent of its interior coloured decoration'.[55]

A decade later, Portsmouth councillors felt a civic building that reflected the town's 'increasing prosperity [and] growing importance' should be commissioned. In this it is clear the town was inspired to proceed by the examples of the northern 'manufacturing districts'. According to Portsmouth's *Evening News*, those towns

> are apt to think that Municipal enterprise is confined to their borders. They pride themselves chiefly on their Town Halls and many of the Yorkshire and Lancashire towns have constructed stately buildings for the conduct of their local affairs. The people of Preston are proud of their imposing Gothic pile; the massive Corinthian Town Hall of Ashton holds first place among the local lions, Oldham, Huddersfield, Halifax and Warrington are all well provided for, but … the Corporation Buildings of Bolton take the palm.

Having the benefit of studying the northern edifices, Bolton was deemed the most impressive and without wasting any time or effort on a competition, simply invited Hill to repeat his Bolton design on a larger scale (**3.20**), a course approved by *Building News*.[56] Hill, always adept in his dealings with clients, thoughtfully reassured the Portsmouth councillors at their foundation stone laying ceremony that 'he had every reason to believe that, with [their] cordial cooperation and assistance' he should be able to surpass the Bolton model.[57]

WILLIAM HILL (1827-1889)

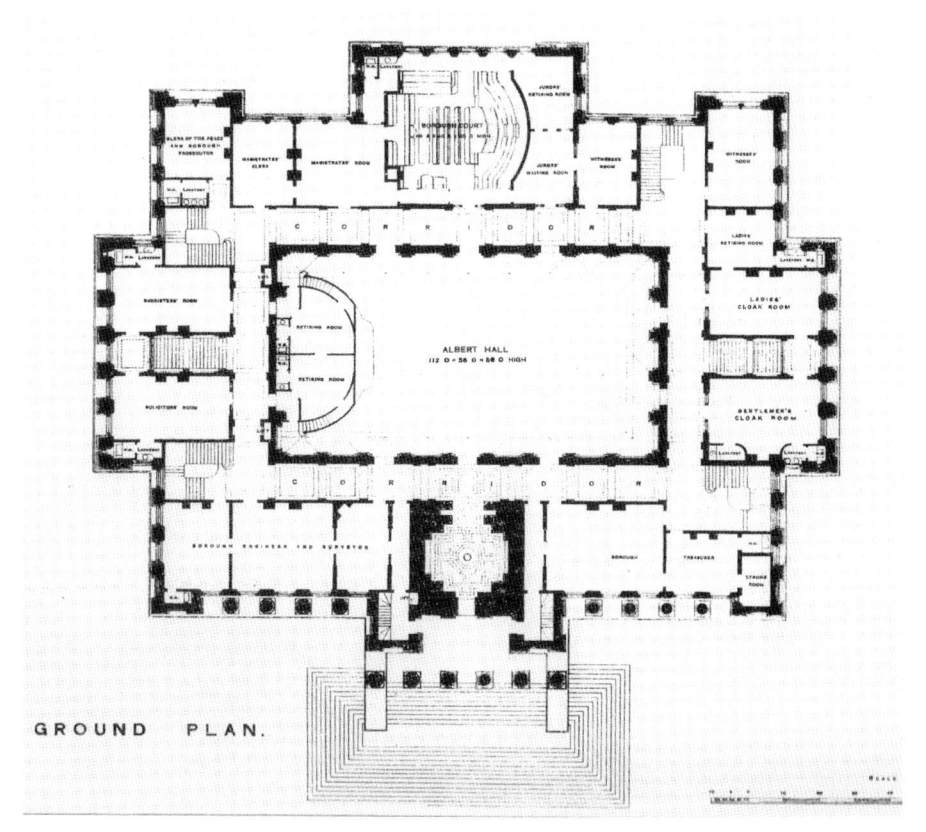

3.19: Bolton, Town Hall. (Building News, *24, 1873, after 672.*)

It was, according to Pevsner, 'One of the grandest gestures of municipal pride (there is little or nothing else of the period in provincial England south of the Midlands to compare in scale)' adding 'but, in its heavy Italianate Classical style, very old-fashioned for the date.'[58] Indeed, by the time of its completion in 1890, Brodrick's Leeds design was 38 years old. The principal development from Bolton is the introduction of ten corner domes to enliven the sky-line – perhaps a reflection of the rising tide of the English Baroque Revival – instead of the more angular ventilation shafts of Bolton, themselves based on those of Brodrick.

Hill's office
Hill's first office was at 59, Albion Street, Leeds; by 1859 he had moved to 71 Albion Street and in June 1865, he announced his move to 11, Park

Chapter 3

Square,[59] by then the town's most prestigious location for professional offices. Like most successful architects at this time, he took in pupils who paid a premium. He advertised for one in September 1856 and again in 1859.[60] Around 1863, George Francis Danby (1845-1929) entered his office initially as a pupil and continued as an assistant until 1872.[61] Another pupil was Stephen Ernest Smith (1845-1925) who spent three years with Hill from 1864 before going to the Royal Academy. Both Danby and Smith subsequently enjoyed solid careers in Leeds.[62] Also trained in the office was Hill's son, William Longfield Hill (1864-1927), who inherited the practice.

We have already considered how Hill learnt of competitions around the country, but an equally significant aspect of this important development in professional practice is the issue of transporting the entries. In this respect, an interesting vignette of the office has survived as his proposals for the 1857 Chichester Cemetery contest failed to arrive on time and he sued the Midland Railway Company to whom they had been entrusted.[63] It was a case that seemed to generate much interest as it was reported in several London and provincial papers. The County Court decided in Hill's favour and awarded him £25 – the amount he sought – although he calculated his loss at around £36 in addition to the chance of winning the competition. This was made up of: 3 days of his own time at 3 guineas per day; 19 days for 2 clerks which he charged at a total of £19 guineas; an unspecified [perspective] artist's time at 5 guineas and £2 for the frame for the last item. And how were his distant victories supervised? It seems he placed a trusted clerk of works at each and, one assumes, he paid an occasional visit using the railway network. In the case of the Stockport MNC chapel, he advertised for a clerk,[64] although it is not clear how others were chosen.

In 1868, Hill entered into partnership with the Sheffield architect Salmon L. Swann that lasted at least ten years. However, this was an unconventional arrangement in which Hill continued to run his Leeds office and Swann his former office in Sheffield. During the decade, some buildings are described as being by 'Hill and Swann', but both men also undertook large amounts of independent work. It is this writer's opinion that in reality few, if any, designs were produced jointly and the work was largely divided geographically.

In 1856 he joined the Lodge of Fidelity in Leeds,[65] a lodge popular with the architect community. This came very shortly after the foundation stone laying of the Flood Almshouses in Holmfirth, an event with a very large Masonic presence, which perhaps, was the catalyst for his joining. He was made a Fellow of the RIBA in 1871, proposed by Thomas Oliver of Newcastle, Henry John Paull of Manchester and William Perkin, his former master.[66]

WILLIAM HILL (1827-1889)

3.20: Portsmouth, Guildhall/Town Hall, 1886-90. (Building News, *51, 1886, after 456*.)

Hill's demise

In 1874, he moved to 'The Heath', a substantial house he had designed in Adel, on the fashionable northern fringes of Leeds, where he lived with his family in some style. He died there on 5 January 1889, aged 61, survived by four children. He left £8,181/5/4d. Two days later, his death was announced to a meeting of the Leeds and Yorkshire Architectural Society by Henry Perkin, the society's president and son of William, Hill's former master. 'During the past thirty-seven years he has held a leading position

Chapter 3

among the architects of this town ... [was] an esteemed member of the [LYA] Society ... and the oldest practising member of the profession, he believed, in Leeds.'[67] His buildings reveal an impressive stylistic range – all handled with aplomb – and a study of his career has revealed not a single hint of impropriety or even publicly expressed criticism; there were few in the profession at the time of whom this could be said.

He was buried at Adel under a somewhat ostentatious memorial of his own design that he had erected following the death of his wife in 1884. It was sculpted by 'Hodgson' and consists of a cross under a Norman arch flanked by angels. Portsmouth's palatial town hall remained incomplete – to be opened by the Prince and Princess of Wales eighteen months later, accompanied by as dazzling a display of municipal ceremonial as might be imagined – a project that was a world away from the modest cottages at the opening of his career, one that graphically revealed the rewards for diligence and prudence.

I wish to acknowledge valuable assistance from D. Colin Dews concerning Hill's Nonconformist chapels and from Mike Hope for information about the Portsmouth Town Hall commission; Gwen Brown generously contributed genealogical information about the Hill and Longfield families.

Abbreviations
B   *The Builder*
BN   *Building News*
HC   *Huddersfield Chronicle*
LI   *Leeds Intelligencer*
LM   *Leeds Mercury*
MNC   Methodist New Connexion
MNCM   *Methodist New Connexion Magazine*

Notes
1 Following Portsmouth's elevation to city status in 1926, the building was generally known as the Guildhall.
2 *LM*, 8 Jan. 1889.
3 One of Hill's near contemporaries on the West Yorkshire architectural scene was William Henry Crossland. His father was also described as a delver, but was sufficiently wealthy to be able to send his son to study in G.G. Scott's office. (I am grateful to Janet Douglas for this information.)

4   This comes from Hill's obituary in *B*, 56, 1889, 34.
5   William was not listed as at home at the time of the 1841 Census.
6   The writer is grateful to John Goodchild for information about the school.
7   For Perkin and Backhouse, *see* C. Webster (ed.), *Building a Great Victorian City: Leeds Architects and Architecture, 1790-1914*, Northern Heritage Publications, 2011, 386-93.
8   *B*, 56, 1889, 34.
9   *LI*, 8 June 1850.
10 This statement needs qualifying. Certainly the Longfields were in Portland Place for the census of 1851, while Hill and Eliza were there for the one in 1861. However, the 1853 *Directory* records none of them there while Hill – presumably with Eliza – was living with two of Eliza's brothers, in Crimble Street, Leeds (pp. 93, 111). However, the 1857/8 *Directory* shows Mr and Mrs Hill, plus Eliza's brother Thomas, were at Portland Place. It is this writer's belief that the entries in the 1853 *Directory* are a misprint and that through the 1850s all of them were at Portland Place.
11 *LM*, 23 Nov. 1850.
12 G. Brandwood, 'Many and Varied: Victorian Provincial Architects in England and Wales' in K. Ferry (ed.), *Powerhouses of Provincial Architecture*, The Victorian Society, 2009, 10.
13 Another firm that did was Bellamy & Hardy of Lincoln, *see* Brandwood [n. 12], 12.
14 C. Cunningham, *Victorian and Edwardian Town Halls*, Routledge, 1981, 101.
15 For the early history of the MNC, *see* G. Packer (ed.), *The Centenary of the Methodist New Connexion*, George Burroughs, 1897.
16 Brandwood [n. 12], 12.
17 *See* A. Petford, 'Unitarianism and Ecclesiology in the North', *Chapels and Chapel People*, Chapels Society, 2010, 16-29.
18 Goodhall, for example, was the architect of Rose Street MNC and Sycamore Street MNC school/chapels Nottingham, both 1895 (*MNCM*, 1895, 274, 403), as well as the earlier Beeston MNC, 1875 (*MNCM*, 1875, 40), and Kimberley MNC, 1884 (*MNCM*, 1895, 115).
19 For Simpson, *see* I. Sergeant, 'James Simpson' in Webster [n. 7], 135-58.
20 Packer [n. 15], 144.
21 N. Pevsner, *The Buildings of England: Yorkshire, the West Riding*, Penguin, 1959, 458.
22 D. Colin Dews, 'Leeds and the Methodist New Connexion (part 2)', *Proceedings of the Wesley Historical Society*, 51:4, 1998, 119.
23 Ex inf. Colin Dews.
24 Norman Pickering, 'The Methodist New Connexion in Cumbria', *Cumbria Branch Bulletin*, 39, 1997, 25.
25 *HC*, 12 Jan. 1867.
26 *LM*, 21 July 1866.
27 R.H. Harper, *Victorian Architectural Competitions*, Mansell, 1983, 237.
28 A complete list of Hill's known buildings and projects can be found in Webster [n. 7], 376-81.
29 Harper [n. 27], 237.
30 *LM*, 23 Feb. 1856.

31 *LM*, 17 Nov. 1857.
32 *LI*, 30 July 1859.
33 *LM*, 6 Feb. 1855.
34 *LM*, 17 Mar. 1855; *B*, 31, 1873, 446-7; Cunningham [n. 14], 278, includes Alton as a competition victory for Hill, but does not say which of several Altons it is. This writer could find no other reference to it.
35 *LI*, 19 Feb. 1859.
36 *LI*, 12 Oct. 1861; Harper [n. 27], 237; *B*, 36, 1878, 242; *LM*, 2 Nov. 1878.
37 *B*, 56, 1889, 34.
38 *LM*, 6 May 1865.
39 *HC,* 26 Apr. 1856.
40 Ibid.
41 R. Macleod, *Style and Society*, RIBA Publications, 1971, chap. 5.
42 *Sheffield & Rotherham Independent*, 10 July 1876.
43 Both were advertised in *LM*, 1 Jan.1859.
44 *HC,* 26 Sep. 1856.
45 Hill's account of the fiasco appeared in *B*, 14, 1856, 210; *see* also Cunningham [n. 14], 82-3.
46 *Bolton Weekly Journal & District News*, 7 June 1873, quoted in D. Linstrum, *Towers and Colonnades; the Architecture of Cuthbert Brodrick*, Leeds Philosophical & Literary Society, 1999, 83-4. Much of the rest of the saga of Hill's Bolton job comes from Linstrum.
47 Linstrum [n. 46] gives the entrants at 39 (p. 84), Cunningham [n. 14] at 38 (p. 236).
48 Butler Wilson, Brodrick's first biographer, recounts that he was 'informed by a Leeds architect who was in Hill's office … and who assisted him in the preparation of the drawings that [the similarities between Leeds and Bolton] is accounted for by the fact that Hill knowing the Corporation of Bolton had approached Brodrick, and expressed their admiration for the design of Leeds Town Hall, decided to follow the lines of that building as closely as possible'. (T. Butler Wilson, *Two Leeds Architects: Brodrick and Corson*, West Yorkshire Society of Architects, 1937, 31-2.)
49 *Blackburn Standard*, 1 Mar. 1865.
50 Linstrum [n. 46], 84.
51 *Blackburn Standard*, 1 Mar. 1865.
52 For a full account of the hall, *see B*, 31, 1873, 446-7; *BN*, 24, 1873, 644.
53 Cunningham [n. 14], 271.
54 *B*, 31, 1873, 417.
55 *BN*, 24, 1873, 644.
56 'Portsmouth is to be congratulated on the choice of so suitable a design for its new Town Hall', *BN*, 51, 1886, 456.
57 *[Portsmouth] Evening News*, 15 Oct. 1886.
58 N. Pevsner & D. Lloyd, *The Buildings of England: Hampshire and the Isle of Wight*, Yale U.P., 2002, 445.
59 *LM*, 7 June 1865.
60 *LM*, 27 Sep. 1856; 15 Jan. 1859.
61 W.T. Pike (ed.), *The West Riding of Yorkshire at the Opening of the Twentieth Century*, Brighton, 1902, 365.

62   For Danby and Smith, *see* Webster [n. 7], 365-8, 397-9.
63   The court case was reported in some detail in *LM*, 17 Nov. 1867.
64   *LM*, 7 Dec. 1865.
65   A. Scarth & C.A. Bain, *History of the Lodge of Fidelity*, Beck & Inchbold, 1894, 224.
66   A. Felstead *et al.*, *Directory of British Architects 1834-1900*, Mansell, 1993, 445.
67   An obituary appeared in *LM*, 8 Jan. 1889, repeated in *B*, 56, 1889, 34. Both articles claimed Hill started his practice in 1851, but there is evidence, quoted earlier, that it started in the previous year.

4.1: Enoch Bassett Keeling: unknown photographer, c.1884. (*Bernard Stanley*.)

4

Acrobatic Gothic, freely treated: the rise and fall of Bassett Keeling (1837-86)

James Stevens Curl

Enoch Bassett Keeling[1] (**4.1**) was born on 15 March 1837 in Sunderland, County Durham. The register of the Sans Street Wesleyan Chapel, Bishopwearmouth,[2] shows he was baptised by Robert Jackson on 16 June, and that he was the son of Isaac Keeling[3] (1789-1869 – Minister of the Sans Street Chapel and Superintendent[4] of the Sunderland Wesleyan Methodist Circuit, 1836-9), who had entered the Ministry in 1811, serving first at Belper, Derbyshire, then in Gainsborough, Lincolnshire (1812), Burnley in Lancashire (1813), and various other places in quick succession before his brief stay at Sans Street. His subsequent career[5] left the family very little opportunity to settle anywhere for long: he was also for a time President of the Methodist Conference,[6] but retired from the Ministry in 1863. A volume of his prolix sermons appeared after his death.[7]

Bassett Keeling, aged 15, was articled to Christopher Leefe[8] Dresser (*c*.1808-after 1891[9] – architect, civil engineer, and surveyor, who practised from 30 Park Row, Leeds, and appears in the Leeds *Directories* of 1847 and 1851 as an 'Architect', but in 1845 as a 'Land Surveyor and Agent'[10]). Keeling

Chapter 4

4.2: Mary Newby Keeling (*née* Harrison), probably 1870s. W. Wright, photographer, 188 & 190 Bethnal Green Road. (*Bernard Stanley.*)

also attended the Leeds School of Practical Art, and was awarded a medal for drawing in 1856 (his draughtsmanship was vigorous), although he is recorded as 'Edward' instead of 'Enoch'.[11] Keeling served five years as pupil to Dresser, then settled in the capital, where he was to remain, commencing practice as an architect and surveyor in December 1857.[12]

Keeling (he appears to have disliked 'Enoch', always signing himself either 'E. Bassett Keeling' or 'Bassett Keeling' [which might explain the 'Edward' referred to above]), then lodging at 3 Upper Terrace, Upper Street, Islington,[13] was elected an Associate[14] of the Institute of British Architects[15] at a meeting on 9 January 1860 chaired by George Godwin (1813-88), editor (1844-83) of *The Builder* and no mean judge of ability. His sponsors were three Fellows: William Tite[16] (1798-1873 – who had strong Nonconformist connections); Philip Hardwick (1792-1870); and David Brandon (1813-97).[17] Keeling must have felt he had prospects, for on 8 March in the same year he married (in the Church of St Pancras according to the 'Rites and Ceremonies of the Established Church by Registrar's Certificate') Mary Newby[18] Harrison (1841-82[19] – a minor), who resided in Euston Square and was the daughter of William Gallimore Harrison, gentleman[20] (**4.2**). Witnesses were William Liver and Lucy B. Keeling. On the marriage register

BASSETT KEELING (1837-86)

4.3: Interior of St Mark's, St Mark's Road, Notting Hill, 1862-3, showing the extraordinarily thin, spiky interior (dem.). (Building News, *10, 1863, 717*)

Chapter 4

4.4: Contract drawing no. 3 for St Mark's, Notting Hill, by Keeling, 1862. (*RIBA Library Drawings Collection.*)

Keeling gave as his address The Polygon[21] (the development at Somers Town designed [1793 – demolished 1894] by Jacob Leroux [*fl.* 1753-99]), yet we know from records and from the 1861 Census[22] that he lodged elsewhere at least since 1859. On 23 December 1860 Edgar Bassett Newby Keeling was born to the young couple at 3 Upper Terrace: Keeling himself was the informant, on 19 January 1861,[23] the same year in which the family moved to 3 Napier Terrace, Upper Street, just to the east of Milner Square, an address they occupied until 1865 or 1866.[24] There is therefore a question mark as to why Keeling claimed to live at The Polygon.

The ecclesiastical buildings

Little is known of Keeling's architectural career at this time, although he had an office at 32 Fleet Street (adjacent to Falcon Court) in 1861-3, and a notice for a tender was published for alterations to premises of Naylor & Co. in Cavendish Square.[25] In 1862 or 1863 he moved his practice to 1 Verulam Buildings, Gray's Inn Lane, an address he was to retain until 1873.[26] He had obtained the commission to design St Paul's church, Stratford, in East London, and a contract was signed with Dove Bros on 28 April 1862.[27] Constructed of stock bricks relieved by stone dressings and bands of coloured bricks, the nave-arcades (on cast-iron columns, a Keeling trademark) were enlivened by polychromy, and the scissor-truss roof suggested something of what was to come in later churches. Seating 1,000, the building cost £4,000 and was consecrated on 10 December 1864:[28] it demonstrated that Keeling could produce large churches at low costs, keep to budgets, and get the job done in good time.[29]

Keeling's second church, St Mark's, St Mark's Road, Notting Hill, was consecrated earlier, on 27 November 1863,[30] the foundation-stone having been laid on 1 November 1862.[31] Again, the contractors were Dove Bros. St Mark's[32] was an extraordinary building, with internal red, white, and black bricks, and the arcades were carried on cast-iron columns vigorously decorated with polychrome designs. In addition, the arrises of the arches and of the scissor-braced trusses were boldly notched, and the interior, with its steeply-raked gallery-fronts, was spikily individual (**4.3**). It certainly did not appeal to all tastes, and was later denounced as an 'atrocious specimen of coxcombry';[33] building-committees were accused of 'irresponsibility in the choice of architects';[34] but shortly after the building was completed, it was more soberly described as a 'Gothic structure ... with a continental touch in it'.[35] Keeling's contract drawings (**4.4; 4.5**) show a restless, prickly design. Nikolaus Pevsner said of St Mark's, with its 'madly asymmetrical' façade and 'wild use of multi-coloured brick', that it was endowed with 'all the ham-fisted ugliness'[36] which Keeling could command. However, he was only seeing the building in a toned-down version: the galleries had been removed in 1896 and 1905, mostly for ideological reasons, without taking into account Keeling's structural system, so the fabric had to be strengthened by encasing the columns in concrete, re-tying the arcades to the aisle walls with concrete structures, and replacing the magpie-polychrome flying buttresses with stock-brick piers.[37] St Mark's was demolished in the 1970s.

Despite the fact that Keeling was one of Goodhart-Rendel's 'Rogue Goths',[38] and that much of his work was savaged by critics, there is no doubt that his abilities brought his name to the attention of the powers-that-were in church-building circles, not least because he was able to provide St Mark's with 1,380 sittings at a contract price of £6,011, including font, pulpit, and altar-fittings.[39] Not everyone was against Keeling or his work, for in 1864

Chapter 4

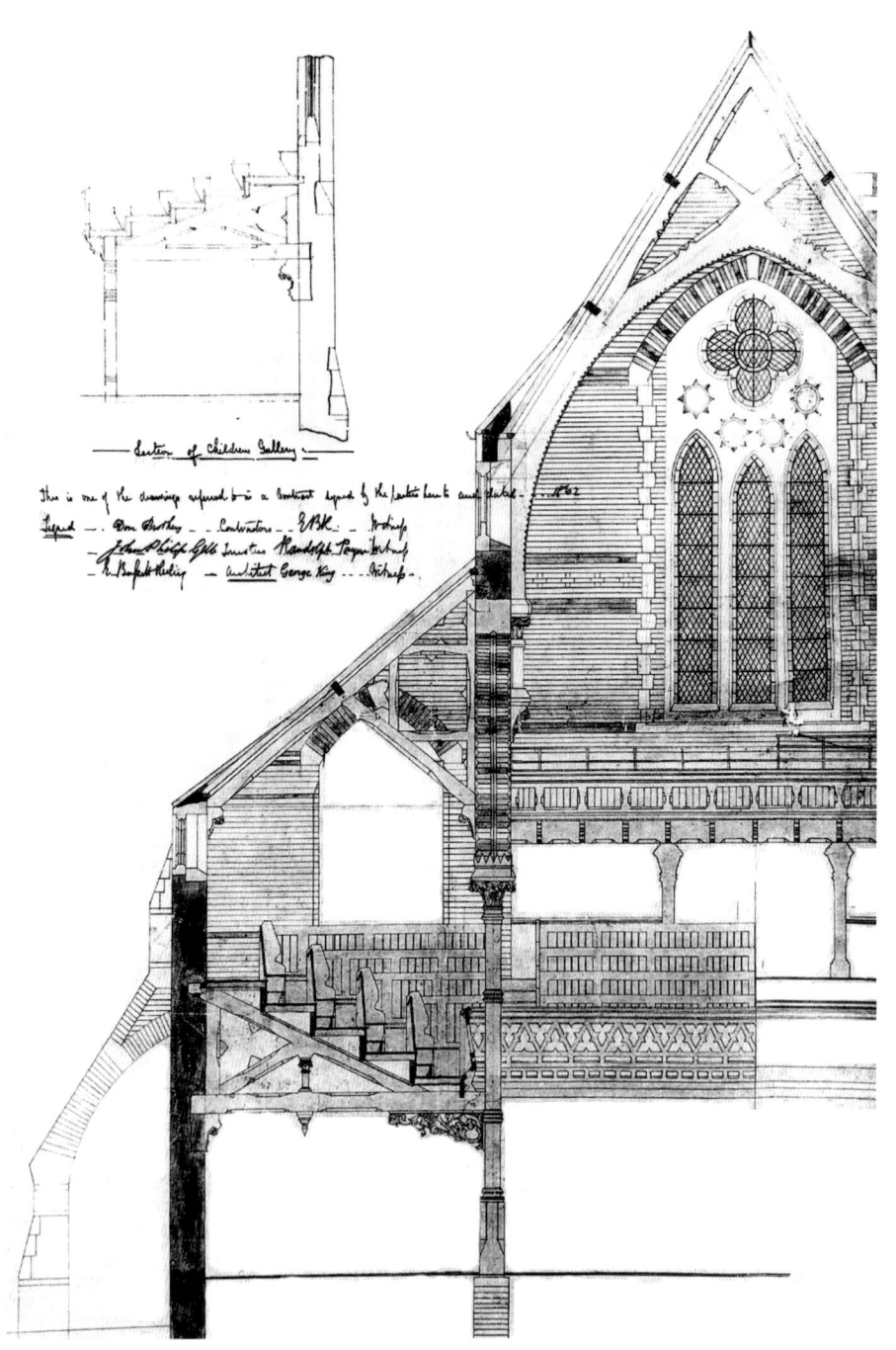

4.5: Contract drawing No. 8 for St Mark's Church, Notting Hill, by Keeling, showing the cast-iron supports for the galleries and nave-arcades. Note the polychrome notched brickwork and displays of structure. (*RIBA Library Drawings Collection*.)

the *Building News* adopted a respectful tone when referring to his designs, pronouncing them to be in the 'modern style of eclectic Gothic' and 'successful' at that,[40] which seems to have led to other architects producing details derived from Keeling's precedents. When St Mark's was demolished, John Sambrook and I visited a scrapyard in Kentish Town to inspect the cast-iron columns (newly freed from their concrete casing) but the capitals turned out to be cast-iron bells to which decorative metal foliage had once been attached. Sambrook opined that the columns with foliated capitals of wrought copper fixed to copper bells, as well as other aspects of the design by Henry Godwin (1831-1917) for St Jude's, Courtfield Gardens, Kensington (1870), were influenced by the work of Keeling, who had the ability to create richly decorative effects by simple means at modest cost.[41] I agreed with his views, but what clinches matters is that the contractors for St Jude's were George Myers & Sons of Lambeth, who also worked for Keeling.

In 1863 the foundation-stone for a small Wesleyan chapel at Waterloo Road, Epsom, Surrey,[42] was laid, and the building, stylistically 'Gothic with Continental modifications',[43] was erected to Keeling's designs. Three more churches date from the following year, when Keeling entered into a partnership with one John Richard Tyrie (b. 1838 in Fore Street, Edmonton): the precise nature of this business connection is obscure, for Tyrie[44] was not an architect, and his hand cannot be detected on any of the drawings produced by the firm of Bassett Keeling & Tyrie, which was, in any case, dissolved by the end of the year. The three churches designed by Bassett Keeling & Tyrie were St George's, Campden Hill, Kensington; St Paul's, Upper Norwood; and a Wesleyan chapel at Dalston.

The site of St George's was purchased in December 1863, and the foundation stone was laid in February 1864,[45] the contractors being Myers of Lambeth. The building's interior was faced with yellow stock bricks relieved with blue, red, and black bricks and Bath and Red Mansfield stone,[46] and the nave arcades had red and black brick voussoirs, notched at the arrises, carried on cast-iron columns, the springing-blocks set in cast-iron dishes forming the abaci of the capitals. William Pepperell (*fl.* 1850s-after 1872) could think of no ecclesiastical building where iron was better treated: the detail was 'sharp and clear', and the columns, somewhat 'Moorish' in appearance, did not seem so slender as to look 'unequal to their task of supporting the brick arches and clerestorey' as well as the gallery (which he considered 'suggestive of a conventional ship's side with ports complete' and very 'graceful', but 'sufficiently angular to be quite in keeping with the church'[47]). Gallery principals were attached to the columns, about

Chapter 4

Opposite: 4.6: The somewhat frantic interior of St George's, Campden Hill, 1864, drawn by John Richard Jobbins (*fl.*1839-66). (Building News, *11, 1864,* 729.)
Above: 4.7: 'Continental Gothic, freely treated': exterior of St George's, Campden Hill, 1864, drawn by J. R. Jobbins. (Building News, *11, 1864, 563.*)

CHAPTER 4

4.8: St Paul's, Anerley Road, Upper Norwood, 1864-6 (dem.). (*LMA. GLC Photographic Unit 68/9526.*)

halfway up the shafts, by means of wrought-iron bands carried on cast-iron haunches, and the larger springing-blocks (necessitated by the geometries of the junctions of nave-arcades, large transept arches, and galleries) were supported on clusters of three cast-iron columns on either side of the nave. Pepperell also admired the nave roof with its 'saw-tooth cut and intersection ribs', and commented upon how necessary the gallery was as an aesthetic and structural tie between the columns of the nave and the aisle walls (**4.6**). The exterior (**4.7**), like that of St Mark's, is in a style which was described as 'continental Gothic, freely treated':[48] the tower was surmounted by a broach-spire, removed by orders of the District Surveyor of the London County Council as a result of damage sustained in the 1939-45 war and replaced by a pyramidal copper cap of 1949 designed by Milner &

Craze.⁴⁹ St George's was consecrated by the Bishop of London in 1864,⁵⁰ and newspaper reports waxed lyrical about the 'strong polychromy' of the 'superb edifice', one the 'most magnificent pieces of architecture' ever seen by the journalists involved.⁵¹ Some contemporary critics noted Keeling's 'straining after originality that produced a fretful effect rather than the calm grandeur we look for in a church', yet acknowledged that 'the building has many admirable points, and, as a whole, is certainly picturesque'.⁵² One went so far as to pronounce St George's to be one of the most successful exemplars of 'modern' eclecticism, 'and though perhaps a little free in treatment, evidences an appreciation of ... continental Gothic which is not too common'.⁵³ The raked fronts of the galleries, with their open framing, the whole set well back from the columns, were praised as enhancing rather than detracting from the architectural effect of the interior.⁵⁴ In the course of the nineteenth and twentieth centuries, however, the interior was subjected to drastic changes (including the removal of most of the galleries,⁵⁵ casing of the columns in concrete partly as a reaction to what Pevsner felt was an 'excessively patterned' treatment,⁵⁶ and much else⁵⁷). Pevsner's verdict that St George's had an 'atrocious front' was typical of opinions of Keeling's work, much of which was unloved by Ecclesiologists and never taken seriously by

4.9: St Paul's, Upper Norwood, showing the nave-arcades and the 'triumphal arch' structure demarcating the chancel, with columns of Red Mansfield stone and bases and carved capitals of Bath stone. (©*Crown Copyright. NMR. BB70/6702.*)

architectural commentators (who tend to follow each other and look with their ears). Such strictures have contributed to Keeling's critical eclipse.

The second church designed (1864) by the short-lived firm of Bassett Keeling & Tyrie was St Paul's, Anerley Road, Upper Norwood, said to be in the 'Early French Gothic' style, 'freely treated':[58] it was consecrated by the Bishop of Winchester in August 1866. The street elevation was powerful, faced with Red Mansfield, Bath, and Kentish ragstones, and the tower was surmounted by a tall, slated spire. Contemporary critics commented upon the west window, with its robust plate-tracery and figure of St Paul within a *mandorla* recess, flanked by two roundels (**4.8**). The nave-arcades were 'sufficiently high to admit of side galleries' (the latter were never realised), carried on cast-iron columns, painted in 'neutral blue and green relieved with black', and rested on massive pedestals of blue Staffordshire brickwork, with 'Portland stone caps under the columns'.[59] Transepts were omitted, and the nave had a roof common with the chancel: to separate the two elements, Keeling employed a cross-wall up to wall-plate height only, complete with chancel-arch surmounted by a small gable, giving the splendid effect of a triumphal-arch (**4.9**). The chief glory of the interior, however, was the survival, intact, of the original painted stencil-patterns over all the brick walls, and it is tragic that this fine work by an underestimated architect was demolished in the 1970s. Another feature of the building was the characteristic Keeling treatment of robust carpentry, expressing structure in a far more convincing way than managed by most of his contemporaries (**4.10**).

One of the signatories on the contract for building the church, inspected at Dove Bros' premises in 1971, was James Tally Vining,[60] solicitor, who originally hailed from Yeovil in Somerset, and seems to have had some sort of connection with the Tyrie clan. It may be coincidence, but James Edward Tyrie was living at Knight's Hill, Norwood, when his bankruptcy hearings occurred in 1865-6,[61] and it could be that his brother, Keeling's partner, endeavoured to help, but only £2,000 in assets were recorded,[62] so this disaster may have had some bearing on Keeling's own tragedy, as ominous clouds began to gather over his future.

The firm of Bassett Keeling & Tyrie was also responsible for the Wesleyan chapel at Mayfield Terrace, Dalston (**4.11**), perhaps Keeling's best essay for the Methodists. Dove Bros were again the contractors, and the contract sum was £4,135.[63] The foundation-stone was laid in 1864: the building contained a chapel, 'good-sized classrooms for church purposes', a committee-room, the chapel-keeper's residence, and accommodation for the heating apparatus. The chapel was designed to seat 1,277: provision was made for a 'minister's

4.10: St Paul's, Upper Norwood, detail of Keeling's robustly designed exposed structure supporting the gallery at the (liturgical) west end. Note the cast-iron column, the pedestal on which it stands, and the carpentry above. (©*Crown Copyright. NMR. BB70/6709.*)

Chapter 4

WESLEYAN CHAPEL MAYFIELD TERRACE, DALSTON
BASSETT KEELING, ARCH' | VERULAM BUILDINGS GRAYS INN

4.11: Wesleyan Chapel, Mayfield Terrace, Dalston, 1864, as depicted in an illustration by J.R. Jobbins. With its plate-tracery and polychrome brickwork, it was an example of Keeling's colourful 'Continental Gothic, freely treated', style. The contract drawings are signed 'Bassett Keeling & Tyrie, Verulam Buildings', even though Jobbins's image omits any reference to Tyrie. (*Author's collection.*)

vestry and dressing-room, etc., attached', and the building was described as 'Gothic of the Early French character, freely treated', with some 'elements of the modern eclectic school, rendered in the simplest and most available materials, viz; picked yellow stock brick walling, relieved with bands, arches, etc., in blue Staffordshire, black and yellow malms, Bath stone dressings, with a few sunk columns in Red Mansfield'. The main building was covered in 'blue and red Bangor, in bands, and the staircase apse in Witland Abbey slates … 'The architects were 'Messrs. Bassett, Keeling and Tyrie [*sic*] of Gray's Inn, whose design was selected in a limited competition with six others'.[64] That mine of information, the *Architect's, Engineer's, & Building Trades' Directory* for 1868[65] reveals that Keeling designed several Wesleyan chapels apart

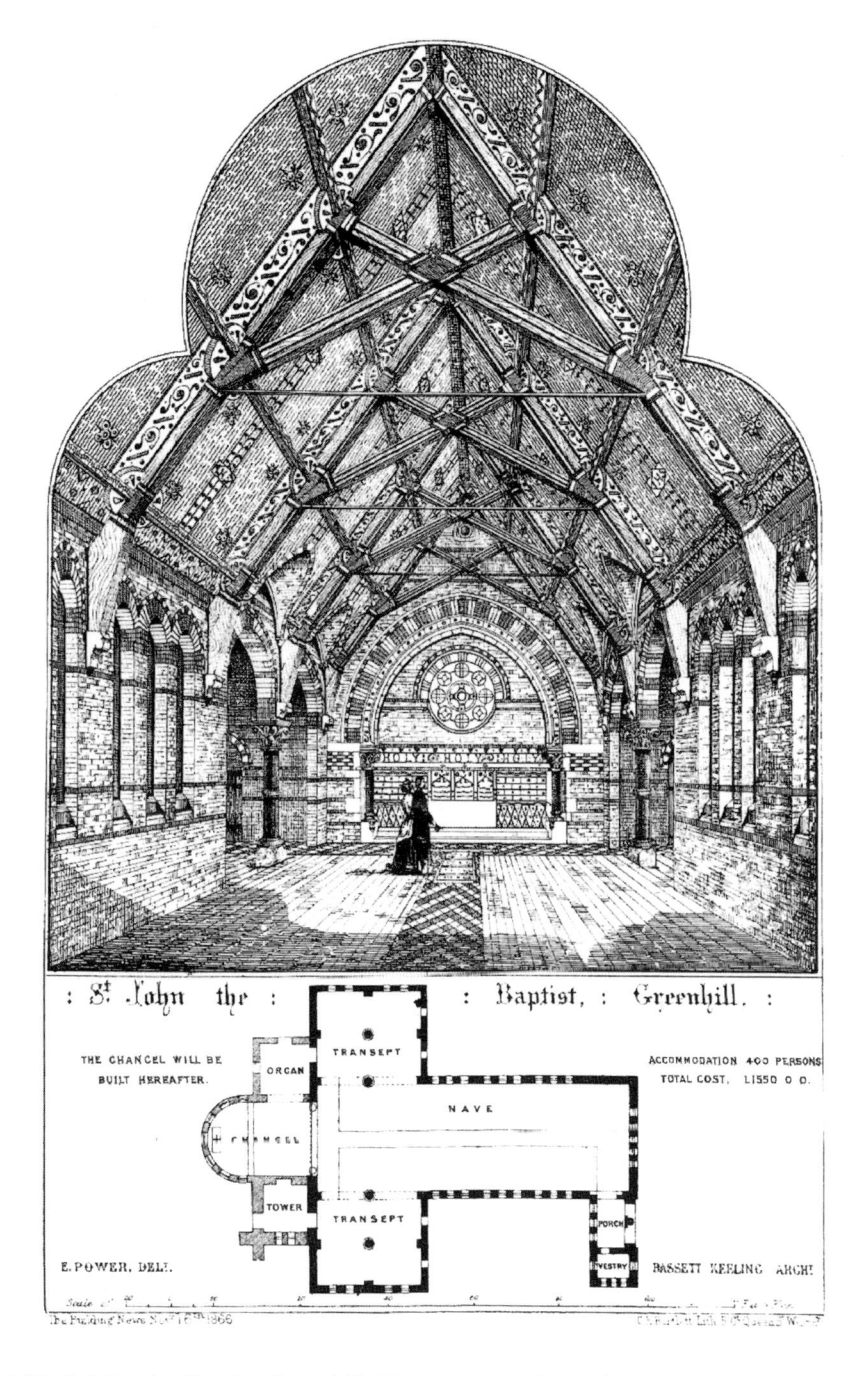

4.12: St John the Baptist, Greenhill, Harrow, 1866, drawn by Edward Power (b. 1840) and lithographed by G.H. Bartlett. (Building News, *13, 1866, 763*.)

CHAPTER 4

from those at Epsom and Dalston mentioned above: these were at Strood, Kent (the spirelet, 1887, and hall, 1898, were added to designs by James William Nash [b.1851][66]); at Reigate, Surrey, in Free Gothic, much gone over by Frederick Boreham (1839/40-1901);[67] and at Scartho,[68] Grimsby, Lincolnshire. In addition, he was responsible for the Wesleyan Day Schools, Southwark; carried out substantial and decorative repairs to the Wesleyan Chapel, St John's Square, Clerkenwell;[69] and submitted a design in a limited competition for a Wesleyan chapel at Kensington which was exhibited in 1863.[70]

Keeling severed his partnership with Tyrie around the time St Paul's, Upper Norwood, was nearing completion, possibly due to the financial problems experienced by the Tyries into which he may have been drawn. Working alone, he was responsible for four more suburban churches: the first was St Andrew's (originally All Saints), Glengall Road, Peckham (1865, consecrated 1866), of ragstone with Bath and Red Mansfield dressings, massive plate-tracery, and nave-arcades carried on short columns of polished red and green Devonshire marble. The elaborate pulpit incorporating marquetry attested to the architect's interest in craftsmanship using wood. Keeling exhibited a fine watercoloured drawing of the church at the Royal Academy in 1867. St Andrew's is now the Celestial Church of Christ.

The next work was the delightful little church (it only sat 400 persons) of St John the Baptist, Sheepcote Road, Greenhill, Harrow (consecrated 1866, but replaced[71] from 1904 as Keeling's structure was not only subsiding, but was too small for a growing congregation), for which Dove Bros were again the contractors, the contract sum being £1,550 (**4.12**). Its short tower with pyramidal cap earned it the nickname of 'candle-snuffer'.[72] Christ Church, Old Kent Road (1867-8), followed, then St Andrew and St Philip, Kensal New Town (1868-70). Of the last building, Pepperell observed that Keeling, 'forbidden the versatility of device he … displayed … elsewhere, has given a free adaptation of early French Gothic',[73] but both churches were badly damaged in the 1939-45 war, and the later building was demolished.

Outside London, apart from chapels, Keeling is known to have designed only one Anglican church, that of St John the Evangelist, West Lane, Killingworth, Northumberland, not far from Newcastle upon Tyne. He was appointed by a committee in May 1866 at the insistence of the incumbent, James Samuel Blair (1830-90), a Yorkshireman, whose wife, Alice Buxton[74] Blair, seems to have been related to the Keeling family, and in any case the Keelings would have been known locally from the days of Isaac Keeling's ministry in Sunderland.[75] St John's survives, but is incomplete, consisting of a nave with south aisle (the north aisle was never built and there is no

BASSETT KEELING (1837-86)

4.13: The Brighton Club, 1863, as designed by Keeling. The use of iron was typical of Keeling's interest in modern techniques, prefabrication, and kits-of-parts. (Building News, *10, 1863, 733*.)

tower nor is there a bellcote), and chancel with polygonal apse. The exterior is of polychromatic masonry with some idiosyncratic detail, and the work of building finished in 1869. Inside the church is a memorial brass to Blair.

Two fine drawings by Keeling, for different churches, are held in the RIBA Library Drawings Collection, but so far their proposed locations have not been determined.[76]

The Strand Music Hall and other disasters

Even before the completion of his first major church, Keeling was appointed architect to two commercial ventures: these were the Strand Music Hall and premises for the the Brighton Club & Norfolk Hotel Co. Ltd.[77] The Brighton venture involved the purchase of the old-established Norfolk Hotel, its remodelling and extension, and the combination of the hotel business with a 'first-class' club (with all facilities found in clubs in London's West End). The *Building News*[78] illustrated the proposed club 'in course of erection' as designed by Keeling (**4.13**), whose initial was incorrectly given as 'J'. All the capital was taken up, but 'the back part only of the buildings' was 'being proceeded with', which suggests that all was not well with the venture. And so it turned out, for Keeling had to sue

CHAPTER 4

4.14: The Strand Music Hall, 1863–4, main façade to The Strand, displaying all the angular spikiness typical of Keeling's work of the early 1860s. (*Building News*, *10, 1863, 869.*)

the company to recover fees, having carried out professional work, yet had been dismissed without being paid: the costs of the project were estimated at £26,000, 'but in fact the work had not been done down to the present time'.[79] In due course the jury at the Court of Common Pleas, Westminster, sitting before Lord Chief Justice Earl, found for Keeling, who was awarded £300, a sum considerably short of the £1,300 he would have expected. Matters are further clouded by a suggestion made in court that Keeling had accepted a Bill of Exchange for £500 'in consideration of' the 'promotors' of the company appointing him architect to build a new hotel on the site of the old one before the company was actually established.[80] This does sound as though someone, somewhere, was trying to work a 'fast one'. After Keeling's dismissal the company appointed Horatio Nelson Goulty (1830-69) architect for 'alterations to Norfolk Hotel', the tender coming in for acceptance at £6,825, a much less ambitious scheme.[81]

If the Brighton Club venture proved an unfortunate connection for Keeling, his involvement with The Strand Music Hall Co. Ltd. was a calamity. The company was formed in 1862 to erect an establishment on the site of the old Exeter Exchange in The Strand,[82] and two architects were appointed: Bassett Keeling and Hyman Henry Collins (1833-1905 – who had commenced independent practice around 1854). Keeling, however, was solely reponsible for the design, as Collins was later very anxious to point out, claiming that he (Collins) was only responsible for 'duties … of a constructional and financial character, together with a general supervision of the works'.[83] Furthermore, Collins stated that he was unsympathetic towards 'Eclectic Design', and although he could testify to the 'almost Herculean labour' Keeling had expended on the work, the great amount of study involved, and the 'intense application' with which Keeling watched the progress of the building, he was 'sure' Keeling would 'take in good part the kindly criticism of those who' thought he had been 'bold in the practice of mistaken rules'.[84] With 'friends' like that, Keeling needed no enemies. It was said of Keeling that 'he knew how to provide places of architectural entertainment for Sundays without either profanity or popery',[85] a reference to his 'Rogue' churches, but the Strand Music Hall was subjected to a continuous barrage of abuse. Some sneered that the building was an attempt to 'adopt the Continental or modern eclectic Gothic feeling, or whatever better name can be found for it', and John Pollard Seddon (1827-1906) mocked 'Acrobatic Gothic',[86] declaring that Keeling had 'played the fool with the recognised styles of architecture', parodying 'its best features' with 'puerilities in the detail', all of which ensured 'grave censure' could not be withheld from the 'author of the eccentricities which are displayed in every portion of this building'. Seddon also accused Keeling of having a 'genius for practical joking', and indeed his entire article is damning in the extreme: the 'hair-stand-on-end style', the 'knobs, bosses, and balls, notches and chamferings with villainous spiky iron-work', 'frantic' notchings, and many more 'faults' were denounced in forthright terms.[87]

Now the façade to The Strand of the Music-Hall was certainly Gothic (**4.14**), and this fact seems to have annoyed commentators. The general contractors were Messrs Trollope of Pimlico, and the carving was by James Tolmie (d. 1866)[88] and James O'Shea (*fl. c.*1845-68), both names to be reckoned with: furthermore, the use of beaten copper to decorate the capitals inside the building drew on Francis Alexander Skidmore's (1816-96) precedents at the University Museum in Oxford, so what had gone so wrong as to arouse such a storm of execration? For the design of the interior (**4.15**) Keeling was not inhibited by the conventional sobriety associated with the British Sunday (although some of his churches were certainly loud and full of 'Go'), and he deliberately set out to be 'original'. The hall was described as a 'palace à l'Aladdin'[89] and much more: some 40 to 50 critical notices appeared in various papers and journals, many of them hiding in cowardly fashion behind pseudonyms. An older or more prudent man might have allowed the criticisms to wash over him, but Keeling, perhaps over-confident (his church designs had not been universally panned by any means), anwered back, and did so with some wit. He poked fun at 'Acrobatic Criticism', and suggested that 'comic talent' had been hired to liven up the po-faced pages of *Building News*.[90] He offered a robust defence of his work, and denounced his critics as 'saturated with pedantry and blinded by dogmatism': his 'poor unfortunate edifice was arraigned before a self-constituted professional tribunal, and charged as a building, but still, being a music-hall' that it was Gothic, that it was not Classic, that it was neither Gothic nor Classic, that it tried to be Gothic, but was not, that it was a practical joke, that it was a serious mistake, that it exactly expressed its purpose, that it did nothing of the kind, and that, being a music hall, it did not bear comparison with 'Mr Woodward's insurance office in Bridge-street, Blackfriars; the half-timbered and weather-tiled houses of Sussex and Kent; St Paul's Cathedral; Mr Webb's shops in Worship-street; Sir C. Barry's West-end clubs; Mr Bodley's churches at Cambridge and Hayward's-heath; Bridgewater-house; and Wren's churches generally'.[91] He would not be forgiven for this outburst.[92]

The condemnations would not have mattered so much to Keeling's career had the music hall been a commercial success. However, John Hollingshead (1825-1904) observed that, 'in spite of its position', it was a 'failure from

4.15: Sectional view of the interior of The Strand Music Hall, London, 1863-4: an extraordinary example of 'Rogue' Gothic and 'Go'. (Building News, *11, 1864, 748*.)

the day of its opening ... The architecture of the place had something to do with it. A decorator's studio, overloaded with samples picked up from all nations was the only thing the place suggested'.[93] The hall closed on 2 December 1866, the contents were auctioned, and the building sold, to be partly reconstructed as the old Gaiety Theatre, but was demolished when Aldwych was created. Apart from the damage to Keeling's reputation, a more immediate problem was his financial involvement in the venture. At the Court of Bankruptcy in Basinghall Street on 17 March 1865, again before Mr Commissioner Holroyd, Keeling (who had been declared bankrupt on 25 January 1865), described as of 1 Verulam Buildings, Gray's Inn, and 3 Napier Terrace, Islington, architect, applied to pass his examination and for an order of discharge, which was granted. Debts were returned for £3,021, inclusive of certain liabilities upon shares, and Keeling 'attributed his difficulties' to losses in connection with the music hall.[94]

CHAPTER 4

The reasons for the opprobrium heaped upon the music hall and its architect were complex. What might have worked for Evangelical Anglican and Wesleyan church-building committees was not necessarily going to work for a music hall. The interior of the building had cast-iron columns, capitals of beaten metal, cast-iron brackets supporting the heavy cornice, raked balcony-rails, an astonishing ceiling with coloured-glass panels set in zinc frames and glass prisms set in the soffits of the hollow ribs, and a stage that defied description. Now some of Keeling's churches also had cast-iron columns or piers, raked balcony-fronts, roofs of frantic carpentry, and bags of structural polychromy in the brickwork, so why were heavy critical guns (albeit often camouflaged by pseudonyms) turned on the hall? The problem seems to have stemmed from attempts to mix medievalism with modernity, traditional with new materials, Gothic with iron and glass, and the application of a style associated with ecclesiastical architecture to a building offering profane, low entertainment.

Bankruptcy must have put enormous strains on Keeling and his family. Apart from Bassett and his wife, there were other mouths to feed and bodies to clothe, including Edgar Bassett Newby Keeling[95] (1860-1916), Gilbert Thomson Keeling (1862-after 1894), and Norman Buxton Keeling (born 1866). After the bankruptcy the family appears to have lived in extremely cramped conditions in Verulam Buildings, Gray's Inn, while Bassett attempted to revive his fortunes by designing more buildings.[96] For a brief period (1870-1) the Post Office *Directories* record that the Keelings lived at 3 Lloyd Square, on the Lloyd Baker Estate in Clerkenwell, and on 7 July 1870 an oak reading-desk, a music-stool, and a presentation copper inkstand designed by Keeling were exhibited at 9 Conduit Street. Sambrook and I indicated that Keeling's career (and indeed whereabouts) became somewhat obscure in the early 1870s, but since we carried out our preliminary studies, some further information has come to light. For example, in 1871 Keeling responded to a criticism of a 'panel in marquetrie executed by W. Clayton from designs by Mr. E. Bassett Keeling' which somebody had denounced as 'crude and inharmonious in colour'. Keeling stated he had 'no knowledge of W. Clayton', and suggested that 'surreptitious use' had been made of one of three drawings made by him (the only ones he had ever made for marquetry work) for panels for the pulpit of St Andrew's church, Camberwell, and which had been made by one Steinitz of Camberwell Hall,[97] so he could hardly be blamed for defects in works not realised under his supervision.

Keeling resigned from his membership of the RIBA in 1872, and it seems he may have attempted to make money designing artefacts for workshops, and indeed he could have been responsible for starting the firm that became

Keeling, Edgar, & Co., with which his son, Edgar Bassett Newby Keeling, was involved from the age of 19 or 20. According to Keeling's obituary in *The Architect*,[98] he was for a time 'headmaster of a local school of art', but its location has proved elusive: Sambrook and I thought this might have been in the Leeds area, but we had no success in establishing this, and subsequently I have formed the opinion that Keeling was involved in design (with possibly some teaching), manufacture, and property speculation in London. We do know that he submitted designs for the Metropolitan Railway Building Competition, Faringdon Road Estate, which he won in 1871: his proposals were described in architectural magazines.[99] Keeling had a business address at 22 Basinghall Street from 1876, and remained there until 1881: for a brief period (1877-8) he was in partnership with George Vidgeon Jebb Blackburne (d.1928).[100]

Another son was born to Bassett and Mary Keeling in 1875: this was Cyril Bernard Keeling,[101] whose birth certificate reveals the family inhabited Norfolk Villas, Bulwer Road, Chipping Barnet, Hertfordshire (now subsumed into Barnet, London), and thereafter the Keelings appear to have lived in the northern suburbs of London. In 1879 they[102] resided at 19 Aden Grove, Green Lanes, Stoke Newington, and from 1882 at Dunwood House,[103] 5 Paradise Row (now part of Stoke Newington Church Street), but in 1882 Keeling practised from 10 King's Arms Yard, Lothbury, and from 1883 until his death his office address was 2 Tokenhouse Buildings,[104] King's Arms Yard, Lothbury, a building he himself designed and where he achieved a remarkably styleless architecture: it was faced with cold-moulded Lascelles's patent cement, a substitute for the more expensive terracotta (**4.16**), and in the 1880s he also experimented with white glazed bricks, faïence,[105] fireproofing, iron structural elements, and various patent cements, so he must be considered as an innovator.

Final Years

The last phase of Keeling's life started in 1878 with an action tried in the Bloomsbury County Court, before Mr Judge Russell, in which Keeling was the plaintiff, suing the defendant, one Lake, to recover a fee of seven guineas for making plans for some proposed bank buildings in Great Russell Street. Blackburne is mentioned as Keeling's 'former partner', and Keeling won his case with costs.[106] From this time he specialised in the design of commercial buildings and housing: his work owed very little to his spiky ecclesiastical buildings of the 1860s. One of his first essays of this period to be noticed was 16 Tokenhouse Yard, Lothbury (1880), where he filled an awkwardly shaped site with an ingeniously planned building incorporating

CHAPTER 4

4.16: Tokenhouse Buildings, King's Arms Yard, 1881-2, where Keeling had his own office, from a sketch by John Sambrook, 1973. (*Author's collection.*)

a stepped curved-glass and metal structure at the rear to admit light and air: so unusually innovative was the design that *The Builder* accorded it considerable coverage[107] (**4.17, 4.18**). It was from 10 King's Arms Yard, Lothbury, that Keeling applied for Fellowship of the Surveyors' Institution in 1881 (he also gave the Dunwood House, Clissold Park, Stoke Newington,

4.17: No.16 Tokenhouse Yard, Lothbury, 1880, Telegraph Street front. (*The Builder, 39, 1880, 204.*)

Chapter 4

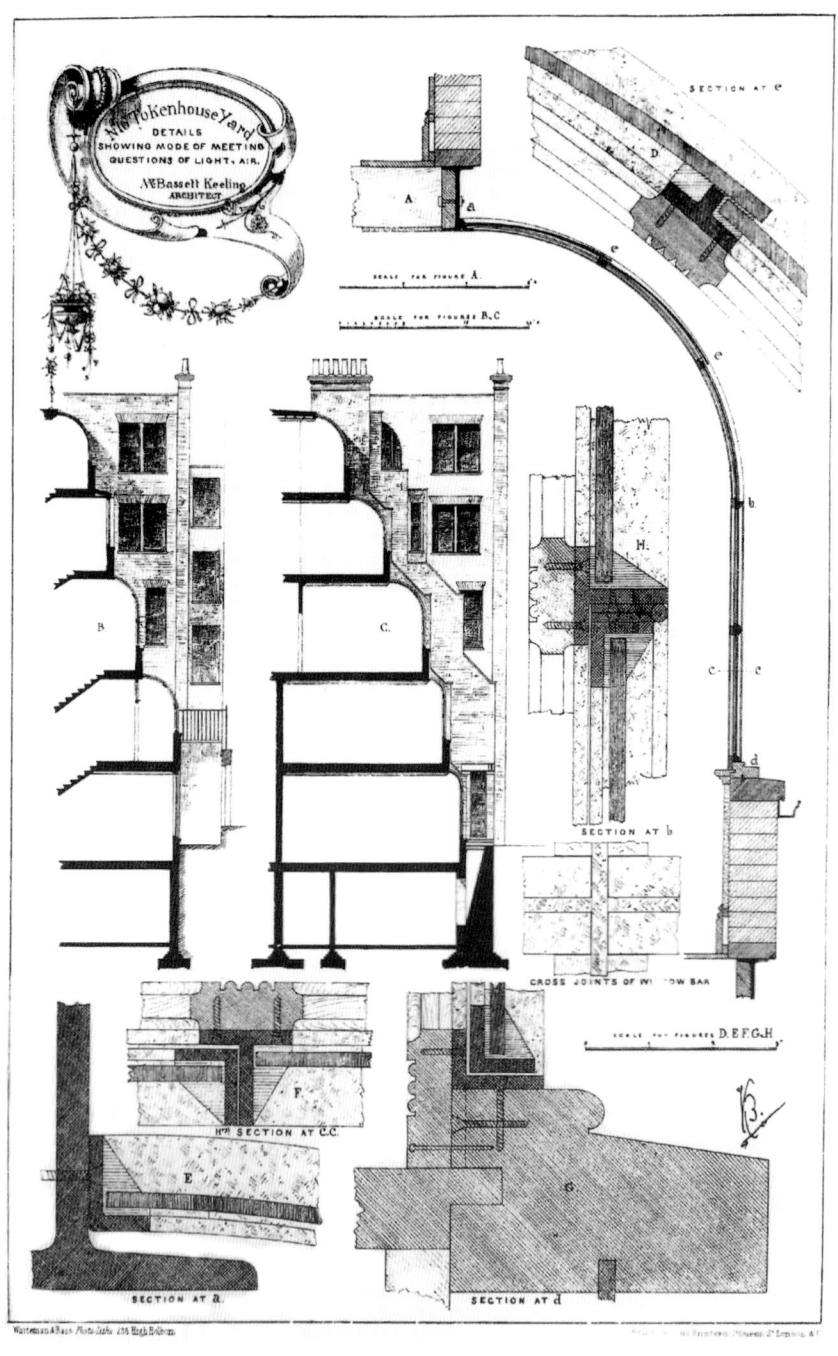

4.18: Details showing Mode of Meeting Questions of Light and Air, no. 16 Tokenhouse Yard. (The Builder, *39, 1880, 206.*)

address), and was proposed by Edward I'Anson (1812-88), his seconders being George Barnes Williams (1817-87),[108] Robert Vigers (1826-1912), Allan Francis Vigers (1858-1923), Ralph Clutton (1843-1912), and Charles Barry (1823-1900), all of whom had close connections with the City of London: he was duly elected in 1882.[109]

In the late 1870s and early 1880s Keeling's convivial nature led him to join the Urban Club which met in the rooms over St John's Gate, Clerkenwell: this 'association of gentlemen connected with literature, arts, sciences, and professions' had been established in 1858 under the name of 'The Friday Knights' because the Club (which was named after 'Sylvanus Urban', editor of the *Gentleman's Magazine*) met on Friday evenings for 'discussion of familiar subjects'.[110] Keeling himself delivered an affectionate valedictory poem at the last dinner before the Club vacated the Gate (its home for the previous 21 years) in 1879.[111] He also provided verses on the occasion of the annual 'Boar's Head Feast' at Ashley's Hotel, Maiden Lane, Covent Garden, on 16 January 1880, the first dinner held by the Club[112] after it had removed itself from the Gate, and a eulogy upon William Shakespeare on 23 April 1880. Keeling proposed the Toast of 'Art' at one dinner, which was printed in full.[113] Such conviviality, however, was not without its outgoings, and Keeling seems to have been somewhat extravagant, travelling to and from home in a cab, thereby earning the nickname 'Bird of Paradise' among cabbies.[114]

Tragedy struck again when Mary Newby Keeling died in December 1882 at Dunwood House aged 41, the cause of her demise being 'General debility Shock after Childbirth and Post partum Hæmorrhage'.[115] The 'informant' was Gilbert Keeling. The child born in 1882 was Bassett Keeling, but he died in 1884 aged '1 year 5 months' at 5 Paradise Row, with his father present at the death, the cause of which was 'Leucocythemia[116] 2 months' with 'sudden convulsions'.[117] Both Mary and young Bassett Keeling were buried in Abney Park Cemetery.[118]

Keeling produced several designs at this time apart from the interesting and inventive buildings off Lothbury. One project was the huge eight-storey Princes Mansions, Victoria and Palace Streets, Westminster (**4.19**), intended as 'residences in flats for the aristocratic and affluent classes',[119] the elevations of red brick and Lascelles's Patent Concrete (coloured to resemble seasoned Mansfield stone) 'very freely introduced throughout the frontage from the ground line to the surmounting dormers ... Each block has separate entrances consisting of double-arched projecting porches in elaborately moulded stone ... All floors ... of iron griders and cement' were intended to be fire- and sound-proof,[120] and the latest thing in hydraulic

CHAPTER 4

lifts gave access to the various floors (in addition to fire-proofed stairs). The journals of the period announced that the architect was 'Mr Bassett Keeling FSI' of 'Tokenhouse Buildings, Lothbury'. The contractors for this 'immense pile',[121] part of which was built over the Metropolitan District Railway, erected on land owned by the Ecclesiastical Commissioners, were 'Messrs Perry & Co., of Tredegar Works, Bow', and the total cost was around £168,500.

His last major building was on an acutely angled site between Northumberland Avenue and Craven Street, begun 1884, to be entirely used 'for the requirements of the Admiralty', the elevations being of Bath stone and polished granite. For this project Keeling collaborated with the architects George Dennis Martin (1850-after 1894) and Edward Keynes Purchase (1862-1923), and the contractors were again Perry & Co.:[122] it demonstrates how competent Victorian architects could make use of every square inch on a very tight, narrow site.

Two of Keeling's sons, Cyril Bernard and Percy, were sent to a boarding-school in Margate after their mother died, and a touching letter from him to them, dated 30 May 1886, survives in the family archive,[123] in which he wrote of the benefits of the sea air and that a small school would be a

4.19: Princes Mansions, Victoria Street, Westminster, 1884 (dem.), photograph c.1890. (*Author's collection*.)

4.20: The Jerusalem Coffee House, 1879-80: printed from three drawings signed by Keeling. (The Builder, *39, 1880, 80.*)

happier experience than he had endured at a 'large public School of over a hundred boys': he also observed that his childhood home 'lacked many of the the tender associations with which' Cyril and Percy would 'look back to dear old Dunwood', which perhaps explains to some degree his love of conviviality.

Keeling died at 5 Paradise Row on 30 October 1886, aged 49, following hæmatemesis lasting 36 hours, the final stage of cirrhosis of the liver.[124] Present at his death was his son, Norman Buxton Keeling, and the body was interred on 4 November 1886 in Abney Park Cemetery in the same plot occupied by his wife and child. No trace of any memorial has been found, and the grave appears to have been re-used. His passing was reported in several papers and journals,[125] and mention made of the New Jerusalem Coffee House at Cowper's Court, Cornhill (**4.20**), the Auction Market Restaurant,

Chapter 4

Tokenhouse Yard (in the basement of 'Mr Somers Clarke's fine building'[126]), and, of course, Tokenhouse Buildings, which seems to have caught the eye of more than one serious critic. *The Builder* also mentioned the Strand Music Hall and the barrage of abuse heaped upon it, but nevertheless the hall 'had the merit of originality and effectiveness, and it was not only at the time something novel in its way, but had even some influence on the style of other buildings erected soon after it; and it is not every architect who could say that of one of his works'.[127] Quite so.

The Keeling saga did not end there, for Gilbert Thompson Keeling attempted to carry on his father's practice from Tokenhouse Buildings. Bassett Keeling had been consulted by a Thomas Sterling (or Stirling) Begbie (1822-99),[128] of Walbrook, concerning the design of a National Concert Hall on a site at Vauxhall Bridge Road, and subsequently a company was formed to build it: it was agreed that if Bassett Keeling were successful in 'forwarding' the sale of the site he was to receive £500, but this would be waived if he were appointed architect to the company. Gilbert Thompson Keeling then prepared plans for a hall estimated to cost £80,000, with £60,000 for the site, but was unable to obtain any fees, and was offered £75 'to get rid of him', as it was claimed Keeling senior had prepared these plans before his death. Keeling, who discovered from advertisements that the architects, George & Peto,[129] had been appointed architects for the hall, then brought an action for non-payment of £1,500 in fees due to him, and at the Lord Mayor's Court, 16 March 1888, the jury found in Keeling's favour, but he was only awarded £500.[130] Shortly after this episode, Gilbert Keeling abandoned architecture, and became a tram-driver in Ramsgate. Bassett Keeling, who did not leave a will, left a personal estate of only £209 0s, 6d.. plus some interests in property, and the letter of administration regarding the estate was granted to Gilbert Thompson Keeling on 4 December 1886.[131]

As the late Gordon Lansdowne Barnes (1917-85) once observed to me: 'Poor Old Bassett Keeling'.

Dedication
This essay is dedicated to the memory of John Sambrook (1933-2001).

Abbreviations
B   *The Builder*
BN   *Building News*
ILN   *Illustrated London News*
RIBA   Royal Institute of British Architects

Notes

1. This essay is based on research carried out in the early 1970s and late 1990s by John Sambrook and myself, culminating in three papers by us: two appeared in *Architectural History*, 16, 1973, 60-9, pls 26-31; and 42, 1999, 307-15; and one in *The Architect*, 2, 1972, 40-2. An article by me appeared in *Country Life*, 180, 1986, 1030-2. I am grateful to John Sambrook's widow, Isabelle, for passing on his notes to add to my own for the purposes of this essay. I also acknowledge help given by Bernard Stanley (Keeling's great-grandson, who was kindly introduced to me by Sir Nikolaus Pevsner), Lucas Elkin of Cambridge University Library, Jeremy Smith of London Metropolitan Archives, and Simon Edwards of the RIBA Library & Information Services.
2. Microfilm copy in the County Record Office, Durham County Council: ex info. Dr W.A.L. Seaman, then County Archivist.
3. Born Newcastle-under-Lyme, Staffordshire, died Ripon, West Riding of Yorkshire. *See*, for Isaac Keeling, *Minutes of Conference ... of People Called Methodist,* London: Conference Office, 1870, 6-8. Reference from Dr P. Nockles, John Rylands University Library, Manchester.
4. In 1837 Keeling's brother, Ralph, accepted an invitation to 'labour amongst' the Methodists of Sans Street, and became Chairman of Chapel Meetings as well as Acting Superintendent of the Circuit when Isaac was called elsewhere in 1839.
5. Ex info. by Dr P. Nockles.
6. As n. 3.
7. *See* Isaac Keeling, *Sermons ... With Memorials of his Life, Character, and Correspondence* by Mrs [(M.A.] Smallpage & G.R. Osborn, W. Willan (eds), Hamilton Adams, 1871.
8. Incorrectly given as 'Leese' in previous notes on Keeling (it was assumed that the 'f' was a long 's').
9. The Census returns reveal he was born in New Malton, North Riding of Yorkshire, that he married late, that he lived in Torquay in 1891, and was an engineer. Interested in electricity and other applied scientific matters, he gave papers to learned societies during his time in Leeds. Dresser was listed in local Leeds directories from 1842 to 1882-3 (ex info. 26 Oct. 1972 by A.B. Craven, City Librarian, Leeds).
10. C. Webster, 'The Architectural Profession in Leeds, 1800-50: a case study in provincial practice', *Architectural History*, 38, 1995, 176-91. Dresser, however, does *not* appear to have been closely related to the more famous Christopher Dresser (1834-1904).
11. *A Report of the Proceedings at the Annual Conversazione, held at the ... Mechanic's Institution and Literary Society, June 3rd, 1857,* Charles Goodall for Leeds School of Art, 1857, 11. Reference from Mrs A.D. Fell, at the time Assistant Librarian, Leeds Polytechnic, 14 Nov. 1972.
12. Form A, the Surveyors' Institution, General No. 695, sessional no. 71, 1881-2.
13. Upper Terrace was on the east side of Upper Street, between Cross and Florence Streets.
14. His recommendation for Associateship was read on 5 Dec. 1859.
15. The Institute received the Royal Charter of Incorporation in 1837, but was not

CHAPTER 4

authorised to add 'Royal' until 1866.
16. Knighted 1869.
17. Antonia Brodie *et al.*, *Directory of British Architects 1834-1914*, 1, Continuum, 2001, 1054-5; RIBA Nomination Papers A, iii, 59, fiche ref. 5/E2. Keeling's registration-number was 1834, 82. See *R.I.B.A. Notices* and *Proceedings* (1859-60, 1871-2).
18. The Newbys were from Cartmel, north Lancashire (now Cumbria): there is a funerary monument (1834-45 – by Fawcet of Lancaster and Liverpool [*fl.* 1834-70]) to James Newby (d. 1834) and his family in Cartmel Priory.
19. Mary Newby Harrison was born on 6 Nov. 1841: her mother was Frances Ann Harrison (*c.* 1820-*c.* after 1851), formerly Newby, and her father, William Gallimore Harrison (*c.* 1812-after 1861), was described as a 'Farmer' on the birth certificate dated 6 Dec. 1841, sub-district Endon & Norton, Registration District of Leek, Staffordshire.
20. Harrison was described as a 'Silk Merchant', of Dunwood Lodge, Longsdon, Leek, Staffordshire (1841 Census, PRO ref: HO 107, 1005), which contradicts 'Farmer' in the birth certificate of the same year. In the 1851 Census (PRO ref: HO 107, 2008. fol.126) a Walter Keeling, aged 15, born in Etruria, Staffordshire, was staying with the Harrisons at Dunwood Lodge, so it would appear the two families knew each other (in 1851 Harrison became a 'Retired Silk Merchant', and at the 1861 Census he was a 'Land Proprietor') (PRO ref: RG9, 1945, fol.18). Several members of the Keeling clan lived in Etruria in the mid-nineteenth century.
21. But omitted any number.
22. RG9/138 (p. 63), 16 Apr. 1861. Keeling was recorded as 'Mar.' and as 24 years old, which fits his date of birth.
23. Details from the marriage and birth certificates.
24. Post Office *Directories* at the Guildhall Library, City of London.
25. *B*, 19, 1861, 132T.
26. Post Office *Directories* at the Guildhall Library, City of London, but these were a year out of date on publication.
27. When working on the *Northern Kensington* volume of the *Survey of London* I visited Dove Bros, and found the firm still possessed contract drawings for several Keeling buildings, some of which are reproduced in this essay. Sambrook and I looked through them, noting Keeling's emphatic draughtsmanship. Many drawings were photographed at my expense, and others by the Greater London Council Photographic Unit of the Department of Architecture & Civic Design (these are now in the London Metropolitan Archives), although the drawings themselves are now in the RIBA Library Drawings Collection.
28. *BN*, 11, 1864, 952; *B*, 23, 1865, 18.
29. Illustrated in Curl & Sambrook, 1973 [n. 1], fig. 26a.
30. *B*, 21, 1863, 866.
31. *B*, 20, 1862, 790.
32. F.H.W. Sheppard (gen. ed.), *Survey of London*, 37, *Northern Kensington*, Athlone Press for the GLC, 1973, 245-7 and *passim*; Curl & Sambrook, 1973 [n. 1], 60-9, fig. 27.

33. *BN*, 17, 1869, 121.
34. Ibid.
35. *B*, 20, 1862, p. 790. According to the printed catalogues of Architectural Exhibitions in Conduit Street, Keeling submitted three exhibits relating to St Mark's church (ex info. my former colleague, Peter Bezodis).
36. N. Pevsner, *The Buildings of England: London except the Cities of London and Westminster,* Penguin, 1952, 299.
37. The faculties were dated 1896 and 1905, and the strengthening of the structure took place (1954-5) under the direction of Milner & Craze. Ex info. Romilly Bernard Craze (1892-1974), the professional partner from 1931 of Sir William Frederick Victor Mordaunt Milner (1896-1960), 8th Baronet from 1931.
38. H.S. Goodhart-Rendel, 'Rogue Goths of the Victorian Era', *Journal of the RIBA*, 3rd ser., 56/6, 1949, 251-9.
39. *BN*, 10, 1863, 716.
40. *BN*, 11, 1864, 560.
41. H. Hobhouse (ed.), *Survey of London*, 42, *Southern Kensington: Kensington Square to Earl's Court,* Athone Press for the GLC, 1986, 375-8.
42. The job would appear to have gone to Keeling through his Methodist connections, but it is significant that Keeling's cousin, Henry (b. *c.* 1834 – whose father, Enoch [b. *c.* 1791], was cashier to the Wedgwood factory at Etruria, Hanley, Stoke-on-Trent), was a 'Chemist and Druggist' at Epsom: in 1862 was born in Epsom a boy, also named Enoch, son of Henry and Mary (b. *c.* 1836 – *née* Miles) Keeling. Information from 1841 and 1861 Census returns and birth certificates.
43. *BN*, 10, 1863, 736-7, reported it was 'in course of erection', was polychrome (local bricks, 'relieved by bands of black and blue Staffordshire bricks, with Bath stone dressings'), producing 'a pleasing picturesqueness and warmth of effect', and cost £1,300. It ceased to function as a chapel in the early years of the twentieth century, and passed to the Ancient Order of Foresters in 1914 when a new Wesleyan complex was completed on a different site. Keeling's building was demolished in the 1970s.
44. Tyrie's address is given as 1 Verulam Buildings, Gray's Inn, and The Ivors, Norbiton, Kingston, Surrey, in the Court Section of the 1865 *Directory* held in Guildhall Library, City of London. Thereafter, his history is obscure. His father was David Tyrie (*c.* 1799-1862), described as 'Gentleman', 'Merchant', and 'Stockbroker' in directories, certificates, etc., whose last address was 4 The Crescent, Camden Road Villas, Islington (re-numbered as 151 Camden Road). The 1841 Census shows that the Tyries still lived in Edmonton, and that there were several children, including James Edward Tyrie (b. *c.* 1835) and John Richard Tyrie: James Edward Tyrie, stockjobber in the City, of 30 Cornhill, and Knight's Hill, Norwood, was bankrupted on 9 June 1865 (*The Times,* 17 June, 7 July, and 16 Dec. 1865), and discharged in 1866 (*The Times,* 9 May 1866, 12, col. 3, and 7 Dec. 1866, 9 col. b).
45. *ILN*, 1245, 13 Feb. 1864, 147.
46. *BN*, 11, 1864, 560.
47. W. Pepperell, *The Church Index: A Book of Metropolitan Churches and Church*

Chapter 4

       Enterprise, W. Wells Gardner, 1872, 33-4.
48. *BN*, 11, 1864, 560.
49. Records of the Church Commissioners, file 28273, and ex info. Romilly B. Craze.
50. *ILN*, 1289, 26 Nov. 1864, 527.
51. *West London Observer,* 26 Nov. 1864, 4c.
52. James Thorne (1815-81) in *BN*, 11, 1864, 901.
53. *BN*, 11, 1864, 560.
54. *BN*, 11, 1864, 726.
55. Part was removed as early as 12 Mar. 1885. The side galleries were excised by a faculty of June 1897: their removal (on the grounds that they were 'never occupied in the evenings', and that with their absence the 'cleanliness, ventilation, and facilities for warming would be greatly increased') destabilised the structure.
56. Pevsner [n. 36], 244.
57. The alterations to the arcades, removal of the galleries, and obliteration of Keeling's polychrome decorations were carried out under the direction of Arthur Heron Ryan-Tenison (1861-1930), who ought to have known better. See B.F.L. Clarke, *Parish Churches of London,* Batsford, 1966, 107. Canon Clarke said of the interior that it had been 'completely de-Keelingised'.
58. *ILN*, 1395, 1866, 392.
59. Ibid.
60. Vining seems to have moved house every two or three years: in 1856-8 he was at Orsett House, Orsett Place (later Orsett Terrace), Westbourne Terrace; in 1859-61 he lived at 4 The Crescent, Camden Road Villas, where David Tyrie also resided from 1861 until his death; in 1862-5 Vining's abode was 15 Dulwich Road, Forest Hill; and from 1866 he lived at Prospect Villas, London Road, Forest Hill.
61. *The Times,* 17 June, 7 July, and 16 Dec. 1865. The address is given on p. 11 col. 4 in the issue of the last date. The case is recorded in the Alphabetical Declarations of Insolvency, vol. B6, 80, 108-11, in P.R.O., and Tyrie hearings took place in the Court at Basinghall Street presided over by Mr Commissioner Holroyd, who also presided on 6 Dec. 1866 at which Tyrie's debts were stated to be 'about £14,000', an enormous sum then.
62. *The Times,* 7 Dec. 1866, 9, col. 6.
63. *B*, 22, 1864, 520; *BN*, 11, 1864, 532.
64. *B*, 22, 1864, 590, under the heading 'Dissenting Church Building News'.
65. *The Architect's, Engineer's, & Building Trades Directory,* Wyman & Sons, 1868.
66. J. Newman, *The Buildings of England: West Kent and the Weald,* Penguin, 1976, 552, where Keeling is not mentioned. The building was sold for redevelopment in the 1970s.
67. I. Nairn & N. Pevsner, rev. B. Cherry, *The Buildings of England: Surrey,* Penguin, 1971, 430, again with no mention of Keeling.
68. Neither this building nor Keeling feature in N. Pevsner & J. Harris, revised by N. Antram, *The Buildings of England: Lincolnshire,* Penguin, 1989.
69. *B*, 24, 1866, 568. 1848-9, designed by James Wilson of Bath (1816-1900), but destroyed in the 1939-45 war.

70. Printed catalogues of the Architectural Exhibitions in Conduit Street, 1863. Information provided by Peter Bezodis.
71. To designs first of all by John Samuel Alder (1848-1919) in a thinnish Second Pointed style, extended in 1925 to designs by Alder & Turrill (the latter being John Turrill).
72. W.W. Druett, *Harrow through the Ages*, King & Hutchings, 1956, with later edn S. R. Publishers, 1971. *See* also *Harrow Gazette Local Intelligencer*, 4 Oct. 1865, 1 Mar. 1866, 1 June 1866, and G. Rowles, *History of the Parish of St John the Baptist, Greenhill*, Rowles, 1954.
73. Pepperell [n. 47], 4.
74. Bassett and Mary Keeling's son, Norman Buxton Keeling, was born in 1866: the address given on the birth certificate is Verulam Buildings, Gray's Inn.
75. Ex info. Revd Jeremy Sampson, incumbent in 1972.
76. Reproduced in Curl & Sambrook (1999) [n. 1], 310. The drawings are identified as Y14/19.1&2.
77. The Brighton Club and Norfolk Hotel Company (Limited) advertised for shares in the *Brighton Gazette & Lewes Observer*, 2212, 6 Aug. 1863, 1, col. 2, stating its 'Temporary Offices' were at 2 Guildhall Chambers, City, and 107 King's Road, Brighton.
78. *BN*, 10, 1863, 732-3.
79. *BN*, 11, 1864, 121.
80. *The Times*, 11 Feb.1864, 10, col. 6.
81. *BN*, 11, 1864, 391. *See* also *Brighton Gazette,* 6 Aug. 1863, 4, col. 6; ibid., 3 Sep. 1863, 5, col. 3. Goulty had Nonconformist connections, and was related to John Nelson Goulty (d.1870), a well known Minister.
82. *BN*, 10, 1863, 868; *B*, 20, 1862, 768.
83. *BN*, 11, 1864, 795.
84. Ibid.
85. Goodhart-Rendel [n. 38], 256.
86. *BN*, 11, 1864, 780.
87. *BN*, 14, 1867, 97-8.
88. *BN*, 10, 1863, 868.
89. *BN*, 11, 1864, 811.
90. Ibid.
91. *BN*, 11, 1864, 864.
92. J.S. Curl, *Victorian Architecture: Diversity & Invention*, Spire Books, 2007, 235-42.
93. J. Hollingshead, *Gaiety Chronicles,* Archibald Constable, 1898, 18.
94. *The Times,* 18 Mar. 1865, 13, col. 5; *London Gazette*, 31 Jan. 1865, 486; 28 Apr. 1865, 2305.
95. According to the directories held in the Guildhall Library, City of London, the firm of Keeling, Edgar, & Co., Mediæval and Art Metal Workers, Gas-Fitting Manufacturers, and Brassfounders, was in business at 14 Elm Street, Gray's Inn, in 1881, and by 1888 the firm was called Keeling (Edgar), Teale, & Co. (Art Metal Workers, Hardwood Door Manufacturers, Etc., Wholesale & Export). The firm continued at Elm Street until at least 1894, and by 1900 was relocated at Ravenscourt Square, Hammersmith, where it remained until *c.*1906, then in

CHAPTER 4

1914-15 it was at 92 Twyford Avenue, Acton, and presumably folded shortly after the start of the 1914-18 war.

96. These included 'Model Cottages at Stratford; Mansions and Villas at Willesden; and other Private Works', according to *The Architect's, Engineer's, & Building Trades' Directory*. A tender of £1,185 for a detached villa on the Stonebridge Park Estate, Willesden, designed by Keeling, was accepted in 1868 (*B*, 26, 1868, 200).
97. *BN*, 19, 1871, 78, 154.
98. *The Architect*, 36, 1886, 294.
99. *BN*, 20, 1871, 193.
100. In 1874 George Hugh Spencer Blackburne (d.1920), son of G.V.J. Blackburne, architect, and his wife, Emma (they married in the new church of St Matthew, West Kensington, in October 1872), was baptised in Christ Church, Fulwood, near Preston, Lancashire. G.V.J. Blackburne, son of William George Blackburne and Harriet Jebb, had an address at 12 Blomfield Street, EC2, in 1880, but thereafter emigrated to Australia, where he became a clergyman (*see* Index to Ecclesiastical [Wills] Files 1926-30: Supreme Court, Brisbane, Australia). G.H.S. Blackburne became Medical Officer and Bacteriologist in Western Australia, and is buried in Albany Memorial Cemetery. I acknowledge the help of A.E. Clarkson in this matter.
101. Grandfather of Bernard Stanley.
102. There were several daughters as well: Minnie, Lucy, Julie, Maggie, and Ada.
103. An allusion to the Staffordshire home of the Harrisons.
104. In 1884 Dove Bros and Horace Dove, auctioneer, had an office at 4 Tokenhouse Buildings.
105. A fine example of Keeling's use of Burmantofts Leeds faïence was at the 'White House', Telegraph Street, Moorgate, shown in 'Rambling Sketches 1883' by Thomas Raffles Davison (1853-1937) (*British Architect*, 20, 1883, 173, with a description on 172).
106. *B*, 36, 1878, 521.
107. *B*, 39, 1880, 204-15. The rear elevations were faced with white glazed bricks, and the two fronts were of Portland and Corsehill red sandstone to the height of the first floor, with kiln-burnt red brickwork above. The contractors were Charles Aldin & Sons.
108. Of Frederick's Place, Old Jewry, London EC.
109. n. 12.
110. W.J. Pinks, *The History of Clerkenwell*, edited by E.J. Wood, Charles Herbert, 1880, 257.
111. Ibid., 27.
112. For the Urban Club, *see* John Jeremiah, *Notes on Shakespeare, and Memorials of The Urban Club*, Clayton & Co., 1876.
113. Sir J.R.S.Vine & W.E. Church, *A Record of The Urban Club and its Old Home at St John's Gate, Clerkenwell. With a Report of the Club's 21st Annual Dinner*, Waterlow & Sons, for The Urban Club, 1879 [this date is probably 1880], 16-18.
114. Ex inf. Bernard Stanley 26 Mar. 1974.
115. Death certificate. Mary Keeling was probably worn out: by the time of her death she had had at least ten children.

116. Leucocythemia, leucocythæmia, leuchæmia, or leucæmia is a desease in which the white corpuscles of the blood are greatly increased in number, with enlargement of the spleen and lymphatic glands, and changes in bone-marrow: it was sometimes called 'splenic anæmia'.
117. Death certificate.
118. In grave no. 72467 section L.9, 5th row (ref. 283E 62669 Gregory).
119. *B*, 46, 1884, 912.
120. Ibid.
121. *B*, 51, 1886, 232.
122. *B*, 46 1884, 668; *The Architect*, 37, 1887, 81. This was plot 21, and various changes to the designs were reported in the Minutes of the Works and General Purposes Committee of the Metropolitan Board of Works, vol. 102 (10 Dec. 1883-10 Mar. 1884), 187 items 80-1, 306, item 47, 442, item 50.
123. I owe this to Bernard Stanley, son of Fanny Gladys Ann Keeling (daughter of Cyril Bernard Keeling) and Joseph Stanley.
124. Death certificate. Members of the family confirm that Keeling was a very heavy drinker, and it is likely his convivial disposition together with his bereavements and financial problems exacerbated intemperate habits; nevertheless, 49 is very young to succumb to drink, so Keeling may have suffered other medical complications.
125. *B*, 51, 1886, p. 753; *British Architect*, 26, 1886, 483 (which states that Keeling 'enjoyed an extensive City practice'); *The Times*, 12 Nov. 1886, first entry in the deaths column.
126. No. 7 Lothbury (completed 1866-7), designed by George Somers Clarke (1825-82) in the Venetian Gothic style. Keeling's restaurant (destroyed) was decorated with Burmantofts faïence, and was much praised in the journals of the day. See *British Architect*, 21, 1884, 101-2, 114.
127. *B*, 51, 1886, 753.
128. Begbie had interests in shipping, and was a blockade-runner during the American Civil War, sailing close to the wind on several occasions.
129 Ernest George (1839-1922), in partnership 1876-90 with Harold Ainsworth Peto (1854-1933). See *Morning Post,* 26 Jan. 1888, 4, and 27 Jan. 1888, 6; *Standard*, 24 Jan. 1888, 6.
130 *Estates Gazette*, 31 Mar. 1888, 169, 173.
131 P.R. 17290 Mddx. Act. 32A.

5.1: St Andrew, Roker, County Durham, 1906–7, interior. (*Ruth Baumberg*.)

# 5

Edward Schroeder Prior (1852-1932): rogue architect?

Stewart Abbott

> ... artistic and personal individuality, reference to vernacular architecture, respect for materials, and love of nature are the threads that run through Prior's writings and architecture; and they provide the basis for understanding his life and work.[1]

The legacy of Edward Schroeder Prior is extensive and, in addition to a succession of ground-breaking buildings, includes publications, educational work, and a major contribution to the intellectual debate about style and materials via his role in the Art Workers' Guild. However, today he is largely unknown outside a small group of admirers and academics. He is best-remembered for his church of St Andrew at Roker, Co. Durham, and his butterfly-plan houses built in Devon and Norfolk.[2] There has, to date, been no major published study of his achievements even though he had a lasting influence in the first half of the twentieth century through his work in the training of architects as the Slade Professor of Fine Art at Cambridge (1912-32). J. Mordaunt Crook, in *The Dilemma of Style*, refers to the Roker church (**5.1**) as part of a new phase of the Gothic Revival

CHAPTER 5

dominated by the principles of the Arts and Crafts Movement: 'Late medieval English prototypes were synthesised, abstracted, harmonised with modern materials, and fused with ingenuity and passion.'[3] It is this very eclectic mix of influences that makes Prior of interest to us today as his work can now be viewed as forming links between the Gothic Revival, the Arts and Crafts Movement and emerging ideas of Modernism that would be developed in the first half of the twentieth century. When re-assessing his significance in this essay it is the recorded working processes of Prior combined with his 'history' publications and educational legacy that are of more interest than the outward visual and stylistic characteristics of his buildings which may appear to be eccentric and appear not to conform to a clear recognisable style in the context of nineteenth-century definitions.

It appears to be the stylistic nonconformity or wilful visual characteristics of his buildings that led to his being labelled a 'rogue' architect by H.S. Goodhart-Rendel in a paper given at the RIBA on 8 March 1949.[4] Goodhart-Rendel puts Prior's qualification to be considered a rogue as showing a 'brave and constant egregiousness that makes it impossible to regard him as a school man in any sense.'[5] Today we have developed a different understanding of the concept of individuality, but Goodhart-Rendel is pointing to conformity as an 'accepted norm' if an architect's work was to be taken seriously. Prior's work certainly displays individuality although this writer would argue that it was not deliberately wilful but rather was based on a view of independence from a recognised stylistic base, with stress put on functionality and rationalism in his buildings combined with a sympathy for, and use of, local vernacular traditions and materials. Lynn Walker, in her PhD thesis on Prior, sums up his independence and individuality: 'Prior showed an adherence to principles, the cohesive principles of the Arts and Crafts Movement, that provided the guidelines for overcoming the stylistic confusion of nineteenth century architecture.'[6] He continued to experiment with new techniques and materials throughout his life and was always alert to the demands of 'functionality' in his buildings.

Goodhart-Rendel's 'rogue' label has coloured how Prior's work has been considered since then. The sharp judgement now seems glib and narrow, seeking an effect rather than being a carefully considered judgement. If anything, it was based on the visual characteristics of his buildings without reference to the process of design: the clothing of, rather than the body of, the building. Indeed to label him as *any* sort of Victorian architect may not help us either. It might be easier to understand his work if we consider him in an international context – rather than a narrow English one – as he was in sympathy with movements outside the United Kingdom. He was searching for forms of construction that were looking forward in function but with reverence for the past on a local level. Prior was not a loner but in close touch with fellow architects, often working in collaboration with his fellow art-workers. Walker points out that 'Rogue architects were supposed to be outside the mainstream of architecture; their extreme individuality prevented them from having any real influence on their contemporaries, and if one takes the argument a step further, barred them from having any influence on future generations of architects.'[7] The rogue label is now being challenged in this essay, largely through a discussion of his buildings in Dorset and Hampshire.

Training and publications

Prior was born in 1852, the son of John Prior (1812-55), a successful, but short-lived barrister. He was educated at Harrow from 1863 to 1870 from where he achieved a scholarship to Gonville and Caius College, Cambridge. A disappointing third in his classical tripos was, to some extent, offset by achievements on the athletics field. His architectural pupilage was served between 1874 and 1879 in the office of Norman Shaw where one of his fellows was W.R. Lethaby. As a pupil, Prior wished to learn more than simply drawing and his developing interest was with construction. Shaw advised him to master drawing first and leave construction until later. However, from this point construction and function appear to have been a focus for his work. He set up his architectural practice in 1880 and in a career that lasted half a century, produced a series of memorable, innovative buildings. He was elected Master of the Art Workers' Guild in 1906 and, as Slade Professor, he set up the School of Architecture at Cambridge.

As a writer he is also exceptionally important. His 1900 publication *A History of Gothic Art in England*, with illustrations by Gerald Horsley, was deemed to be 'one of the finest expositions on medieval work' that had been published by then. It is a compelling and comprehensive survey that reveals the thoroughness of his research and attention to detail. It was recognised as a standard text in the USA as well as the UK and Walker suggests that it complemented G.G. Scott junior's *An Essay on the History of English Church Architecture* of 1881 in providing a comprehensive knowledge of Gothic architecture.[8] In the first chapter Prior attacked nineteenth-century restoration 'For the next generation to ours any direct acquaintance with the great comprehensive Gothic genius, except by means of parodies, will be difficult.'[9] He continues 'Where not completely rebuilt, Gothic monuments have been re-surfaced; their paintings have been re-painted; their sculptures re-chiselled. At its worst … this has been causeless and ignorant substitution.'[10]

He states that he wishes to be objective in his approach and avoid the propaganda of Pugin, Ruskin and Morris.[11] Prior argued that a less dogmatic approach was needed, one based on locality and the vernacular, rather than a single set of principles.

In *The Cathedral Builders in England* published in 1905, Prior follows his examination of Gothic art with a detailed study of the country's cathedral heritage from 1066 to his own day. The book is illustrated with prints, drawings and photographs, some of the prints made from medieval sources being in colour. He proposed that the summit of Gothic art was between 1250 and 1290, a period when 'national manners draw together, and as to the detail of construction, a wide uniformity prevails in the practice of the whole of West European architecture.'[12] He cites 1275 as the year when there was the greatest uniformity in the practice of Gothic throughout Western Europe and describes the results as 'continental' and 'regal'.[13] He observed a deterioration of Gothic art since that high point as a divergence between style and craft reached in the nineteenth century.

> Art, which had been a natural expression of life, has in the last three centuries become a matter of taste, not the necessity, of craft. It has grown fanciful and fastidious, wants ever a new dish to tickle its appetite: shows disgust at what went before and destroys it at all hazard.[14]
> The fervour of the ecclesiologist was especially deadly in his aesthetic exaltation of Gothic art. The tenet that the style of this building was the most religious, has worked untold havoc. The idea has handed churches over to the constructional archaeologist, who not content with our Cathedrals as they came down to us, has wished to make them what they ought to be. ... In the parish-churches what has been done under architects has really now destroyed the medieval quality entirely.[15]

In his final paragraph of *Cathedral Builders* Prior tackles issues of nineteenth-century 'Revivalism' which in many instances he did not admire. He was critical of what he saw as intervention by architects, which hid the original Gothic constructions of previous generations.

> If the most modern conceptions of religious responsibility in art are not those which made the Cathedral a monument of ancient religion, at any rate they are less repellent to it than the patent insincerity of the trade-art that has been admitted. ... as long as the outward shapes were those shown in books as Gothic, it has condoned the absence of inner grace, of honesty and craft-love – and this in religious art! The irony of the situation has been that admiration for the religious arts of the Middle Ages has now pretty well put them out of sight.[16]

Prior's view was uncompromising and deeply held and was ever looking for a return to the building practices of old that had created the pre-'Revival' buildings he so admired.

His last major publication was in 1912, *An Account of Medieval Figure-Sculpture in England,* with illustrations by Arthur Gardner. It was a comprehensive survey of architectural sculpture, stressing that it was designed as an integral part of the structure and lost meaning when it was seen in isolation. He opens his Introduction with: 'It must be accepted that medieval figure-sculpture was part and parcel of the larger part of medieval building, and that its period in England was that of the later Middle Ages – roughly the four hundred years from 1130 to 1530.'[17]

Quay Terrace, West Bay, Bridport, Dorset, 1884

The buildings under consideration for 'roguish' qualities are those in Dorset and Hampshire and span the full extent of his practice. Prior's first commission, however, was Carr Manor, Leeds (**5.2** and jacket), for Dr Thomas Albutt in 1881, a job passed to him by his former teacher, Norman Shaw. It was a tactful remodelling of an existing seventeenth-century house for which Prior adopted a Pennine vernacular tradition. It is a competent essay, but entirely orthodox for its date. However, it provides a useful context for an examination of Quay Terrace of just three years later, revealing a radically novel set of design principles in the latter.

Prior's family was prominent in the Bridport area of Dorset and this

5.2: Leeds, Carr Manor, 1881. (*Ruth Baumberg.*)

Chapter 5

5.3: West Bay, Dorset, Pier Terrace, 1884. (*Author*.)

helped secure a number of commissions; his marriage in 1885 to the daughter of the rector of nearby Symondsbury brought further useful links. Bridport had a port close by that had been in decline for some time, especially after the arrival of the railway at Bridport in 1857. Thus the Bridport Railway Company built a feeder line in 1884 in the hope of developing trade again and the port area was renamed West Bay. The *Bridport News* reported a

5.4: West Bay, Pier Terrace, 1884. Only part of the later addition to Prior's Terrace is shown on the right. (*Author*.)

proposed development, saying that 'a gentleman who visited the Harbour was so impressed with the beauties of the whole district, that he suggested a plan for building suitable houses, which he will probably carry out on an extensive scale.'[18] Walker suggests that Prior was this gentleman. Several proposals and designs were made by Prior but not built.

However, Prior's design for Quay Terrace (now Pier Terrace) of 1884 (**5.3, 5.4**) was executed. This residential building was on the quay-side, end on to the sea, and exposed directly to the elements. Prior proposed concrete for the ground floor of the west front but this was rejected in favour of 'a solid base of Portland stone quarried from the rocky peninsular across the West Bay.'[19] The exterior construction and decoration of the original plans were modified but the interior remained as initially planned.

Walker quotes Baroness Mary Stocks who was a Quay Terrace resident for 75 years:

> Intended for occupation by landladies and lodgers, it was in this respect commendably functional. Each house contained a semi-basement kitchen, scullery and living room for landlady and family; on the first floor a sitting-room and two small bedrooms for lodgers, above that another sitting room and bedroom for more lodgers and a w.c. for all lodgers. The w.c. was of identical design with the Peeresses' lavatory ... now widely recognized as the most cherished period-piece in the Palace of Westminster. Above this was an attic comprising one large double bedroom and two small ones. ... Below the scullery was a cellar and w.c. opening on to an area with steps up to the ground level.[20]

The roof was of Taylor's patented tiles, while the chimneys were of Portland stone. The exterior was part tile hung, offering protection from the storms, above rustic rubble stonework, thus showing Prior's interest in local materials and practical construction. It is hard to place it stylistically as part of any recognisable nineteenth-century tradition, and clearly indicates Prior's early individuality. Walker comments that 'the enormous size of Quay Terrace, which contributes to "its curious massive warehouse quality", was conceived in relation to the tall-masted ships that still visited the harbour.'[21]

Holy Trinity, Bothenhampton, Dorset, 1884-9

By the early 1880s the fifteenth-century church at Bothenhampton – a Dorset parish with a population of around 500 – had fallen into disrepair and in 1884 Prior was asked to provide a replacement (**5.5, 5.6, 5.7**). Some insight into his design approach can be found in a lecture he gave in 1896 as part of a project he had set his students at the Architectural Association in which they were to design a church in an exposed part of Westmorland. In

Chapter 5

5.5: Holy Trinity, Bothenhampton, Dorset, 1887-9. The site is exposed to the Atlantic gales but the low profile of the building aids stability during storms. (*Author.*)

5.6: Holy Trinity, Bothenhampton, 1887-9. The Incorporated Church Building Society initially objected to the method of roof construction and proposed a wooden support system instead. After some modification and much argument in favour of his scheme by Prior, the stone supports were agreed. With the three-foot-thick walls and embedded roof rib arches, clear sightlines are possible for both congregation and priest and the building remains stable in all conditions. (*Author.*)

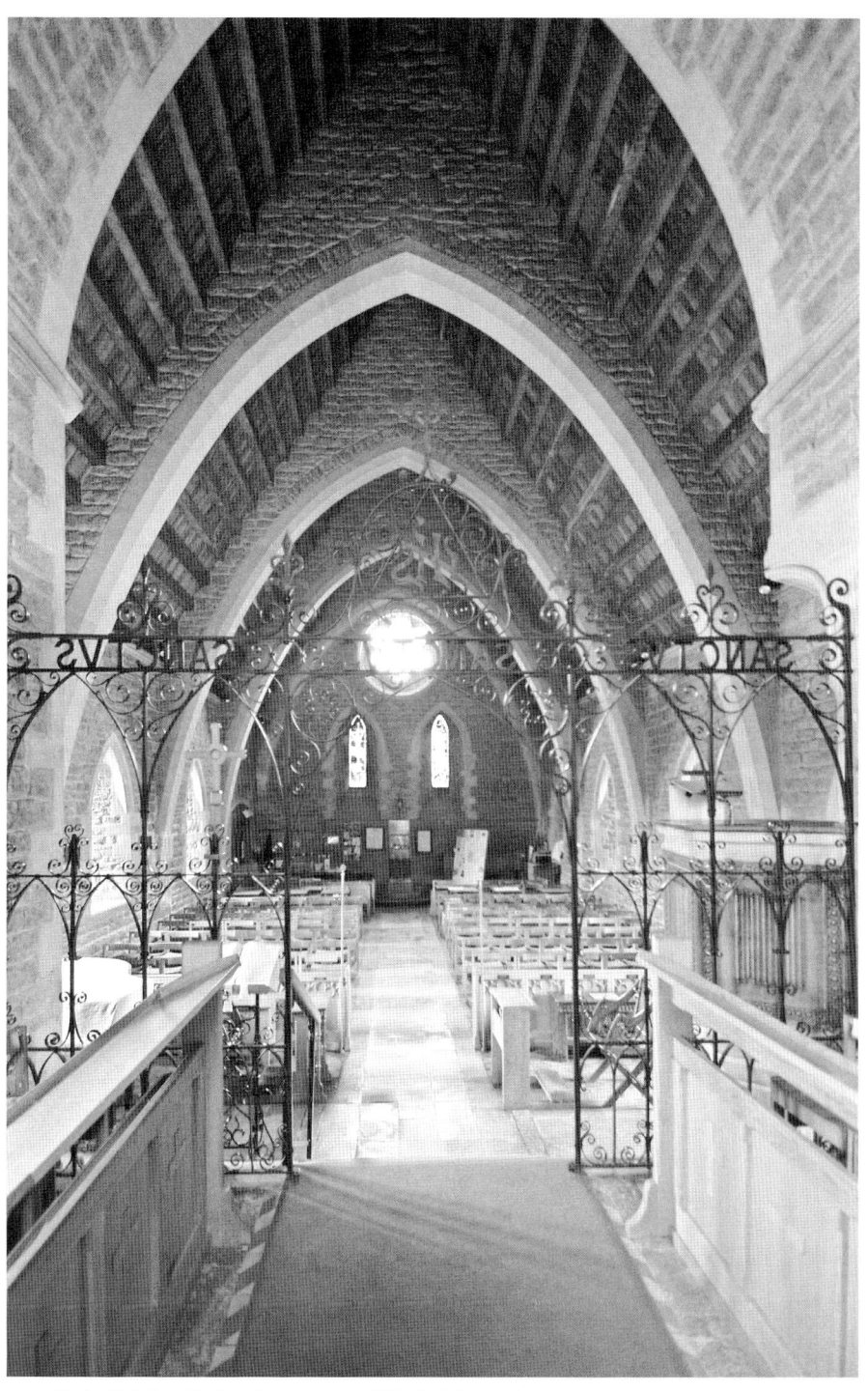

5.7: Holy Trinity, Bothenhampton, 1887-9. (*Author.*)

it he explained his own response to the Atlantic gales in Dorset and urged his students to look carefully at the solution he evolved for the church's roof.

He stated clearly to the students his philosophical starting point for such a project: 'he belonged to the same school of architectural thought as Mr Lethaby ... the school which believed that architecture was rational building.'[22] At a time when rational architecture was still widely seen to be Gothic, Prior's pragmatic interpretation emanating from a vernacular base was at odds with the followers of Pugin and Ruskin who steadfastly saw Gothic as the only rational form of architecture. At one level this was a battle of styles but Prior's outlook was different and seated in a localised rather than a national tradition and form. This was summed up in the *A.A. Notes for November 1896*:

> He [Prior] would ask them [the A.A. students] to imagine that this was not their first design, but one of a series. Of themselves they knew nothing, but others had built churches ... [in the area] for hundreds of years; and so a great amount of experience had been built up, and they depended on this experience to conceive their church. This was the true use of tradition. A building was erected. When built, it was evident that the forethought of the builders had been lacking in some particulars. The builders of the next church saw this and corrected these faults, they also did not reach perfection, and so each set of builders profiting by their predecessors' failures, approached more nearly the perfect building.[23]

This process is one that would have been recognised, in Prior's mind, by medieval masons. Prior was asking his students to adopt it and update it by using materials and technology of the present time rather than being constrained by a reliance on historic materials. This process put forward by Prior for demonstration purposes seems to have formed a set of principles for his own designs and buildings; a rational process primarily with style emanating from the local natural and built environment. The first perspective drawings for Holy Trinity were completed in November 1884 and exhibited at the Royal Academy in 1885.[24] Prior had analysed local building traditions and set three headings: conditions of use; conditions of materials; conditions of sentiment.[25]

> In the numerous conditions of use he placed light, warmth, protection from weather and seating. Materials would be sourced locally; Bothenhampton stone came from J. Gundy's quarry and due to its porous nature would be required to be three feet thick. The site was exposed to Atlantic gales and the choice of roofing tiles could be either very small and close set or large and heavy, which would resist the wind by sheer weight. The latter would require a substantial roof structure for support.

The church took five years to complete partly due to the objections of the Incorporated Church Building Society to the roof construction of the nave. Any grant from the society would be withheld until its Committee of Architects accepted all the proposed constructional details and for Bothenhampton they ruled that the roof was unacceptable. 'The character of the roofing proposed is extraordinary, expensive, & unsafe & not to be recommended according to constitution & decor.'[26] Prior answered their objections and pointed out that the form was common in secular medieval halls. He suggested that the committee called the roof expensive without understanding the conditions under which it would be built and that it was safe, challenging the committee to point out where the lack of stability was to be found.[27] Prior's plans for the roof were rejected again in December 1886 with his old teacher Norman Shaw now on the scrutiny panel and supporting rejection in favour of a wooden roof. The struggle continued with Prior proposing minor constructional modifications but holding firm on the main features. He presented a massive weight of supporting evidence for his construction and the committee finally granted approval in January 1887. Now it is difficult to see what was deemed problematic, other than that a novel, non-ecclesiastical form being used in a church for a small rural parish. Prior had defended his roof thus:

> In an exposed situation, subject to heavy gales, with the ordinary construction of a church roof with framed wood principals is not a useful one. The trusses vibrate under the weight of the wind, and as was found in an instance close at hand, the creaking and straining of the timbers may make noise enough to seriously interrupt the church services. To avoid the discomfort stone arches were used in place of wood principals, and quite successfully for the purpose. It was found, moreover, that on a site where stone could be got close at hand the expense of the arches was, under a builder's estimate, less than that of wood framed trusses.[28]

The third condition of sentiment 'mirrored his deep faith, as well as his concern for solid, but economical, architectural means.'[29] We can return to his advice to students previously mentioned.

> The Expression of the Building. ... It should be unmistakably what it is. A church, a place of common assembly for the worship of God. It should be reverential, simple and honest. Ornate treatment was out of place here, and students should aim at a graceful effect ... not flimsy and not coarse.[30]

For the construction, a local builder Thomas Patten was engaged and the structure was completed in 1887; the interior took a further two years with consecration in January 1890.

Chapter 5

5.8: St John the Baptist, Symondsbury, Dorset. The south transept window with tracery by Prior, 1885. Prior was married in this church. (*Author.*)

St John the Baptist, Symondsbury, Dorset, 1885

In 1885 Prior married the daughter of the rector of Symondsbury and in the same year worked with Lethaby on the south transept window there. Georgian renovation had removed much of the original detail of the church and there was no old tracery remaining in the window. Prior's replacement consisted of four lights, generally in keeping with the rest of the church which he decided was of fifteenth-century date style (**5.8**). Lethaby designed the stained glass depicting the four Evangelists attended by gold-winged angels (**5.9**).

Edward Schroeder Prior (1852-1932)

St Mary, Burton Bradstock, Dorset, 1894-7

The repair and renovation of St Mary, Burton Bradstock, was planned in 1894 and undertaken in late 1896 (**5.10, 5.11, 5.12**); Prior was working on The Barn at Exmouth during this time. Walker records the work as 'an important instance of Arts and Crafts restoration, which, in this case was organized in an almost medieval fashion.'[31] The vicar, the Revd Edward

5.9: St John the Baptist, Symondsbury. The four Evangelists, designed by Lethaby, 1885. (*Author.*)

CHAPTER 5

5.10: St Mary, Burton Bradstock, Dorset, 1897, where Prior rebuilt the north nave aisle. (*Author.*)

Templer, was a cousin of Prior and became clerk of works. There was no contract involved but the skilled labour was provided by Messrs. Bartlett, who had worked for Prior at Symondsbury. Prior's aim was 'to give the sense of personal handicraft, and of personal pleasure in the work, rather

5.11: St Mary, Burton Bradstock, 1897, north aisle. The windows are filled with Prior's Patent Early English Glass. (*Author.*)

EDWARD SCHROEDER PRIOR (1852-1932)

5.12: St Mary, Burton Bradstock, 1897, north nave aisle added by Prior to replace an earlier structure. The aisle is generally considered to blend harmoniously with the rest of the church. (*Author.*)

than mere expenditure of money.'[32] Stone was used from the locality and local smiths and carpenters were used in preference to imported workers. The interior was decorated by some of the parishioners; the green painted dado in the nave was constructed using woodwork from the box-pews, which were replaced by benches (**5.13, 5.14**). A motto was painted along the top edge, punctuated by local animals and plants. 'In this year of our Lord 1897 [bees and flowers] being the 60th year [lobster] of the reign of Queen Victoria [turbot] and the thirteen hundredth year since Columba came to Canterbury was this church repaired.'

Prior reconstructed the south aisle to blend harmoniously with the fourteenth-century nave. Stone windows replaced the wooden ones and the wooden roof was designed to harmonise with that in the nave. The windows were re-glazed including two in the chancel which were opened up using Prior's 'Early English Glass', a form he devised with very thick glass and leading, and which he considered emulated early medieval glazing. He used an abstract design of single wild roses. His work moved the church interior away from its Georgian character to an essentially Victorian model. An examination of the interior reveals the full extent of its fine Arts and Crafts fittings, a product of local skills and devotion, which thus became a

Chapter 5

5.13: St Mary, Burton Bradstock, 1897. Here are windows by Prior filled with his Patent Early English Glass. The decorated dado, made from the redundant Georgian box-pews, was decorated by local residents. (*Author*.)

working example of Prior's understanding of medieval practice in a modern context.

Winchester College Music School, Hampshire, 1901-4

In 1901 Winchester College decided to build a Music School and place the subject on a level with mathematics and science[33] in which 'complete

5.14: St Mary, Burton Bradstock, 1897, detail of the decorated dado. (*Author*.)

accommodation' for the teaching of music must be provided. Prior submitted designs and on 26 March 1902 'The Bursar was requested to inform Mr E.S. Prior that his plans for the new Music School had the general approval of the Warden and Fellows, and to ask him to prepare working drawings.'[34] The school was completed rapidly, opening its doors at the start of the autumn term of 1904 (**5.15-5.18**).

The interior is complex and its structure is determined by function. On the ground floor is an entrance hall, a porter's room and the first level of the concert hall. Stairs lead down to the brass band room, which is located under the main auditorium. Practice rooms are on the first and second floors and are like small cells off corridors. The first-floor corridor ceiling is barrel-vaulted and made of concrete. On the mezzanine there is a gallery overlooking the auditorium, a quartet practice room and a retiring room that doubled as a library and the Music Master's room.

> Although the varied functional requirements of the space seem to have been the determinants of the shape and structure, the heating and air-conditioning system supplied by Sturtevant was not an unqualified success since the inlet and outlet ducts placed between the walls carried the sounds of instruments throughout the building along with the heat and ventilation. Prior made great efforts in his plans at soundproofing including double doors and double-glazing but these were ultimately defeated.

5.15: Winchester College Music School, view of the entrance. A recent extension is visible on the left. (*Author.*)

CHAPTER 5

5.16: Winchester College Music School, agreed design, signed by Prior. (*Winchester College.*)

St Osmund, Parkstone, Poole, Dorset, 1912-16

Prior's best-known church is St Andrew, Roker, County Durham (1906-7). However, as the building has been examined in detail elsewhere,[35] it will not be reconsidered here. Five years after Roker, Prior began work on

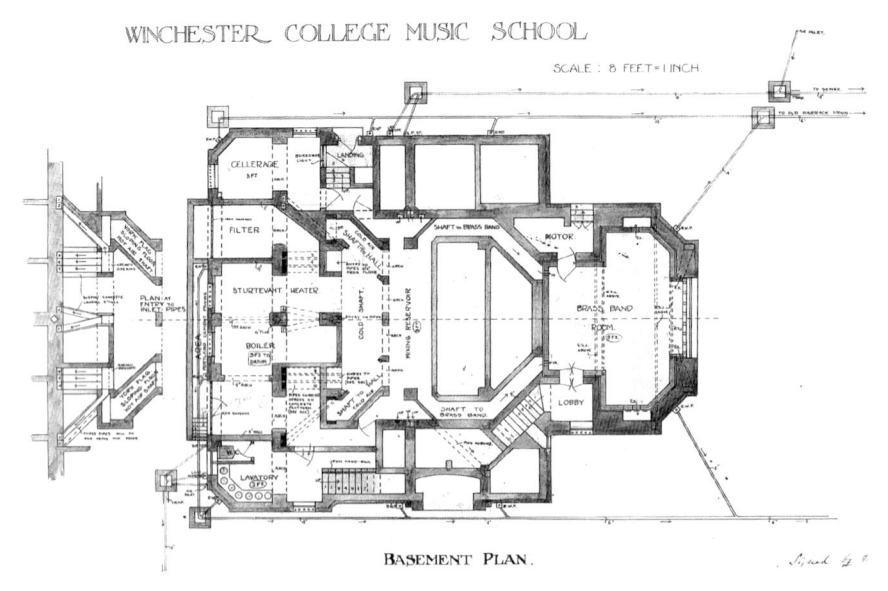

5.17: Winchester College Music School, agreed design, signed by Prior. Basement plan on which the location of the heating and air-conditioning system by Sturtevant can be seen. (*Winchester College.*)

162

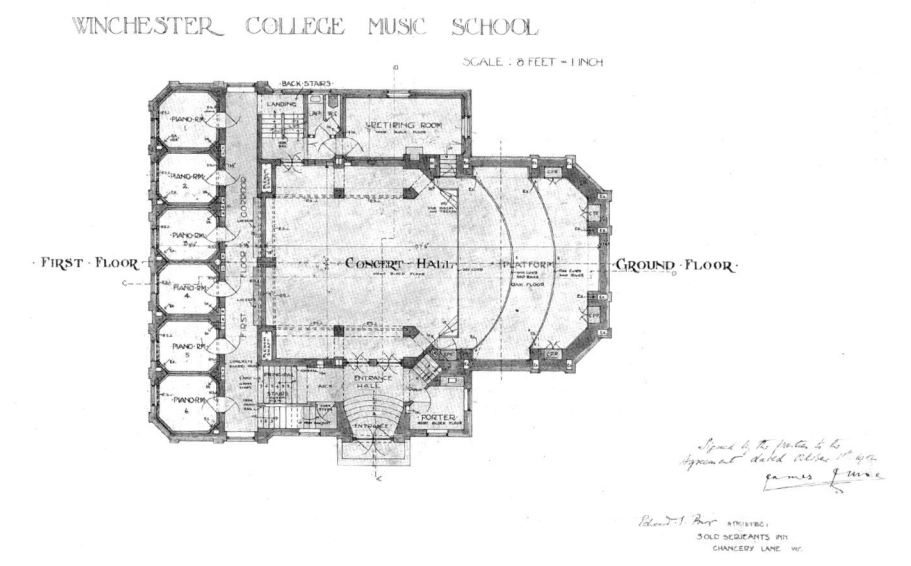

5.18: Winchester College Music School, agreed design, signed by Prior. First-floor plan showing the first level of the practice rooms and concert hall. (*Winchester College*.)

the church at Parkstone, a building of considerable interest (**5.19, 5.20**). Prior was not the original architect but took over an existing project from G.A. Bligh Livesay, a Bournemouth-based man working in partnership with Winter and Allner. They had designed St Osmund's based on 'a Romanesque Basilica on the exterior similar to St Zeno at Verona and internally on St Clemente and St Stephano Rotondo Rome.'[36] Prior and Arthur Grove were appointed joint architects in 1912. Prior adopted the Byzantine Revival style of Livesay and in this was influenced by Lethaby who had written that in early Byzantine construction 'The art of building was made free from formulas, and architecture became an adventure in building once more.'[37] Since his Slade inaugural lecture at Cambridge, Prior's work had been promoted by Lethaby as a revolution in constructional methods and opening a way for new expression in building. St Osmund's was the next church project after Roker and one that continued the use of reinforced concrete in the construction. At St Osmund's, Prior and Grove specified a variety of materials including lightweight concrete and iron in the dome and roof with the walls made predominantly of locally produced bricks. The glass is all of Prior's Early English type and is non-figurative in pale shades of green, pink and blue with some deep ruby and blue hues in the south transept window. Walker comments

Chapter 5

5.19: St Osmund, Parkstone, Dorset, 1912-16. The rose window is heavily leaded and filled with Prior's Patent Early English Glass, as are all the windows in the church. (*Author.*)

> The real glory of the building is the rich surface of brick, ... which is the final and consummate statement of Prior's commitment to the colour, texture and quality of materials. ... he [Prior] had persuaded makers of simple pottery by the shores of Poole harbour to turn their clay to bricks of every colour from purple to vivid orange for his church at Parkstone.[38]

The dome, designed by Grove, was not initially a success as it had to be replaced in 1922. The construction of the church took place in difficult circumstances during the First World War; Prior was by then Slade Professor at Cambridge and dividing his time between Cambridge, London and Chichester. Although not an unqualified triumph, this last design by Prior shows his continued interest in individuality. After the war Prior's architectural practice did not regain momentum and he concentrated his efforts in academic work at Cambridge.

Conclusions

Does Prior deserve the label 'rogue'? To our understanding today this is too blunt and based on a narrow perspective of past years where visual aesthetics were the dominant feature of analysis. Current thinking requires a deeper analysis of how the design was determined and the working practices and philosophy of the architect. Prior's buildings, the vast majority of them are still in use today, were rational and functional, and built for specific locations and needs, often to a limited budget. The fact that Prior never built in London has not helped his reputation. There are no significant national buildings to his credit but instead a considerable wealth of scholarship, which gained him international recognition. Some of his buildings have been written about in detail and all show the results of his collaborative 'Arts and Crafts' working practices. His stress on rational and functionality in his buildings rather than style does not make it easy to approach some of his projects, Holy Trinity at Bothenhampton might appear understated, although more careful examination reveals it to be entirely appropriate for both its purpose and site. The Music School at Winchester College was determined by its function and used concrete and steel in its construction as well as incorporating a heating and air conditioning system. Externally it was constructed using local traditional material, flints in the walls, and incorporating Classical features in exterior style as befits a place of learning.

One of his obituaries noted among his many achievements his role in the foundation of the St George's Art Society:'The relationship between the architect and the craftsman was a subject of intense interest to those young men and there was much talk of the possibility of bringing them together'.[39] He also impressed his students with the importance of materials and their

5.20: St Osmund, Parkstone, 1912-16, the south façade. Livesay's design is the eastern section and Prior's the western. (*Author.*)

prominence.⁴⁰ Together with many other Arts and Crafts practitioners, he spoke tirelessly of the movement's theory and practice, and these ideas spread throughout Britain and into Europe where they can be detected in hybrid form in the Bauhaus. Prior's work deserves to be studied anew with a fresh approach and understanding; he saw no future in the pursuit of style but worked for a more rational approach to architecture and construction based on scholarship and understanding of the past. His buildings do not parody the past but, at best, articulate tradition.

Prior was not a prolific architect yet his design successes were considerable: 'Roker ... and Brockhampton [represent] the highest achievement of the [Arts and Crafts] Movement in ecclesiastical architecture';⁴¹ *The Barn* is 'breathtaking',⁴² its plan 'started a fashion ... it was much copied;'⁴³ 'every one of Prior's buildings repays study with delight and interest'.⁴⁴ This was no slight achievement for a man who was 'first and foremost an educationist'.⁴⁵

Acknowledgments and thanks to Suzanne Foster, Archivist to Winchester College for her time and help with new materials that came to light during cataloguing of the College Archive, and sincere thanks to Winchester College for its kind permission to print images 16-18.

Abbreviations
ABN   *Architect & Building News*
B   *The Builder*
ICBS   Incorporated Church Building Society

Notes
1. L.B. Walker, 'E.S. Prior 1852-1932', unpublished PhD Thesis, Birkbeck College, University of London, 1978, 17.
2. T. Garnham, *St Andrew's Church, Roker*, Phaidon 1996. There is a brief outline of Prior's work before the comprehensive study of St Andrew's.
3. J.M. Crook, *The Dilemma of Style*, John Murray, 1989, 149.
4. Subsequently published as 'Rogue Architects of the Victorian Era', *ABN*, 22 Apr. 1949, 359-62.
5. Ibid.
6. Walker [n.1], 10.
7. Ibid., 8.
8. Ibid., 485.
9. E.S. Prior, *A History of Gothic Art in England*, George Bell & Sons, 1900, 4.
10. Ibid., 3.

11 Ibid., 5.
12 E.S. Prior, *The Cathedral Builders in England*, Seeley & Co., 1905, 60.
13 Ibid., 61-2.
14 Ibid., 103.
15 Ibid., 108-9.
16 Ibid., 110.
17 E.S. Prior & A. Gardner, *An Account of Medieval Figure-Sculpture in England*, Cambridge U.P., 1912.
18 *Bridport News*, 27 Apr. 1883, quoted in Walker [n. 1], 314.
19 Walker [n. 1], 318.
20 Ibid.
21 Ibid., 319.
22 *A.A. Notes*, Nov. 1896, vol. 2, 120.
23 Ibid., 120.
24 R.A., *Summer Exhibition Catalogue*, 1885.
25 *A.A. Notes*, Nov. 1896, vol. 2, 120.
26 Lambeth Palace Library, ICBS file 09129, letter from ICBS to Prior, 2 Nov. 1886.
27 Ibid., letter from Prior to ICBS, 10 Nov. 1886.
28 *B*, 93, 1907, 562.
29 Walker [n. 1], 335.
30 *AA Notes*, Nov. 1896, 122.
31 Walker [n.1], 347 with a note that the description was found in an undated newspaper clipping from Miss Bessie Prior's scrapbook, *c.* 1897. The description was probably given to a local paper by Revd Templer.
32 Walker [n.1], 347.
33 I am indebted to Suzanne Foster, Archivist to Winchester College, for her help with documents and the original plans reproduced here.
34 Winchester College, A4/4/2.
35 P. Davey, *Arts and Crafts Architecture*, Phaidon, 1999, 80-2.
36 Walker [n. 1], 559.
37 W.R. Lethaby, *Architecture: An Introduction to the History and Theory of the Art of Building,* Williams & Norgate, 1912, 155.
38 Walker, 561.
39 *RIBA Journal*, 89, 1932, 859.
40 Ibid., 858.
41 A. Service, *Edwardian Architecture,* Thames & Hudson, 1977, 123.
42 Ibid., 23.
43 *ABN*, 131, 1932, 238.
44 Davey [n. 35], 87.
45 *B*, 143, 1932, 328.

6.1: Harold Peto, on the bridge at Iford Manor, Wiltshire. (*Private collection*.)

6

Harold A. Peto (1854-1933): architect, interior designer, collector and aesthete

Hilary J. Grainger

Despite Harold Ainsworth Peto (**6.1**) always styling himself an architect, and indeed having been trained as such, consideration of his work to date has tended to focus on his significant contribution to the development of the Italian school of Edwardian gardening at the turn of the twentieth century as exemplified by his own garden at Iford Manor, Bradford-on-Avon, Wiltshire.[1] But as the recent appraisal of his sixteen years in partnership with the leading domestic architect Sir Ernest George (1839-1922) has revealed, Peto's talents and importance extended far beyond garden design.[2] Described as 'a man of extreme artistic culture and taste',[3] Peto was an architect, interior designer, collector, connoisseur, traveller and aesthete. While these areas of expertise were to come into play, either individually or in combination, at different points throughout his career, it was not until the completion of three well-publicised designs for villas and gardens, begun after 1900 in the south of France, that the confluent articulation of Peto's interdisciplinary talents could be appreciated fully. Although a more balanced

Chapter 6

view of Peto's career is now possible as a result of a better understanding of his work with George, it seems opportune to explore the ways in which his later independent architectural commissions might throw further light on his earlier practice which remains somewhat opaque on account of the paucity of surviving office documentation. In so doing, this chapter seeks to establish Peto's wider importance for late nineteenth- and early twentieth-century English architecture and design.

Background and training

The fifth son of the celebrated mid-Victorian public works and railway contractor Sir Samuel Morton Peto (1808-89), Harold was born into a life of wealth and privilege, tempered by social responsibility and religious belief. His father operated at the highest levels in the worlds of construction, commerce, art, politics and Nonconformity, both at home and abroad, and belonged to that 'heroic class of Victorian contractor'[4] which combined business acumen with a highly developed sense of social and professional responsibility. Sir Samuel's career and building ventures are well documented,[5] but some details are nevertheless germane to an understanding of the shaping of Harold's character and taste.

During the 1840s Sir Samuel began a long and fruitful relationship with the people of Suffolk after purchasing the old Elizabethan Somerleyton Hall, which he remodelled in an Anglo-Italianate style 'of massive splendour and taste.'[6] The palatial nature of the interiors, Classical in idiom, revealed Peto's wealth and his devotion to the arts, while the 'truly elegant'[7] winter garden, with its huge central fountain, made more than a passing reference to the Great Exhibition, for which Peto acted as a guarantor. In 1855, when reputedly the largest employer of labour in the world, Sir Samuel built two impressive houses on the east side of Kensington Palace Gardens, looking 'across open grassland to the Round Pond'[8] and it was here at no. 12 that Harold was born on 11 July 1854, at the height of his father's financial success. His early years, however, would be spent at Somerleyton. Although we can imagine the young Harold in this sumptuous environment, surrounded by some of the finest examples of mainstream art that money could buy, we have no knowledge of his childhood experiences.

Somerleyton was sold to Sir Francis Crossley in 1862, when financial clouds were gathering over Peto's affairs. The family lived briefly in Scotland before moving to Kent in 1868, where their close neighbours were Fearnon and Henry Avray Tipping (1855-1933), then living at Brasted Place – both of whom would remain lifelong friends of Harold. The London house was sold in 1868 and, since Lady Peto was a woman of independent wealth, the family 'went abroad' staying in France, Switzerland, Italy and Germany until 1872 during which time Sir Samuel travelled the world in connection with his railway contracts.

Little is known of Harold's early education. His older brothers, Morton, Frank and Herbert had followed a practical training with a view to going into business – considered by Sir Samuel to be the way to make money. In the autumn of 1869 Harold followed his brother Samuel Arthur to Harrow but left in the summer of 1871 after several bouts of illness and was perhaps unsuited to the regime. During their school holidays he, Arthur and Frank visited the rest of the family, who were wintering in the south of France, before moving to Switzerland in early 1870.

In 1871, at the age of seventeen, Harold began his architectural training with John Louth Clemence (1823-1911) in Lowestoft, where Sir Samuel's ambitions to make the fishing port a fashionable seaside resort had begun to unfold south of the harbour with the building of the Royal Hotel in 1847. In addition to being a local architect, surveyor and one-time mayor of Lowestoft, Clemence was, at that time, also works manager of Lucas Brothers, builders, at their premises at South Wharf. The firm had worked for Sir Samuel on railway contracts, undertaken the building work at Somerleyton Hall and later constructed the harbour and esplanade, railway station, St John's Church, 1853,[9] and several hotels in the town. By 1868 the brothers are thought to have taken over part of Peto's London business, being listed at 5 Great George Street, London, and Belvedere Road, Lambeth, as well as in Lowestoft. Harold's RIBA fellowship papers record that in 1871 he spent time at the Lowestoft works, where he must have learned a good deal about the practical side of building, before moving to the offices of architects Lewis Karslake & Mortimer at 5 Great Queen Street, WC2, at which point Lucas Brothers were involved in the construction of the Royal Albert Hall. Nothing is known of how Harold's time was spent in London, but in the spring of 1871 he met with his family in Venice and recalls spending three months visiting 'several towns in North Italy and Germany'.[10] Later, in 1874, he accompanied a group from the Architectural Association to northern France, doubtless to deepen his knowledge of foreign work.

George & Peto, architects

From 1876 until 1892 Peto was in partnership with Sir Ernest George (1839-1933) who was to work with three successive partners, Thomas Vaughan (1836-75), Peto and Alfred Bowman Yeates (1867-1944). Although George enjoyed a long and productive career, by far his most spectacularly successful period was that in partnership with Peto. Indeed, half of George's

Chapter 6

total architectural output dated from the 1880s, when, claimed his pupil Guy Dawber, he was 'perhaps one of the busiest architects in England, large country houses and other buildings filling his office with work'.[11] While their projects encompassed commercial and some ecclesiastical work, they were above all domestic architects, their métier being country houses. It was reported that 'Young men scrambled to get into the office of "George and Peto", which soon began to be known all over the kingdom as a fashionable training ground',[12] dubbed 'The Eton of offices'[13] and 'that cradle of the English Domestic Revival'.[14] Pupils and assistants included Sir Edwin Lutyens, Sir Herbert Baker, Guy Dawber, F.D. Bedford, Herbert Wigglesworth, J.J. Joass, D. Kennedy, Dan Gibson, Hart and Waterhouse, R.S. Weir, Read and Macdonald, Ethel and Bessie Charles and many others.[15]

By 1876 George was in the ascendant, having been acknowledged as an architect of considerable promise. He and Vaughan had risen to some prominence with a series of clever and individual buildings in west London, their partnership working on the familiar art-and-business arrangement, George undertaking the more artistic branch of the profession'.[16] Early success was sealed with designs for a villa and wine stores in Spain for the Duke of Wellington and by their arresting country house début at Rousdon in Devon (1874-83) for Henry William Peek, of Peek Frean & Co., the biscuit manufacturers. But tragedy struck in March 1875 when Vaughan died prematurely, leaving George to work alone for a time. It was not long, however, before 'It was proposed ... that Harold Peto ... should join me, and at the age of twenty-one he became my partner and we worked together sympathetically for many years'.[17] The proposal doubtless came from Sir Samuel, now retired, who, through his professional connections, would have been well placed to know that George was looking for a partner. Furthermore, in 1871 George and Vaughan had undertaken work at the Pimlico premises of Peto Brothers, Builders, the firm established by Harold's brothers (William) Herbert and Morton Kelsall. In 1875 Harold had moved to 19 Gillingham Street, Pimlico, London SW1, to live with Herbert next to the building yard. While there is no suggestion that he was involved in any practical way with the firm it is likely that his proximity to the business would have furthered his vocational training. In March 1876 his independence was sealed when he entered into partnership with George, fifteen years his senior.

For George's part there must have been some risks involved in taking on a young and untried partner, but the advantages were clear. Most importantly, the Peto family provided a direct entrée into the London building world historically through Sir Samuel, and contemporaneously through Peto

Harold A. Peto (1854-1933)

Brothers. Their business connections with Doulton would lead both to commissions and to George & Peto's extensive employment of terracotta. Although not employed regularly by George & Peto, Peto Brothers also played a crucial role in the advancement of the partnership, most notably through their timely speculation in the early 1880s in Harrington and Collingham Gardens, Kensington. It was here that George & Peto confirmed their success and where Harold was undoubtedly the intermediary between architects, builders and clients.[18]

Furthermore, George favoured partnership, arguing 'that the complete architect is hardly to be found in any one individual'[19] and in Peto, George found the perfect complement to his strengths. The *Builder's Journal* later observed, 'There is no less assertive practitioner than Ernest George, and in his partner he found the antithesis to himself'.[20] Despite his conspicuous talent, not only as an architect but also as a watercolourist and etcher, George was by nature modest and retiring. In contrast, Peto was reputed to be quite a complex and at times, difficult man. His father had been a patron of the arts whereas Harold developed into an aesthete with a horror of vulgarity, his perfectionism leading him into an almost overriding obsession with good taste and refinement, which deepened as he grew older. His taste was unfaltering from the outset; his brother Basil recalls Harold having bought a 'mahogany double sculling boat. As one would expect from Harold's taste in such things, it had very special cushions and other such fittings and he was very proud and careful of it'.[21]

Commissions followed swiftly in Peto's wake. The firm's client base expanded rapidly to encompass a wide social spectrum with jobs for the landed gentry, the professional classes and industrialists, all of which are well documented. However, the fact that no office papers survive renders it difficult to establish a definitive account of the division of labour in the partnership. What is clear is that George was unquestionably the principal designer throughout. Stanley Adshead recalled that 'Peto was rarely seen, but it was understood that he spent most of his time with clients. Ernest George did all the designing and the dozen or more draughtsmen simply traced and fitted together his designs under personal supervision.'[22] He would appear to have taken on the role of 'business man, with qualifications for determining estimates, supervising works and materials and meeting the many legal and other problems and difficulties that arise in building operations'.[23]

Correspondence suggests that Peto and George became close friends as well as business partners. Their partnership brought not only companionship, which George certainly valued, but also allowed each the opportunity to take holidays abroad without jeopardising the success of the business. In many

Chapter 6

respects they were soulmates, George recognising Peto as 'One who is in hearty sympathy with the Old World.'[24] When proposing him for fellowship of the RIBA in October 1883, George described his partner as having 'exceptional ability and artistic qualifications for the practice of architectural knowledge of construction and taste in form and colour',[25] later recording that he 'was not a draughtsman, but had all the feeling of an artist; and to his originality of thought, soundness of judgment and refinement of taste he added also a capacity for the conduct of affairs that cannot be divorced from the practice of our craft, with its many sides.'[26] Indeed, the confidence and excellence of many final schemes, while emanating initially from George's pen, owe much to Peto's rare combination of taste and business management. What is quite clear and now documented comprehensively, is the enormous impact that the Petos had on the pattern of practice.

Relationships with clients

Details of Peto's day-to-day professional commitments remain tantalisingly fugitive. The few client diaries and letters that have emerged suggest that he made frequent and regular site visits and was certainly involved with detailed aspects of the commissions; an early example being the frequency with which he returned to Clandon Park, Guildford, Surrey, to supervise work on the estate for the Earl of Onslow. Letters show Peto taking a particular interest in the quality of materials employed and the levels of craftsmanship to be secured throughout. Although prone to a certain degree of impatience, Peto was generally charming to clients, although some revealed a degree of frustration in their dealings with him – an example being Edmund Hanbury, of Truman, Hanbury & Buxton, Brewers, who, together with his wife Amy, commissioned 'Poles' in Hertfordshire in 1890-2. They confirmed that it was George who took the major responsibility for the work. They liked him very much, regarding him as 'a first rate artist and designer, much taste'.[27] Conversely, Hanbury found Peto irritating with his 'nuances'[28] and 'a sham gentleman'[29] to boot.

George believed that the wants of the client 'should have the most careful consideration even when they seem opposed to our views of what is best'.[30] Peto, however, was altogether more assertive in his approach, revisiting houses long after completion in order to satisfy himself that interior schemes remained unchanged, much to the chagrin of Mrs Harrison at Shiplake Court, Henley, who was reported constantly moving furniture in anticipation of a visit. Furthermore, Peto could be positively disparaging, characterising Edward Steinkopff, one-time proprietor of the *St James Gazette,* who had commissioned rebuilding work and redecoration at Berkeley Square, Mayfair, in 1891, as a 'vulgar exacting nouveau riche'.[31]

In 1890 the painter G.F. Watts commissioned the firm to design a house and studio, 'Limnerslease' on the Hog's Back, Compton in Surrey. Mary Seton Watts records Peto's visit on 6 January 1891. Her diary entry provides rare and revealing insights, which appear to run counter to the notion of Peto as being a man of firm opinions. Struck by his 'fine, grey eyes', she recalled him as being

> very pleasant, though as an architect we could not quite find out that he had very definite ideas. He admired nothing here. When Signor pointed out the staircase with its curve which he admires, he only said 'What a curious thing the desire for curves was' – He seems rather to think he would like to build a Greek temple in London, but on the whole we could not think he had 'anything to say on architecture'. He did not even comment on the red chalk drawings in the studio. He talked pleasantly upon many things ... It was very nice going round the house with him, he especially pointed out what a pity it was that the pleasant rough plastering of the walls was lost in the finely polished mortar veneer – in America they sometimes keep it – Oh I said I have been longing to try that in the drawing room – the texture of it is so pleasant.[32]

In contrast, Mary Watts records George's visit on 17 April when more practical aspects were discussed, perhaps prompted by differences of opinion between George and Watts over details. 'We went to meet Mr George who walked out to see the house – Signor pitched into him rather smartly about the soilpipe chiefly & architects who will try to hide things, & make them look what they are not – He denied the charge & says they have no shams but the brick wall behind the stucco and oak of our walls, they consented to doing that to make the house warmer'.[33]

There is also a fleeting suggestion that Peto might have taken the lead in some commissions, Basil Peto recalling that in the summer of 1881 he was doing a lot of overtime in Harold's office, 'where he [Harold] was working on a big specification for an elaborate house for his friends, the Middletons, which was never built, as the father – old Middleton died'.[34] William Middleton, a friend of Sir Samuel had bought Shrubland Park in Suffolk in 1848, where he had Sir Charles Barry design a huge Italian terraced garden and had presumably been planning a new house.

Interior design

Peto's most conspicuous talents lay in interior design and it is here that his signature is most clearly apparent. It was an area in which both he and George excelled. Clear evidence suggests that while George designed furniture – both freestanding and fitted – for houses, Peto bought furniture

Chapter 6

6.2: George & Peto, the yacht, *Cuhona*, for Sir Andrew Barclay Walker, 1883, George & Peto's perspective. (Building News, *45, 1883, 50*.)

and furnishings on behalf of clients. Both men were themselves collectors, George writing to Peto from Algiers in 1889 – 'So we have thirteen years of work and play together? I wonder how much more work there is in either of us, or both collecting'.[35]

In this respect, George & Peto formed part of the tradition which had grown in England since the Gothic Revival and which they, in turn, were to advance. As Robert Kerr pointed out, the remit of the architect had widened in the 1880s, and George & Peto clearly relished the new interdisciplinary challenges. Specialist knowledge and expertise was called for and there was no partnership better qualified to provide it. The firm was an attractive proposition for those from a wide range of social backgrounds anxious to furnish 'in good taste', but who preferred to employ the services of their own architect rather than being passed on to decorators or relying on fashionable interior design manuals. It was not, however, without its frustrations for Peto, who, recalling the tribulations encountered when trying to buy paintings from a count in Verona in 1888, wrote, 'Those who have not experienced what time and patience it takes to buy pictures abroad would never imagine it'.[36] He further recalled that while on the same fortnight's holiday in Italy, 'a little Italian Customs House Officer' challenged his attempted export of a number of paintings, despite their legitimate provenance. He 'refused the offer of 50 francs, but was prepared to accept a few of Sir A. Walker's cigars'.[37] Andrew Barclay Walker, the Liverpool brewer and philanthropist was a regular client of George & Peto. In 1883 they designed the interior of Walker's yacht, *The Cuhona* (**6.2**) which included a specially designed sideboard, writing tables, chairs, piano casing and even wine glasses. They also made additions and alterations to his house, Gateacre Grange, Woolton, Lancashire providing aesthetic interiors for which Peto bought china.

While George favoured Northern Renaissance styles, Peto's preference for Italian Renaissance was detectable as early as 1878, when he and George altered and redecorated the outer hall, dining room and library at 6, Grosvenor Place, London SW1, for future Prime Minister, Henry Campbell-Bannerman, brother of Peto's brother-in-law, James Campbell. The hall, painted in the early Italian manner, with its large stone chimney-piece, suggested Peto's hand, while the Renaissance decoration in the dining room, with a walnut mantelpiece and buffet, carved by James Knox of Lambeth, was most likely by George.

Interestingly, it appears that Peto was also responsible for some interior design commissions under his own name, notably the complete refurbishment of 36, Bow Street, Covent Garden, opened as a temperance establishment for The Kiosk and Coffee Stall Company of which the Duke of Westminster was president. The *Coffee Public House News* reported in December 1880 that the 'house had been entirely rebuilt, and from roof to basement every attention had been made for the convenience and enjoyment of the public'.[38] Notable was the introduction of electric light on the Siemens Brothers' system, illuminating both the exterior and interior. A second commission, dating from 1887-8, attributed to Peto, was the interior design of the new shop and factory for Henry Heath, the hatter, at 105-109, Oxford Street, W1, designed by Messrs Christopher & White and built by Peto Brothers. The arresting terracotta exterior was notable for the beavers, sculpted by Benjamin Creswick, which formed the decorative finials surmounting the large and small gables of the façade announcing the trade represented therein.

Peto's own interiors in Collingham Gardens, Kensington, during the 1880s reveal a great deal about his taste. A lifelong bachelor, Peto lived alone, first at no. 9 between 1885 and 1889. The house was furnished exquisitely with acquisitions from different periods, bought by Peto on his travels and included 'many good bits of German glass' introduced into the windows, and antique tiles and panels in the hearths (**6.3**). Peto apparently harboured a 'great dislike of "collections", where there are many examples of the same thing, entirely destroying the balance and interest of a room'.[39] This principle is clearly discernible in many of the houses that George & Peto

CHAPTER 6

6.3: George & Peto, hall, 9 Collingham Gardens, Kensington, London, photograph by Bedford Lemere, c.1888. (*Private collection*.)

designed and furnished – Shiplake Court, Henley, 1889-91 and 'Poles', Ware, Hertfordshire, 1890-2, being fine examples.

While George was busy furnishing his house, 'Redroofs', Streatham Common in 1889, Peto exchanged the intimacy of no. 9 for the loftier rooms of no. 7 Collingham Gardens (**6.4**). Here the interiors were remarkable for their rich, dark, panelled rooms, furnished with fine *objets d'art*, which would have delighted Pater, but not so Aymer Vallance, who believed that Peto 'had forgotten to allow for the vast difference there is between the clear air of Italy and the murk of London. He had selected nothing but was a faultless work of art of its kind, but for all the rich and imposing effect of each individual piece, in their new environment the ensemble was only gloomy and oppressive.'[40]

The long sitting room occupied a storey and a half on the first floor, in the original warehouse/shop fashion of northern European wharfside houses, taking the form of a panelled gallery hung with antique tapestries (**6.5**). This room undoubtedly influenced George & Peto's 'studio' at the Yellow House, 1892, for Harold's great friend, the furniture historian and

Harold A. Peto (1854-1933)

6.4: George & Peto, 7 Collingham Gardens, 1885, was the only house on the east side faced entirely with terracotta, occupied by Harold Peto, 1889-92. (*Martin Charles.*)

Chapter 6

6.5: 7 Collingham Gardens, 1885. The first-floor drawing room, looking towards the street front, photograph by Bedford Lemere, 1891. (*Private collection.*)

collector, Percy MacQuoid.[41] The dining room at no. 7 was decorated with sixteenth-century stamped and gilded leather above an oak dado, forming a contrast with the arched stone inglenook.

Harold's manuscript travel diaries, written between 1887 and 1898, chronicle his visits to Italy, Spain, Germany, America, Canada, France and Greece during his years in partnership, and Egypt, Italy, Ceylon, Singapore, China, Japan, Canada and France after 1892.[42] These dairies are being published gradually and indicate most clearly the influences that shaped his taste.[43] Couched in a lyrical, highly subjective language, they provide an insight into his character, taste and attitudes. For the most part they eschew commentary on architecture in favour of personal responses to, and descriptions of, places and objects, together with some accounts of the social circles in which he moved. It was Italy that captivated Peto's imagination most – 'O Italy you do contain delights little realised by those who stay at home'[44] – and whence he returned most frequently, preferring Florence over Rome, maintaining 'it is so small and displays itself in such a quietly charming way, Rome is vast, overwhelming, and has its own charms; but give me to live near the Medieval city, classic times are too distant.'[45]

But it was his trip to America in 1887 that would confirm his contemporary stylistic preferences. He visited New York, Philadelphia, Baltimore, Washington and Chicago. In the latter he was able to familiarise himself with the new building methods and technological developments that had followed in the wake of the great fire of Chicago of 1871 and had captured Basil Peto's imagination two years earlier. The American diaries, extracts of which have been published recently,[46] focus for the first time on architectural and technological developments. Peto met Basil's friend, New York's prominent builder David H. King junior, and was particularly admiring of his innovative structural system devised in collaboration with architect George B. Post for the latter's remodelling of the Equitable Building, 120 Broadway (1886-9). Astonishingly, the building had been completed in twelve months at a cost of one million pounds. Peto commented on the lifts, electric lighting, ventilation, pneumatic tubes for messages and boiler room with its myriad engines. It was King who introduced Peto to a number of architects in New York, including McKim, Mead and White, with whom King would later work on his celebrated Model Houses in Harlem of 1891.

Peto visited 'some schools building with clever system of ventilation which I carefully noted'[47] and in New York he saw 'much that is commendable in drainage, sanitary matters, heating etc; etc; which I am going to formulate from my rough notes before I leave, so as to have time to clear up any points that occur to me in going through them'.[48] He was much taken with the quality and care of their 'good new work, thoroughness of finish that makes me think our work very rough Everyone ... I expect is willing to spend much more on getting good work done than we are'.[49] He admired in particular the Renaissance style, then enjoying considerable popularity in the opulent American mansions constructed and furnished during the 1880s. This was the 'Gilded Age' that had flourished under the influence of Jacob von Falke, the great proponent of Italian Renaissance interior design, whose *Die Kunst im Haus* of 1871 had been published in English as *Art in the Home*, in Boston in 1878, thereby setting a fashion. Peto thought New York 'loathesome' after 'the dainty charm'[50] of Boston and identified contemporary Americans as living in a 'much more complete and even luxurious way than with us'.[51] Such clients were also developing a taste for the refinement of the Italian Renaissance having seen the palaces of the Old World and they too, had begun to import pictures, furniture and tapestries. They were now building homes of commensurate beauty in which to exhibit them. Peto commented consistently on the quality of materials, woods and fabrics and records looking at 'a collection of American woods' in the Natural History Museum and 'noted some for use'.[52] He also noted the use that the Americans made of plain brown leather for walls studded with large and small brass nails.

Peto met a number of architects, including H.H. Richardson, Robert Swain Peabody of Peabody & Stearns, and Arthur Rotch of Rotch & Tilden. William Ralph Emerson and others are mentioned too, but it was the restraint and subtlety of work by McKim, Mead & White to which Peto was particularly attracted. According to C.H. Reilly, 'McKim had an almost encyclopaedic knowledge of Italian detail and with it acquired an almost faultless taste'[53] and he and Peto clearly had much in common. The Villard House, McKim, Mead & White's first scholarly exercise in Classical architecture of the Italian Renaissance in New York, made an indelible impression. Amongst the contemporary American influences that were to find a strong echo in Peto's later work was the employment of marble. Peto attributed its success in America to the 'proper supply of a steady flow of warm air into the house, making all this use of marble quite delightful, even now in the depth of winter, you only shudder at marble when you are shivering with cold yourself',[54] a point which must surely have exercised him when translating Italian interiors into English contexts, but, less problematic in his French villas.

From the outset, George had always included the latest technology in his houses – at Rousdon, 1874-83, with its Zimdah's pneumatic bells and hydraulic lift,[55] at 1 Collingham Gardens with its modern drainage system and Tobin ventilating tubes, and no. 4 with its 'lavatory with shampooing apparatus'[56] dating from 1886. The kitchen fittings at Crathorne Hall, Yarm-on-Tees, 1903-6,[57] designed with Yeates, bear witness to the fact that he remained conversant with technological advances, a point that was remarked upon in the contemporary press. There is no doubt, however, that Peto's experience of contemporary American developments, both technical and aesthetic, found resonance in work of the early 1890s, where the character of a number of London works suggest that Peto might have had the upper hand. 6 Carlton House Terrace, for C.H. Stanford was one such example; Stanford sought initially to rectify the 'undignified'[58] staircase arrangement, which he felt lacked style. George & Peto reconstructed that whole part of the house in 1891 by creating a magnificent marble staircase with balustrades and wall lining while at the same time redecorating throughout (**6.6**). The fifteenth-century Italian-inspired carving and detailing and the extensive employment of marble parallels reflected American taste of the time, and the two bathrooms echo Peto's admiration for the luxury of American examples

HAROLD A. PETO (1854-1933)

6.6: George & Peto, marble hall and staircase at 6 Carlton House Terrace, London, for C.H. Stanford, 1889-90, George & Peto's perspective. (The Architect, *43, 1890, 311*.)

in that the walls were lined completely with elaborate, yet subdued, cloisonné work, above low marble dados.

The replacement façade of 47 Berkeley Square, rebuilt and redecorated by George & Peto for Edward Steinkopff, in a pure, early Italian Renaissance style, which was quite 'advanced' [59] for its date, suggested the influence of McKim, Mead & White's domestic work in New York and Boston. Again, extensive use of marble was planned for the hall and staircase, where columns and arches of Pavonazzo marble were to be inserted on the main upper landing. Other London projects included interior design work at no. 3 Ennismore Gardens for E.O. Bickfield, and at no. 15 Hyde Park Gardens for Peter Brotherhood.

West Dean Park, Sussex, 1891-3, bore the undeniable stamp of Peto and American luxury, not least the ample use of marble supplied by Farmer & Brindley for the entrance hall. It was here that he and George re-planned, re-equipped, remodelled and redecorated an existing house bought by the immeasurably wealthy school friend of Harold, William Dodge James in 1891. James and his wife Evelyn, although untitled, were nevertheless accepted into royal circles. George & Peto accordingly created an environment suited to the entertaining of the future King Edward and his set. The idiom of the

CHAPTER 6

6.7: George & Peto, West Dean Park, Sussex, 1891–3. Dining room showing the carved sideboard. The Istrian stone chimneypiece suggests the influence of sixteenth-century Italian style. (The Architect, *55, 1896, 124*.)

four old principal rooms on the south façade arranged *en filade* to allow entertaining on a grand scale show Peto producing the kinds of interiors that he had admired in America and which he would replicate later in some of his Riviera villas. The dining room was Italian in style with sixteenth-century portraits around the frieze coming from an old palace in Milan (**6.7**). A carved Istrian stone chimneypiece, with Hopton Wood stone hood and Spanish tiled back, created a focus and there were close parallels with Isabella Gardner's Boston house. Peto advised James on the purchase of the silk panels and also the hall panelling, suggesting the purchase of 'a very fine specimen of 16th century work'.[60] The drawing room was more or less Louis XVI in style.

Independent work after 1892

While clearly inheriting his father's business acumen, Peto appears from

Harold A. Peto (1854-1933)

a comparatively early age to have reacted against mid-Victorian business values. He developed an abhorrence of London and what he termed 'the squalor and rush of modern life'[61] which finally resulted in his move to the countryside. Peto retired in 1892 on the grounds of ill health. The terms of the dissolution of partnership[62] were mutually supportive, in so far as there were provisions for a transitional period of three years during which George might continue to practise as 'George & Peto' and Harold agreed not to work as an architect or surveyor in England. Thereafter, he was at liberty to undertake decorative work, as distinct from architectural work, but only for existing clients of George & Peto. Given that he was only 38, it was always likely that he would wish to continue to work in some capacity. It was agreed, therefore, that he could undertake furnishing work, described as 'the purchasing of furniture or objects of artistic value'[63] for anybody he liked after 1895. As Whalley points out, the precise dating of some of his independent commissions has proved difficult. In 1899, after a long search for a property, Peto moved into Iford Manor where he restored the house (**6.8**) and laid out the gardens, recording his work in *The Boke of Iford* (1917). He appears to have worked alone until 1906, devoting his attentions to garden design and planting, interests in which had developed

6.8: Iford Manor, Wiltshire. The hall, possibly 1899, photographed 1922. (Country Life, *52, 1922, 243.*)

CHAPTER 6

apace after his retirement. Designs, covered comprehensively by *Country Life* at the time, included those for Easton Lodge, Essex, *c.* 1902, for the Countess of Warwick;[64] 'West Dean', for William James, 1911-12;[65] Critchel House, Dorset, 1906;[66] Petwood, Lincolnshire, completed by 1915;[67] High Wall, Oxford, underway in 1912;[68] Buscot Park, Oxfordshire, 1904-13;[69] Hartham Park, Wiltshire, completed 1907;[70] Bridge House, Surrey, *c.* 1903;[71] Heale House, Wiltshire, 1906-11;[72] and Wayford Manor, *c.* 1902[73] and Burton Pysent, Somerset, for Harold's sisters Helen and Sarah respectively. His other notable work was for 'Ilnacullin', Garinish Island, Ireland, for Annan Bryce, 1910-14[74] and his own garden at Iford Manor, *c.* 1899-1933.[75]

Such commissions invariably incorporated Peto's favoured architectural features, namely pillars, pergolas, rotundas, colonnades, pavilions, terraces and bridges. Somewhat surprisingly, given the formal architectural interventions in his gardens, it is testament to Peto's great understanding of plants, and particularly the setting of trees, that his work should have been afforded attention by followers of William Robinson (1838-1935) including Gertrude Jekyll (1843-1932), who included Peto in her account of paved water gardens, referring to his 'thorough knowledge of plants and keenly discerning perception of their best use is so valuable connexion with his matchless work in garden design'.[76] She was particularly admiring of his canal-shaped pool at Bridge House. Jekyll and Lawrence Weaver also illustrated Peto's garden seats at Sedgwick Hall, Horsham, and his Classical summer-house at Iford in *Gardens for Small Country Houses* of 1912.[77]

In 1906 Harold engaged Gilbert Peto, who in 1920, he recalled as having 'been with me for 14 years in the position of my only architectural assistant during which time I executed very important works to Country Houses, laying out numerous gardens and buildings in connection with same; so that during that time he had the most varied experience of work'.[78] The need for an assistant might well have been prompted by the invitation from Cunard in 1905 to design the first-class accommodation for the *Mauretania*.[79] In so doing, Peto joined the distinguished line of architects employed by shipping lines; J.J. Stevenson (1831-1908) at the Orient Line; Richard Norman Shaw (1831-1912) for the White Star Line and T.E. Collcutt (1870-1924) for P&O, all of whom had managed 'to decorate modernity using the vocabulary of a romanticized English past with hints of the exotic "Orient"'.[80]

Cunard's chairman, Lord Inverclyde, intent upon securing the services of an architect, had first drawn up a list known to have experience of the interior design of British ships; this comprised Collcutt, William Flockhart, Dunn & Watson, Niven & Wrigglesworth, J.J. Stevenson, and Mewès & Davies. Inverclyde also favoured Glasgow architect James Millar. The

Chairman of Swan Hunter, the shipbuilders, suggested decorators Messrs Trollope, well known to George & Peto. Furthermore, the decorating firms Waring & Gillow and White Allom also threw their hats into the ring, but Cunard turned finally to Peto. It is thought that he was approached on the recommendation of Aston Webb, then President of the R.I.B.A. After finally resolving the vexed issue of fees and agreeing to work from his 'London' offices with a clerk of works appointed on Tyneside, Peto visited the *Kaiser Wilhelm*, *Lucania* and *Caronia* to increase his understanding of ship decoration, to date limited to the *Cuhona* in 1883. With characteristic intransigence, he insisted on working with one or two directors rather than the entire board, because 'each would think that his taste was best'.[81]

The relationship with Cunard was complex and at times fraught, but Peto's gift lay in creating elegant domestic environments for the wealthy to display their paintings, tapestries, furniture and *objets d'art*. In the designs for the *Mauretania*, he successfully translated these interiors to meet the needs of the modern liner, an opportunity that many felt had been missed in terms of bringing 'ship decoration up to the standard of the "improved" taste of the last few years'.[82] *The Shipbuilder* acknowledged Peto's previous architectural work, describing the grand staircase as 'unequalled in size and beauty in any vessel afloat, and indeed it is worthy of any mansion ashore'.[83] The furnishings and electric light combined to create 'an atmosphere of luxury and beauty hitherto considered impossible in modern steamships'.[84] Responsible for the first class public rooms, stairways, staterooms and overall decoration and furnishing, Peto employed a range of fashionable historic French and Italian styles, in a manner and scale hitherto reserved for 'a private mansion'.[85] His vocabulary reflected British and North American taste of the time. The staircase, in fifteenth-century Italian Renaissance style was opulent, but subtle. The first class dining room was the largest and most impressive interior, occupying a two-storey space for 485 diners (**6.9**). This Peto decorated in French sixteenth-century, or François I style, inspired largely by the Château de Chambord. The smoke room (**6.10**) was fifteenth-century Italian in style, while the library and writing room was in a fashionable eighteenth-century style with bookcases copied from the Trianon library at Versailles. The two 'Regal Suites', comprising dining room, two bedrooms, bath and toilet were decorated in Adam style with silk wall-panels and matching carpets. Also to Peto's design were the 64 special state and en suite rooms and 109 first class state rooms without facilities. Peto worked with Turner Lord & Co. on the majority of the designs, but employed Charles Mellier & Co., who had worked at West Dean, for the lounge, library and some staterooms. The innovative and influential verandah

CHAPTER 6

6.9: Harold A. Peto, general view of upper and lower first-class dining saloon in the *Mauretania,* for Cunard, 1907, decorated by Turner Lord & Co., London. (*Tyne & Wear Museum Service*.)

café was, by comparison, quite modest in idiom, with its wicker furniture and a variety of plants and trees in pots. His work was much admired, not only on account of its taste, but also the meticulous attention to detail.

In the early 1900s, Peto embarked on a series of commissions in the south of France which would break away from the commonplace villas that reportedly 'prevailed on the Riviera.'[86] By virtue of his altering or

HAROLD A. PETO (1854-1933)

6.10: The smoke room looking aft, *Mauretania*, 1907. The room was divided into two spaces, with a panelled screen separating them. A wagon-vaulted glass and enamelled-wood ceiling. In fifteenth-century Italian style, the room was decorated by W. Lord & Co., London. The double doors led out through a vestibule to the Verandah Café. (*Tyne & Wear Museum Service.*)

adding to existing gardens, his work up until this point had denied him the opportunity to orchestrate fully the subtle relationship between house, interior and garden, although he had been involved in the design of a villa in partnership with George, 'La Rinconada', Cannes, 1891.[87] This commission rather suggests that Peto might have been alerted to the opportunities on the Côte d'Azur, having visited Cannes in 1889, although interestingly it was to George & Yeates that Sir Charles McLaren turned for his villa in Antibes in 1907.[88]

Peto's social network stood him in good stead, resulting in the commissions for three villas in landscaped gardens with interior decoration. The sites of all three presented particular challenges to which Peto responded with skill and inventiveness. The Villa Sylvia 1902, for Ralph Curtis, an expatriate Bostonian known both to Peto's friends the painter John Singer Sargent and Isabella Stewart Gardner, was the first of Peto's villas on the Cap Ferrat, Nice. The sloping site dictated the design of a long, narrow plan, and the east wall was set close against the retaining wall of the road in order to take full

CHAPTER 6

6.11: Harold A. Peto, Villa Sylvia, Cap Ferrat, south of France, for Ralph Curtis, 1902. Ascent to the front door. (Country Life, *28, 1910, 97.*)

advantage of the plot and view. Peto's plan was imaginative and beautifully judged.

The villa was entered through a porch on a level with the bedroom floor. The principal feature was the lofty Italian staircase, comparable with those in Italian palaces, which descended to the sitting rooms and ascended to the bedrooms (**6.11**). It was conceived perfectly to give access to the saloon,

Harold A. Peto (1854-1933)

with its coffered ceiling and fine old fifteenth-century mantelpiece with plaster hood (**6.12**), to the library and the English Palladian-style dining room below, and to the bedrooms above. Such was Peto's attention to the suitability of materials, he had a nearby quarry at La Napoule re-opened in order to obtain local stone for the ground floor walls, the upper floor being stuccoed with a rough finish, known locally as 'Crépissage'. The windows, with their delicate double-arched openings in the fifteenth-century Italian manner and shafts of Pierre de la Royal (a marble-like stone polished to look like green slate) were recessed in thick walls. The great overhanging eaves of the pantiled roof, in the 'Southern manner' were combined with plastered chimneys to create a silhouette that accorded perfectly with its Riviera setting. Writing in 1910, H.A Tipping argued

> The Villa Sylvia, therefore marks the determination of the best modern architects and modern designers not merely to create a thing beautiful in itself, looking enticing on the drawing-board, but beautiful rather because of its subserviency to a larger and wider effect, because it belongs to an organised whole, to which each part is a concomitant of the other as much as are the body, head and limbs of a human being. We are getting

6.12: Villa Sylvia, 1902. The saloon. (Country Life, *28, 1910, 96.*)

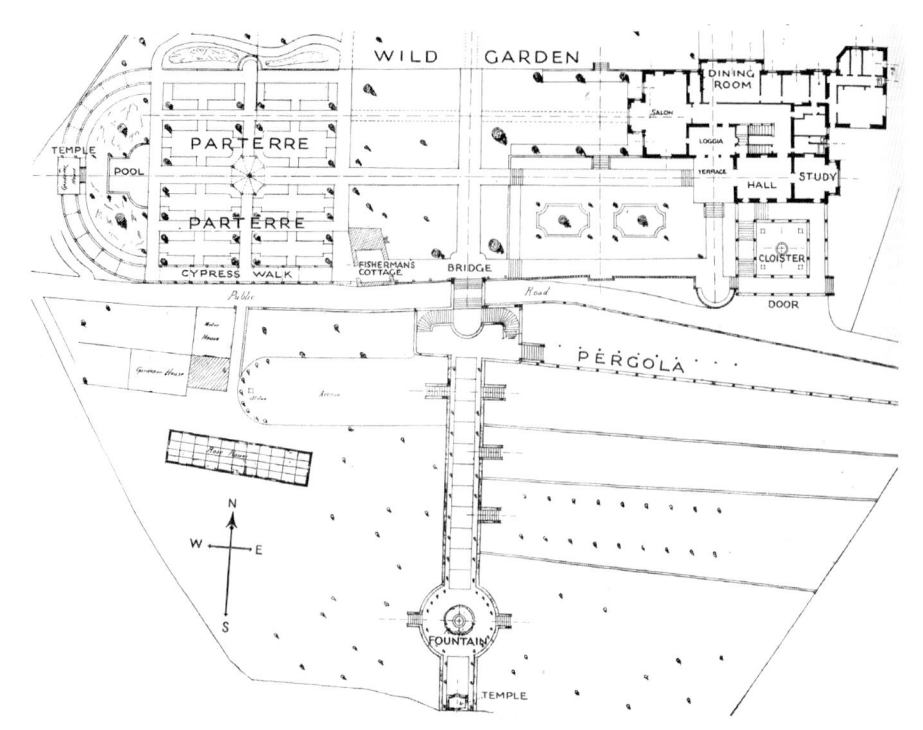

Chapter 6

6.13: Harold A. Peto, plan of 'Maryland' and garden, Alpes Maritimes, south of France, for Arthur Wilson, c. 1905. (Country Life, *28, 1910, 870*.)

more and more to see this principle well carried out in England, and it is agreeable to our national vanity to find that its best and most satisfying manifestations on the Riviera are due to the initiative and taste of an English architect.[89]

The Villa Maryland [90] on the Cap St Jean was completed by 1910 for Arthur Wilson, the Hull shipbuilder. This again posed the problem of a challenging domain, in this instance dissected by a roadway (**6.13**). Described as 'modern ... and fully and efficiently adapted to the mode of living of its day',[91] the villa sounded strong echoes of Florentine and Venetian *palazzi*, in particular the Vanramini Palace, without any sense of historicism (**6.14**). The interiors and furnishings were all the work of Peto, with many pieces having been imported, for example, the ancient door from Spain (**6.15**), the painted panels in the entrance hall 'representing coats of arms, heads of knights in battle array and other kindred subjects, all of which came from the Soncino Castle in Lombardy'.[92] Chairs were Italian, with some French examples dating from the time of Louis XIII. 'Maryland' was acclaimed for combining the spaciousness of the Italian *palazzo*, 'with the comfort and

Harold A. Peto (1854-1933)

6.14: 'Maryland', c. 1905, looking north from the semi-circular bastion. (Country Life, 28, 1910, 865.)

fullness dear to the Englishman. The stiffness and bareness which mar the one scheme, and the clutter and fussiness too often present in the other, are alike avoided' (**6.16**).[93] This feat was not achieved lightly

Peto's 'broad architectural experience' and 'perfect taste'[94] were noted as contributing to the design of the Villa Rosemary, designed for Englishman Arthur Cohen, and the largest of the Cap Ferrat villas. It was built on a

CHAPTER 6

6.15: 'Maryland', *c.* 1905. Ancient door from Spain. (Country Life, *28, 1910, 869.*)

rocky, pine-clad domaine deemed valueless for agricultural purposes which had been acquired by a company that laid it out for building. Apparently 'on Peto's advice'[95] Cohen acquired two and a half acres. Once again, Peto turned what a less experienced architect might have deemed the defects of the site to great advantage by placing the house in a commanding position in the sharp angle of the north-east corner. The entrance porch (**6.17**) was

Harold A. Peto (1854-1933)

6.16: 'Maryland', c. 1905. The entrance hall. (Country Life, *28, 1910, 868.*)

reached by crossing the 'court of the lemons'.[96] The porch, with its Italian features and configuration, relieved an otherwise rather severe elevation, which contrasted with the south side, described as 'joyous with its liberal fenestration, its ample loggias and balconies, its broad marble-paved terrace – all speaking of the social life that is led here both within and without doors'.[97] To that end, Peto constructed the *Squiffa*, a long, open loggia based on examples from Moorish gardens, to mark the extremity of the layout with an architectural accent. Again, Italian in style, the house was executed in local stone quarried from Cap Ferrat. The upper parts of the house were treated with plaster. When soft the surface was scratched in a diagonal pattern revealing a darker colour beneath and creating a simple, but effective decorative described by the writer in *Country Life* as being 'in the [s]graffiti manner'. The plan dispensed with a drawing room to allow for a spacious 'sitting-hall', described as 'stately'[98] with an archway opening on to a broad

Chapter 6

6.17: Harold A. Peto, Villa Rosemary, Alpes Maritimes, south of France, for Arthur Cohen, completed by 1912. The entrance porch on the north side. (Country Life, *31, 1912, 472.*)

staircase of veined marble, readily available in the south of France (**6.18**). The hall itself was furnished mostly with late seventeenth-century pieces, its most dominant feature being the antique Italian hooded fireplace. These three villas show Peto's mature architectural style, drawing its architectural

Harold A. Peto (1854-1933)

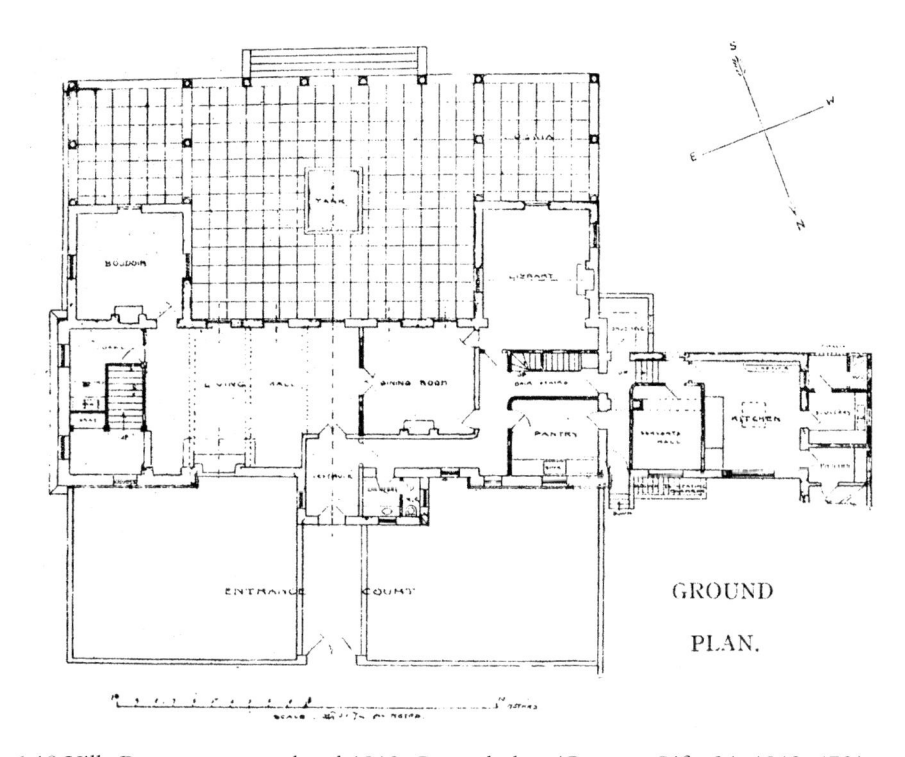

6.18: Villa Rosemary, completed 1912. Ground plan. (Country Life, *31, 1912, 473*.)

vocabulary from the early Italian Renaissance, to create beautifully judged compositions perfectly suited to their locations. They all involved a repertoire of arcades and cloisters, pergolas and bridges often based on Classical Italian examples. The interiors suggest that Peto continued to buy furnishings on behalf of clients. Correspondence from March and November 1913, April 1914 and July 1919 record discussion of architectural antiquities from Prof. Pagan de Paganis in Bologne, P.F. Gouvert in Paris, a specialist in *Décorations de Parcs, Jardins et Interieurs, Anciens & Modernes, Reproductions parfaits dans le Style de l'epoque* and Louis Arnaud, *Antiquaire*, in Avignon, although it is not clear where the items were destined.[99]

Peto also made additions and alterations to other existing properties. At the Villa Salles, Beaulieu,[100] he transformed some of the public rooms, including the music room and salon, for Mme Salles-Eiffel, the daughter of the engineer Gustave Eiffel, who Peto had met on numerous occasions in Paris. He designed architectural features, including a cloister (**6.19**) and

Chapter 6

6.19: Harold A. Peto, the Villa Sallés, Beaulieu, Alpes Maritimes, south of France, for Mme Salles-Eiffel, early 1920s. The cloister garden house. (Country Life, *60, 1926, 970.*)

garden houses, for his garden for Mme Douine at the Villa Cypris, Cap Martin.[101] Work was also undertaken for Baron Van André at the Villa Isola Bella,[102] including a fine example of Peto's characteristic garden houses.

In 1920 Peto wrote 'I do not propose to do further work which would necessitate my keeping such a competent assistant [Gilbert Peto].'[103] Thereafter he appears to have travelled regularly to the Continent, doubtless continuing to advise clients in the Riviera, although an unpublished drawing for a villa, Les Cédres, Cap Ferrat for wealthy merchant banker Ernest Josef Cassel (1852-1921) dates from 1921 but was presumably abandoned on Cassel's death in that year.[104] It shows an imposing, Italianate design on a grand scale (**6.20**). Interestingly, Peto recalls being 'royally entertained by Cassel' in Monte Carlo as early as 1889.[105]

Close examination of these later independent works lends weight to the argument that Peto must surely have played a highly significant role in the positioning of George & Peto's great country houses of the 1880s and early 1890s. Glencot, Wells, Somerset, of 1887 was described at the time as 'a masterpiece'[106] on account of the superb exploitation of the site. Batsford Park, one of their finest houses, for A.B. Freeman Mitford, was described by William Robinson, garden writer, designer and friend to George and Peto, as 'one of the few really good, new houses in England'.[107] He admired particularly the garden pavilions. Such features were common to many of George & Peto's houses and it is not unreasonable to conclude that Peto played a major part in their design. Indeed one of the most remarked upon characteristics of George & Peto's houses, both large and small, was the way in which they took their place in the landscape and in so doing embodied effortlessly those qualities so admired by Arts and Crafts architects of the following generation. Guy Dawber had applauded George's sensitivity and his facility to reproduce this relationship pictorially,[108] but foreknowledge of Peto's later schemes suggests that he made his own notable contribution. So too the interiors of Peto's villas serve to confirm his strong impress on the design, style and furnishing of the earlier houses.

In a letter to Edward James, in the late 1920s, Peto wrote of his Riviera work:

> I enjoyed my time there very much, I felt the beauty so much, and introduced a new feeling into building there, which I am glad to think has affected much that is done there now ... I did what I felt would have been done in the 15th century, if they had been able, and not harassed by pirates and the Saracens, who made all building impossible, except crows nests like Eze'.[109]

By the early 1930s Peto's health was failing and he died at Iford on Easter Day 1933. Ralph Edwards, who met Peto at the London house of his *Country Life* colleague H.A. Tipping, considered him to be the

Chapter 6

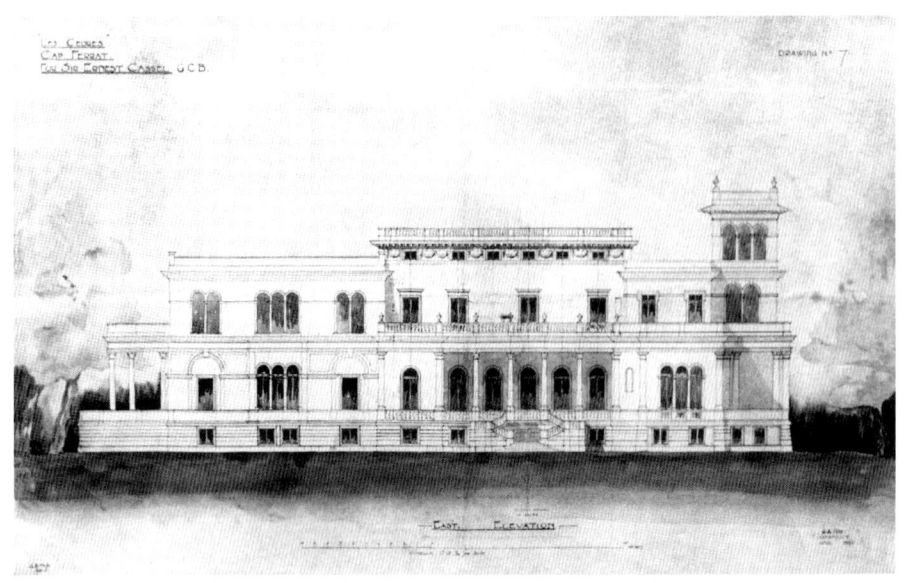

6.20: Harold A. Peto, drawing of Les Cèdres, Cap Ferrat, south of France for Sir Ernest Cassel, dated 1921. (*Private collection.*)

> British aesthete in pose, appearance and voice … . Verging on old age when I met him, he had been granted plenty of time to study the part. I recall him at dinner in Dorset Square with his fastidious air and mincing gait, cambric ruffles at his wrists, his manner and deportment evoking contemporary descriptions of Horace Walpole.[110]

Peto was a man of extreme taste and sensitivity, becoming in later life, something of an arbiter of such matters amongst the drawing rooms of the wealthy. In partnership with Ernest George, he made an invaluable contribution to one the leading architectural practices of the late nineteenth century. His contribution is clearly legible in a number of areas: his business acumen; his influence on the pattern of patronage; his relationships with clients; the importance of his visit to America; his concern for craftsmanship; his respect for materials; his interior design, his consummate skill in marrying houses with sites and above all his exceptional taste, all characteristics and qualities that were perpetuated by many of the pupils and assistants that passed through the offices of George & Peto.

Peto showed remarkable judgment in his French villas. Avray Tipping waxed lyrical about these in a series of articles in *Country Life*, in which attention was drawn repeatedly to Peto's gift for unifying house and garden. Tipping identified the fact that 'while they all breathe the spirit and are instinct with the genius of the designer, the contrast is very considerable, and arises naturally and rightly from Mr Peto's just and sensitive appreciation of every particular situation and of circumstance in the ground and of character and purpose in the client'.[111]

As an independent practitioner, Peto excelled as an interior decorator, and as a garden designer and planter, finding a niche with the design of villas, their gardens and interiors. But it was the rare combination of his talents that was so telling. Peto represented the British aesthete *par excellence*, but above all, he understood the complexities of the interdisciplinary relationship between architecture, interior and garden design. Herein lay not only his great gift, but also his enduring legacy as an architect.

Abbreviations

AR *Architectural Review*
B   *The Builder*
BN *Building News*
CL *Country Life*

Notes

1   R. Whalley, *The Great Edwardian Gardens of Harold Peto*, Aurum Press, 2007; D. Ottewill, *The Edwardian Garden*, Yale U.P., 1989; H.J. Grainger, 'The Architecture of Sir Ernest George and his Partners, *c.* 1860-1922' (unpublished PhD thesis, University of Leeds, 1985, available online: https://www.etheses.whiterose.ac.uk/239/ ; 'Iford Manor and its Garden', *Architectural Review*, 33, 1913, 11-14, 28-30.
2   For full details of George's work, *see* Hilary J. Grainger, *The Architecture of Sir Ernest George*, Spire Books, 2011.
3   *Builder's Journal: An Architectural Review*, 3, 1895, 57.
4   J. Summerson, *The London Building World of the Eighteen-Sixties*, Thames & Hudson, 1973, 11.
5   L. Chown, *No. 1: Brief Biographies of Leading Laymen, Sir Samuel Morton Peto, Bart., M.P.: The Man Who Built the Houses of Parliament*, Carey Press, 1945; *Sir Henry Peto, Sir Morton Peto: A Memorial Sketch*, printed for private circulation, London, 1893; M. Port, *Dictionary of National Biography*, M.M. Chrimes *et al.*, (eds), *Biographical Dictionary of Civil Engineers in Great Britain and Ireland*, Thomas Telford Publishing, 2008, 614-18; A. Vaughan, *Samuel Morton Peto, A Victorian Entrepreneur*, Ian Allan Publishing, 2009.
6   *Illustrated London News*, 8 Feb. 1851, 106.
7   Ibid., 10 Jan. 1857, 24.
8   Basil Peto, unpublished MS diary in the possession of the estate of the late Lady Serena Matheson, 1.
9   Now destroyed. Designed by J.L. Clemence, www.suffolkchurches.co.uk
10 Harold Peto, application for Fellowship of the RIBA, 3 Nov. 1881.
11 E.G. Dawber, 'The Late Sir Ernest George, R.A., a Few Thoughts by Mr E. Guy Dawber, F.R.I.B.A', *B*, 123, 1922, 903.

Chapter 6

12 D. Braddell, entry on George in *The Dictionary of National Biography, 1922-1930*, 308.
13 Braddell quoted in A. Stuart Gray, *Edwardian Architecture: A Biographical Dictionary*, Wordsworth, 1985, 186.
14 Ibid., quoting *The Times*.
15 For full details and biographies of pupils and assistants, see Grainger [n. 2], 437-55.
16 *BN*, 28, 1875, 308.
17 Ernest George, 'An Architect's Reminiscences by Sir Ernest George R.A.', *B*, 120, 1921, 623.
18 For a full discussion of Harrrington and Collingham Gardens, *see* Grainger [n. 2]. For a full discussion of Peto Brothers, builders, *see* Grainger [n. 2] and Grainger [n. 1].
19 As n. 17.
20 As n. 3.
21 B. Peto [n. 8], 29A.
22 A. Powers (ed.), '"Architects I have known", the Architectural Career of S.D. Adshead', *Architectural History*, 24, 1981, 112.
23 As n. 17.
24 George described Peto as such in his dedication of *Etchings of Old London*, Fine Art Society, 1884.
25 George's proposal of Peto for fellowship of the RIBA, Oct.1883. Peto was awarded fellowship on 7 Jan. 1884.
26 As n. 3.
27 Edmund Hanbury, unpublished diary in the possession of Robert Hanbury, 22 Feb. 1889.
28 Ibid., 10 Apr. 1891.
29 Ibid., 31 Dec. 1890.
30 'Presentation of the Royal Gold Medal to Mr Ernest George at the Sixteenth General Meeting, 22 June 1896', *JRIBA*, 3, 1896, 469-72.
31 H.A. Peto, unpublished MS diaries, 2 vols, transcribed (by an unknown hand), Swindon Record Office, 2780, p. 228.
32 Diary of Mary Seton Watts, 1891, held at the Watts Gallery, Surrey.
33 Ibid.
34 Basil Peto [n. 8], 17.
35 Letter from George to Harold Peto dated 1889, in the possession of the estate of the late Lady Serena Matheson.
36 Peto [n. 31], 183.
37 Ibid, 179.
38 *The Coffee Public House News*, 1 Dec. 1880, 491.
39 'Iford Manor and Its Garden - 1', *Architectural Review*, 33, 1913, 13.
40 A. Vallance, 'Good Furnishing and the Decoration of the Home', quoted in the *Magazine of Art*, 1904 (pt 1), 20.
41 For full details, *see* Grainger [n. 2], 244-5, 290.
42 As n. 31. Peto's extensive travel diaries date from 1887 to 1898. Book 1 (299 pp.) covers visits to Bayreuth, Rothenberg, Venice (1896); Pisa, Florence, Siena, Orvieto, Assisi (1887); New York, Boston, Newport, Washington, Philadelphia, Quebec (1887); Spain, Gibraltar, Tangiers, Seville, Granada, Cordoba, Toledo, Madrid (1888); Venice, Torcello, Verona, Lake Como, Cannes, Lucca, Florence, Bologna, Rimini, Urbino, Parma, Piacenza, Milan, Fontainbleau (1889); Greece, Corfu, Athens (1891); Egypt, Luxor (1892); Palermo, Girgenti, Taormino, Venice

Harold A. Peto (1854-1933)

(1895) and Ceylon, Cairo, Colombo, Kandy, Hakgala (1898). Book 2 (92 pp.) covers Singapore, Canton (March 1898), Japan, Nagasaki, Fugi, Tokyo, Kyoto, Lake Biwa, Ishyama, Nara, Atami, Nikko, Chuyengi, Victoria, Vancouver; France, Brittany (July 1898), Kersaillou, St Pol de Léon, Santec.

43 See Grainger [n. 2]; R. Whalley 'Harold Peto's Japanese Diary', *Hortus*, 36, Winter 1995, and Spring 1996; 'Harold Peto's Spanish Diary 1888', *Hortus*, 55, Autumn 2000.
44 Peto [n. 31], vol. 1, 21.
45 Ibid., 26-7.
46 See Grainger [n. 2], 257-60.
47 Peto [n. 31], 55.
48 Ibid., 76-7.
49 Ibid., 51.
50 Ibid., 69
51 Ibid., 75.
52 Ibid., 83.
53 C.H. Reilly, *Scaffolding in the Sky*, Routledge, 1924, 11-12.
54 Peto [n. 31], 80.
55 S.F. Murphy, (ed.), *Our Homes and how to Make them Healthy*, Cassell and Co., 1883, 251-8. See also Grainger [n. 2].
56 *British Architect*, 12 Mar. 1886, 255.
57 'Crathorne Hall, Yorkshire', *CL*, 29, 1911, 598-604.
58 *The Architect*, 43, 1890, 311.
59 T. Raffles Davison, 'The Progress in Recent Architecture: Town Houses: New Designs and Adaptations', *Magazine of Art*, n.s. 2, 1904-5, 159.
60 Peto writing to Edward James in July 1892 quoted in Whalley [n. 1], 42.
61 Peto [n. 31], vol 1, 2.
62 Deed of dissolution of partnership between George & Peto, 31 Oct. 1892, Wiltshire County Record Office, Trowbridge, NRA list no. 6118. Peto assigned half of the partnership, premises, furniture, books, drawings, stock in trade and goodwill to George, for the sum of £5,606 13s. 9d. The deed lists 26 works and contracts in hand at the time of the dissolution and sets out the percentage of the income from them to be paid to Harold Peto. In addition, thirteen outstanding accounts are listed from which Peto would derive half the amount owing.
63 Ibid.
64 'Easton Lodge, Essex', *CL*, 22, 1907, 738-48; 25, 1909, 639.
65 'West Dean Park, Chichester', *CL*, 170, 1981, 1378-81, 1462-5; gardens, *CL*, 6, 1899, 112-18.
66 'Critchel, Dorset', *CL*, 57, 1925, 766, 814; gardens, 57, 1925, 766-74, 57, 1925, 814-23; gardens 23, 1908, 90-6; 57, 1925, 874-81.
67 'Petwood, Woodhall Spa', *CL*, 38, 1915, 198-204.
68 'High Wall', *CL*, quoted in Whalley [n. 1], 21, 27, 64-9.
69 'Buscot Park, Berkshire', *CL*, 87, 1940, 502-7, 524-8; gardens, 40, 1916, 490-7.
70 'Hartham Park, Wiltshire', *CL*, 26, 1909, 196-205.
71 'Bridge House, Weybridge, Surrey', *CL*, 24, 1908, 558-66; 'A Garden at Bridge House, Weybridge', *AR*, 33, 1913, 55.
72 'Heale House, Wiltshire', *CL*, 37, 1915, 272-7.
73 'Wayford Manor, Somerset', *CL*, 76, 1934, 336-41; 123, 1958, 494-6.
74 For an account of Garinish Island, see E. Hyams, *Irish Gardens*, Macdonald, 1967, 60-6; Whalley [n. 1], 123-39; Ottewill [n. 1], 155-6.

Chapter 6

75 'Iford Manor, Wiltshire', *CL*, 22, 1907, 450-61; 94, 1943, 907; gardens, 22, 1907, 450; 52, 1922, 242-8, 272-7; correspondence 133, 1963, 726; 151, 1972, 1214-15; 34, 1913, 484-5; 'Iford Manor and its Garden – I', *AR*, 10, 1913, 11-14; 'Iford Manor and Its Garden – II', *AR*, 10, 1913, 28-30.
76 G. Jekyll, *Wall and Water Gardens*, Country Life, 1913, 175
77 G. Jekyll & L. Weaver, *Gardens for Small Country Houses*, Country Life, 1912, republished as *Arts and Crafts Gardens*, Antique Collectors' Club, 1981, 247.
78 A reference written by Harold A. Peto for his cousin Gilbert Peto in support of the latter's application for post of Chief Architectural Assistant for the Dorset County Council, 15 May 1920. Harold Peto comments further, 'I consider the experience Mr Gilbert Peto had obtained after he left me, whilst in the Army during the War, in the Engineering and Surveying Offices at the Admiralty Works at Southwick, will have given him a most useful extension of knowledge of such practical works which he had less experience of whilst here ... I think most highly of him'. Harold's great-niece, the late Lady Serena Matheson recalls that Gilbert 'by the standards of the time was considered to produce homes in good taste'. She recalled that there was always an air of mystery about Gilbert.
79 For a full account of Peto's work, *see* A. Wealleans, *Designing Liners: A History of Interior Design Afloat*, Routledge, 2006, 46-52; P. Newall, *Mauretania, Triumph and Restoration*, Ships in Focus, 2006, 46-63.
80 Wealleans [n. 79], 25.
81 Meeting between Peto and Lord Inverclyde and Edward Cunard, 24 May 1905, quoted in Newall [n. 79], 46.
82 A letter from the decorating firm White Allom, 10 Mar. 1905, quoted in Wealleans [n. 79], 45.
83 Quoted in M.D. Warren, *The Cunard Turbine-Driven Quadruple Screw Atlantic Liner 'Mauretania': Authentically Reproduced from a Rare Commemorative Edition of 'Engineering', with Additional New Material Selected by Mark D. Warren and with the Assistance of Swan Hunter*, Patrick Stevens, 1987, quoted in Wealleans [n. 79], 49.
84 Warren [n. 83], 18, quoted in Wealleans [n. 79], 52.
85 Warren [n. 83], 17, quoted in Wealleans [n. 79], 49.
86 'Country Homes, Gardens Old & New, Villa Rosemary, Alpes Maritimes. The property of Mrs Arthur Cohen', *CL*, 31, 1912, 468.
87 Illustrated in *BN*, 60, 1891, 669.
88 *B*, 92, 1907, 694.
89 'Chateaux & Gardens of France, The Villa Sylvia, Alpes Maritimes, The Property of Mr Ralph Curtis', *CL*, 28, 1910, 97.
90 'Country Homes, Gardens Old & New, Maryland – II, Alpes Maritimes, The Residence of Mrs Arthur Wilson', *CL*, 28, 1910, 866.
91 Ibid.
92 Ibid., 870.
93 As n. 90.
94 'Country Homes and Gardens Old and New: Villa Rosemary, Alpes Maritimes, The Property of Mr Arthur Cohen', *CL*, 30, 1912, 468-74.
95 Ibid.
96 Ibid., 472.
97 Ibid.
98 Ibid., 473.
99 Letters in the possession of the estate of the late Lady Serena Matheson.

100 'Houses & Gardens of the Riviera, the Villa Salles, Beaulieu, A.M. The Residence of Mme Salles-Eiffel', *CL*, 60, 1926, 964-71.
101 'The Garden of the Villa Cypris, Cap Martin', *CL*, 61, 1927, 342-6.
102 'Country Homes & Gardens Old & New, Isola Bella, Cannes, a Residence of Baron Van André', *CL*, 29, 1911, 450-6.
103 *See* n. 78.
104 Ernest Cassells, born in Germany of Jewish parents, was one of the wealthiest men of his day and was a good friend of King Edward VII. He retired in 1910. His philanthropic benefactions included support for the King Edward's Hospital Fund, the British Red Cross and the founding of an Anglo-German Institute in memory of King Edward VII. In 1919 he founded the Cassel Hospital in Richmond, London.
105 Peto [n. 31], 181.
106 J.W. Gleeson White, 'The Revival of English Domestic Architecture V: The Work of Messrs George and Peto', *The Studio*, 1896, 212.
107 W. Robinson, *Garden Design and Architects' Gardens*, John Murray, 1892, xii.
108 Dawber, [n. 11].
109 Quoted in Whalley [n. 1], 155.
110 R. Edwards quoted in J. Carnforth, *The Search for a Style: Country Life and Architecture 1897 1935*, André Deutsch, 1988, 131.
111 *CL* [n. 98], 450.

7.1: Hugh Thackeray Turner, 1886, aged 33, the year he was elected as a member of the Art Workers' Guild. (*Art Workers' Guild*.)

7

Artist in the craft of building: the architectural work of Hugh Thackeray Turner (1853-1937)

Robin Stannard

Hugh Thackeray Turner's life bore witness to a period of dramatic social and technological change. He belonged to a group of people who benefited from Britain's industrial prosperity, but who were dedicated to improving social conditions and protecting both the built heritage and natural environment of England. He enjoyed a long, varied career, but he is perhaps best remembered for his role as conservationist, working for 29 years as secretary to the Society for the Protection of Ancient Buildings (SPAB) and a further 26 as chairman of the society's committee. This is very much as Turner would have wished. His memorial in Godalming church, carved by his brother Laurence, reads, 'An architect and artist in the craft of building, who devoted most of his life to the saving and repairing of the ancient buildings of England, and to the preservation of the beauties of the countryside.'

In addition to his conservation work, Turner was also an important Arts and Crafts architect, many of his buildings symbolising the essence of what lay at the heart of the movement. He never wrote about his approach to design, but examining his architectural work reveals buildings rich in originality and integrity (**7.1**).

CHAPTER 7

Early life

He was born in 1853, at Foxearth, Essex, the son of a country vicar, the Revd John Turner. He was one of five sons and two daughters. The family moved frequently between a succession of rural parishes including Spalding, Lincolnshire, and Wotton-under-Edge, Gloucestershire, before finally settling at Wroughton, Wiltshire, in 1875. Turner's future career and life were heavily influenced by his upbringing, in which he was encouraged to develop interests in art, antiquities, music, nature, history, and sport. Through his father's work, he developed a keen sense of Christian social duty and a deeply held belief in the importance of honesty and integrity, two traits which would form the cornerstone of his architectural work.

His character had many aspects and the *Survey of London* describes Turner as reticent and modest.[1] He was also meticulous, with an almost obsessive interest in recording detail, a quality that would prove an important asset in his work for the SPAB. Turner enjoyed a full social life and had many artistic and socially aware friends. He also thrived on controversy and debate; in 1938 his friend F.W. Troup described this aspect of character:

> I first met Turner many years ago as a member of the Art Worker's Guild. Here he was a frequent speaker. His comments were always vigorous and to the point. He said what he thought and never lost his temper. He expected his opponents and often succeeded in getting them to reply in the same manner, and he seemed to enjoy controversy about any matter he was interested in. But it was at the executive committee of the SPAB, that I got to know Turner intimately and learned to admire his fighting qualities, which I fear made him not a few enemies in his robust eagerness to save ancient buildings from disfiguration or vandalism.[2]

Education and early career

Throughout his life, Turner remained close to his elder brother Hawes and younger brother Laurence. Both his brothers attended Marlborough College. Hawes then went on to study at Trinity College, Cambridge, before training to be a painter at the Royal Academy. Little is known of Hawes' artistic career and he is best known for his role as Keeper of the National Gallery, a position he held between 1898 and 1914. Laurence studied at Oxford University and was then articled to the Oxford architect John McCulloch. He never practiced as an architect, but instead developed a successful career as a carver, working in stone, wood and plaster. Laurence often collaborated with Turner and also undertook commissions for many of the leading architects of the period, including G.F. Bodley, Sir Herbert Baker, William Weir, Henry Hare, Sir Walter Tapper and Curtis Green. He is credited with playing a leading role in the renaissance of English carving and also taught the subject to a number of Arts and Crafts craftsmen including George Jack.

In contrast to his brothers, Turner attended Newbury Grammar School and then went to work in London as an architect's assistant. In 1874, when he was aged 21, he was articled to Sir George Gilbert Scott. At this time Scott was approaching the end of his long and successful career. Scott's office has been described as 'developing into the prototype of the modern large architectural firm producing a consistent house style.'[3] Little is known of Turner's work for Scott, but the experience gave him a thorough understanding of architecture and practical building. However, like a number of those who trained under the architects of the Gothic Revival, Turner rebelled against the style. Troup, in his appreciation of Turner states that 'Thackeray Turner was trained in Sir Gilbert Scott's office and from his experience there learned much to be avoided and acquired an almost instinctive revulsion of the Gothic Revival, whether for church or any other form of building.'[4]

Turner was keen to set up on his own account and unsuccessfully entered a number of architectural competitions. In addition to working for Scott, in 1877 Turner carried out work for J.T. Micklethwaite and also began work on the design of his first building, the Wroughton Board School, Wiltshire, which was completed in 1881.[5] In 1878, Scott died, and Turner continued to work in the office with Scott's son, John Oldrid. This change does not appear to have suited Turner, because seven months later he left to become George Gilbert Scott junior's chief assistant.

Scott junior was then aged 39 and at the height of his brilliant, but tragically short career. The opportunity of working for him would have held much appeal for the ambitious 25-year-old Turner because Scott was a leading figure in the development of church design and an important figure in the Queen Anne Revival. Scott's other assistant at this time was Temple Lushington Moore (1856-1920), who had joined him as an articled pupil in 1875. On completing his articles, Moore continued working in close collaboration with Scott, remaining a loyal friend and eventually building up his own successful practice to become one of the leading late Gothic Revival church architects.[6]

Little is known of Turner's work for Scott junior, but during the five years he was employed by him, the office was involved in a wide variety of work, both ecclesiastical and secular. Important projects at this time include the new church of All Hallows, Southwark, ongoing work at St Agnes, Kennington, and new residential buildings at both Pembroke College, Cambridge, and St John's College, Oxford. The only building by Scott of which there is positive evidence of Turner's involvement is at the church of St Peter & St Paul at Knapton, Norfolk, in 1882, and it was regarded as one of Scott's most successful church restorations. In 1880, the first signs of Scott's mental condition had appeared. He recovered, but declined again and on 20 July 1883 was detained in the Royal Bethlem Hospital. From then onwards, he fluctuated between periods of sanity and insanity, making the continuation of his architectural work increasingly difficult.[7]

Early work for the SPAB

Turner's work at Knapton drew him to the attention of the SPAB, and on 11 December 1882 he was offered the position as its part-time secretary. He eagerly accepted and on 15 February 1883 began working for the society. For Turner, aged 29, this appointment marked a turning point in his career, sparing him from witnessing Scott's distressing final decline.

Turner's appointment would prove equally important for the SPAB, his professional experience, naturally combative character and methodical nature making him exactly the right person for the role. He brought stability to the society as William Morris' involvement in its day-to-day business decreased. Turner also gave it continuity as its role changed from a protest group in the late nineteenth century to a respected professional body in the twentieth. He was required to work for the society three days a week which enabled him to continue with his private architectural practice which he was encouraged to undertake at the SPAB office. Turner was, however, prohibited from accepting architectural appointments for repair work to buildings in which the society was involved. This cast Turner's role in the SPAB as managing the work of other architects, although with his experience, he would often have been more capable of carrying out the work himself.

His early work for the society involved visiting buildings under threat, taking notes, making sketch plans and then reporting back to the committee where the appropriate response was debated and proposed action agreed. The experience gained from these visits would have an important influence on his own architectural designs.

The founding of Balfour Turner

Although Turner thrived in his role for the SPAB, it was a period of financial difficulty because he was unsuccessful in obtaining sufficient architectural commissions to supplement his part-time salary from the society. This situation changed when, on the 10 June 1895, he entered into partnership with Eustace Balfour, creating the practice of Balfour

Turner. Eustace Balfour was then aged 31 and was acting as an honorary secretary of the SPAB. He came from an aristocratic family, his brother Arthur would later become Conservative Prime Minister, while his sister became Principal of Newnham College, Cambridge. Balfour had married Lady Francis Campbell, whose uncle was the Duke of Westminster.[8] This family connection would prove very important for the future success of the partnership.

Balfour was educated at Harrow, then at Trinity College, Cambridge. It was while at university that he first took an interest in conservation, alerting William Morris to George Gilbert Scott junior's restoration work at Cherry Hinton Church in 1878. The *Builders' Journal & Architectural Record* noted that after graduation 'he became a pupil in the office of Basil Champneys, or rather a student for ordinary forms of pupilage were waived, and after a much shorter term of practical experience than is usually advised to a young architect, he began practice on his own account, and set forth on his career as an architect.'[9]

The instigation of the partnership was likely to have been prompted by Balfour securing the commission to rebuild Ampton Hall, Suffolk (**7.2**), which had been destroyed in a fire. This was a major commission for Balfour, who would have found Turner's wider experience of great benefit. The building is of a very restrained design, constructed of red brick, with stone mullioned windows and crow-stepped gables. Although the design is competent, it lacks the inventiveness of Balfour Turner's later work. The *Builders' Journal & Architectural Record* describes it as 'built on the foundation

7.2: Ampton Hall, Suffolk, 1885. The first major work by Balfour Turner, it was the rebuilding of a Jacobean house previously destroyed in a fire. (*English Heritage/NMR.*)

of an old Jacobean House [and] does not reproduce that which it succeeds, although, as will be noticed, the detail owes much to the tradition of the Jacobean period.'[10] Balfour Turner's office was located in the same building as the SPAB. This would lead to an association between the two organisations that would last 25 years.

Marriage and financial security

It is likely that through the SPAB Turner met the wealthy stockbroker, Thomas Wilde Powell, a partner in the company Heseltine & Powell. Both Powell and Heseltine were strong supporters of the SPAB. The two men also used their wealth to support philanthropic causes, as well the arts and architecture. In 1874-6 Heseltine had commissioned Norman Shaw to design his house, 196 Queen's Gate, London. Four years later Powell engaged Shaw to design his house, 'Piccards Rough' in Guildford.[11]

Powell had three sons and five daughters who were of a similar age to Turner. In 1886, Turner began staying with the Powell family at 'Piccards Rough'; two years later, Turner married Powell's daughter Mary. Powell had very enlightened views regarding women's rights, and following the Women's Property Act, bequeathed substantial sums of money to each of his daughters to ensure their financial independence. In giving this money, he stipulated that it should be used to buy property and support good causes. Powell's concept of using his wealth to support philanthropic causes and contemporary architecture would result in the design of a number of Turner's most important buildings.

On his marriage, Turner and his wife moved to a substantial Georgian townhouse at 20 Gower Street, London, a transformation from his days as a bachelor, sharing rooms with his brother Hawes in Grey's Inn Square. The marriage was a good match, allowing both of them to develop and share each other's creative interests. Turner's wife was an important Arts and Crafts embroideress, who in 1907, founded the Women's Guild of Art, with May Morris.

In 1886, Turner was elected as a member of the Art Workers' Guild and in 1889 he exhibited painted ceramic work at the Arts and Crafts Society Exhibition. He had begun painting china in the late 1870s and would later become an important exponent of the craft. Turner was joined by his wife in the 1890 Arts and Crafts Society Exhibition, where she exhibited embroidery.

Work for the Garrett circle

The move to Gower Street and the connection with the Powell family

Hugh Thackeray Turner (1853-1937)

7.3: York Street Chambers, 1892, Balfour Turner's first major work in London. It was specifically designed to provide accommodation for single women. (*Author*.)

brought Turner into close contact with the Garrett circle. This group centred on the pioneering female doctor Elizabeth Garrett Anderson, and her sister the architectural decorator, Agnes Garrett as well as the suffragist, Millicent Fawcett. Agnes and Millicent lived not far from the Turners, at 2 Gower Street. Others connected with the group included Thomas Wilde Powell; his daughter, the artist, Christiana Herringham; the solicitor, James Beale (for whom Philip Webb designed 'Standen'); barrister John Westlake; Anne Townsend; the Revd Giles Pilcher; and the Queen Anne Revival architects J.J. Stevenson and J.M. Brydon.[12] This group were dedicated to the advancement and care of women. In 1888, they founded the Ladies Residential Chambers Ltd, whose purpose was to provide accommodation for single, working women. Their first project was the construction of Chenies Street Chambers, London, designed by Brydon in 1889. Its success led to the erection of a second ladies' residential chambers at York Street, London (**7.3**). For the design of this building, Balfour Turner were chosen as architects and Turner was invited to inspect the establishment in Chenies Street. York Street Chambers was completed in 1892, and was one of Balfour

213

CHAPTER 7

7.4: Campden House Chambers, Kensington, London, 1896. The design shows greater Arts and Crafts influence than the earlier York Street Chambers. (*Author.*)

Turner's first designs to be built in London. Like Brydon's earlier chambers, its style was Queen Anne.

In 1896, Balfour Turner were appointed to design a second residential block at Sheffield Terrace, Kensington, called Campden House Chambers (**7.4**). Like those in York Street, it was intended that the occupants should live as a community. A communal dining room was located in the basement

Hugh Thackeray Turner (1853-1937)

7.5: 7 Balfour Place, London, seen from Alford Street. Typical of Balfour Turner's flamboyant, Queen Anne Revival-influenced early work on the Grosvenor Estate. (*Author.*)

and featured a vaulted ceiling supported by black granite columns from Alloa. The building housed both men and women. Although not connected to the Ladies Residential Chambers Ltd, the building was managed by Anne Townsend, from the Garrett Circle.

Campden House Chambers reflected current Arts and Crafts ideas as well as the work of Philip Webb. It was built of yellow London stock bricks

Chapter 7

7.6: 10 Green Street, London, 1895, shows much more Arts and Crafts restraint than Balfour Turner's previous work on the Grosvenor Estate. Of particular note is the floral stone carving surrounding the entrance door by Laurence Turner. (*Author.*)

with contrasting red brick quoins and arches. The building features the use of SPAB-influenced red clay tile details to the windowsills and heads. At ground level the walls were constructed in warm-coloured, smooth stonework, arranged in alternating narrow and deep bands. In its 1937 appreciation of Turner, the *Architects' & Building News* said of the building:

> it has been authoritatively stated that, while [Camden House Chambers] embody most of these medieval principles of design, they are still, even today, up to date and practicable. Indeed he foresaw the idea of the 'flat' and the principles governing the design of the block of residential flats forty years before that notion became a popular one.[13]

The Grosvenor Estate

During the late 1880s Balfour Turner had little success in securing significant work, apart from a house called 'Kingswood Hanger' in Gomshall, Surrey, and a house at Hayes Common, London. Turner at this time was financially dependant on his part-time SPAB salary and his wife's independent income for support. This situation changed dramatically when in 1890, Eustace Balfour was appointed as surveyor to the Grosvenor Estate in Mayfair. Balfour's appointment was largely due to the Duke of Westminster being his wife's uncle, and as a result the partnership were given the opportunity to design new buildings on the estate. Although Balfour was in overall control of the partnership, it is generally considered that Turner was largely responsible for the design. Much of the partnership's early work for the estate was centred on the Mount Street and Aldford Street area. The design of their first range of buildings, 1-6 Balfour Place, was tentative, but they quickly gained confidence and subsequent work in Mount Street and Aldford Street shows much more variety and imagination. These represent some of the partnership's most flamboyant designs, drawing on a rich variety of historic references to produce lively street elevations (**7.5**).

By comparison, 10 Green Street (**7.6**), built in 1895, shows much more restraint as well as Turner's Arts and Crafts ambitions. The main visual feature of the street elevation is a pair of double height stone bay windows. These are designed in a freely interpreted Jacobean style, with simplified detailing. The greatest decorative impact is reserved for the entrance, were naturalistic floral stone carving by Laurence Turner rises between the recessed front door and side windows, spreading out across the curved arch above. This shows the influence on Turner of Philip Webb and the architects associated with the Art Workers' Guild, in particular William Lethaby. Much later, in 1932, at the RIBA Lethaby Tribute, Turner recalled:

> When I was living in Gower Street and Lethaby was living in Gray's Inn, I used to spend my time after church, in either calling on Philip Webb or Lethaby ... Webb liked me to bring my children with me, so I used to go to him fairly often. I used also to go to Lethaby, and if he was out of bed, which was not very often .. we used to have extraordinarily interesting discussions on art and architecture.[14]

Chapter 7

7.7: 21-22 Grosvenor Street, London, 1898, a confident, Philip Webb–influenced design in the heart of Mayfair. (*Author.*)

Architectural experiments in Mayfair

As Balfour Turner's work for the Grosvenor Estate continued during the 1890s, so Turner's architectural inventiveness and stylistic sympathies developed; although he never spoke of his design philosophy, from the

Hugh Thackeray Turner (1853-1937)

7.8: 1-10 Eaton Gate, London, 1910, five large town houses, for William Willet, arranged in an ingenious Arts and Crafts composition. (*Author.*)

buildings he produced it is apparent that he was experimenting with several themes. The first of these was the development of the rational and restrained Arts and Crafts design approach adopted at Green Street. This is typified by a simply proportioned set of stables called Balfour Mews built in 1899 and a pair of town houses at 21-22 Grosvenor Street (**7.7**), dating from 1898. A more adventurous and complex example of this approach is a group of townhouses which Turner designed for William Willet at 1 to 10 Eaton Gate (**7.8**) in 1910. Like Green Street, the stone detailing is simplified, with the decorative interest reserved for rich naturalistic floral carving to the bay windows, produced by Laurence Turner.

A second theme explored by Turner was to combine architectural styles of different periods on the same building. This approach is typified by another group of townhouses designed for William Willet at Lygon Place (**7.9**) in 1900. Much of the building's street elevation was designed in a Philip Webb-inspired interpretation of an early eighteenth-century Classical style, with a deeply projecting stone cornice and repetitive two-storey stone bay windows with shuttered sashes. In contrast, a wing to the north,

CHAPTER 7

7.9 Lygon Place, London, 1900, designed for William Willet. An example of Turner's 'style blending.' The leaded lights to the ground-floor bay window allow the Jacobean-influenced wing to merge with the Classical style of the main building. (*Author*.)

which visually collides with the building, uses a free interpretation of a sixteenth-century style. At the junction between the two, the small pane sashes merge with leaded light windows. This concept was likely to have been influenced by Turner's experience of visiting historic buildings for the SPAB, where he would have seen architectural features of several periods on the same building. Many architects, including Philip Webb, used similar ideas to create an impression of a building that had organically evolved over several centuries. Few architects, however, took this concept to the extreme adopted by Turner.

A third theme explored by Turner was to create a formal framework, then within this juxtapose features in an irregular pattern. An example of this is a group of stables in Duke's Yard (**7.10**), built in 1900–2. A harmonious framework is created by a strong stone cornice and a regular pattern of gauged brick arches, then within this, brick pilasters and sash windows are randomly placed. This is another example of how Turner was influenced by historic buildings where the fenestration defied a strict pattern or symmetry.

HUGH THACKERAY TURNER (1853-1937)

7.10: Stables, Duke's Yard, London, 1900-1. A strong cornice and repeated gauged brick arches creates a framework for the irregular placement of pilasters and windows. (*Author.*)

This idea was taken to the extreme at 40-46 Brook Street (**7.11**), designed in 1898-9. Here a strong stone cornice and regular arrangement of crow-stepped gables creates a regular framework for the irregular placement of sash windows. On the lower two storeys, double-height, stone bay windows and arches deconstruct themselves and visually crash together in a seemingly haphazard manner. Also of note is the use of squared off and simplified stone details anticipating much later Art Deco idioms.

The two buildings in Mayfair for which Balfour Turner are best known are also the partnership's most contentious designs. The first of these was Aldford House, Park Lane (**7.12**), built in 1894-7, for the South African mining magnate Alfred Beit. The site was originally intended to accommodate two

CHAPTER 7

7.11: 40-46 Brook Street, London, 1998-9. A regular pattern of crow-stepped gables provides a framework for the haphazard clash of architectural features at the lower levels. (*Author.*)

compact detached villas, but after construction had started, Beit was allowed to extend a single-storey billiard room and winter garden onto the second plot. This late change further compromised the design, which was a curious mixture of Arts and Crafts combined with flamboyant, loose mode, French Classicism. The second building is St Anselm's Church, Davies Street (**7.13**), built in 1893-6, one of only two churches designed by the partnership. It is another example of Turner's eclectic blending of styles and his rejection of the Gothic Revival. It also shows his unwillingness to conform to the contemporary approach to church design.

Hugh Thackeray Turner (1853–1937)

7.12: Alford House, Park Lane, London, 1893, built for the South African mining magnate, Alfred Beit. Arts and Crafts sensibilities combine with ostentatious display: the design was compromised by the later addition of the single-storey element to the right. (*Survey of London.*)

7.13: St Anselm, Davis Street, London, 1893–6. The Classical interior contrasts to the Gothic-influenced exterior. The stone and timber carving was by Laurence Turner. (*English Heritage/NMR.*)

Chapter 7

The most striking feature of the composition was that it combined a fourteenth-century Gothic inspired exterior with a fourteenth-century Classically inspired interior, although neither was a direct copy. *The Builder* states that it was Turner's intention, 'to avoid introducing features in the design which call up remembrances of ancient buildings … as our present conditions of building render competition with such buildings impossible.'[15] Troup, writing in 1938, concluded 'In features and details there is little to suggest copying or following any phase of medieval architecture, except possibly the reticulated tracery of the windows.'[16] Externally, the church comprised a steeply pitched tiled roof, double aisles, clerestory, prominent buttressing, and walls constructed of stock brickwork with Portland stone and red brick dressings. The austerity of the mass of brickwork was matched by the flamboyance of the sweeping curve to the top of the paired buttresses which were terminated by arched openings from which rainwater spouts protruded. The project incorporated a new rectory, linked at high level to the church by a blind and pierced arcade.

In contrast to the Gothic-inspired exterior, the interior is a surprise, spacious and light with an overtly fourteenth-century Italian Renaissance flavour. In the spirit of the Arts and Crafts Movement, stone throughout the building was left with the tool marks showing. Similarly, the walls were finished in a single coat of plaster from the trowel and then whitewashed. The columns and other stonework were made from blue-grey Robin Hood stone from the Forest of Dean. Laurence Turner carried out the carving to the column capitals, and carved the four representations of the Evangelists in the chancels.

The *Builders' Journal & Architectural Record* was enthusiastic pronouncing it 'not only one of the most interesting of modern churches; but the best Church raised in London of late years.' Of the interior it continued:

> The whole church is a very happy conception, it catches a distant atmosphere of the severity Archaic without forcing a comparison with our present fashions; and it certainly shows how some such style as this is amenable to the needs of modern Church-goers, than the incompatible mysticism of the Gothic styles. There is none of the effort in straining traditional Gothic forms to new needs.[17]

However, this positive assessment was not shared by others; Beresford Pite writing in the *Architectural Association Notes* considered it to be 'an insult both to Cockerell's Hanover Chapel and to the gentle memory of St Anselm's, and an exhibition of that pride of bastardy which is so prized today.'[18] It would appear that the church was not universally popular and with a declining local population, in 1937 the Church Commissioners decided on demolition.

Hugh Thackeray Turner (1853-1937)

7.14: Wycliffe Buildings, Guildford, Surrey, 1894. Built for Turner's father-in-law, Thomas Wilde Powell, to provide working-class housing. The design symbolises the essence of Arts and Crafts architecture. (*Author.*)

Turner's close friend Troup unsuccessfully campaigned for the church to be taken down and re-erected on a suburban site, but this attracted little support from fellow architects. H.S. Goodhart-Rendel considered that the church was 'purely a personal record of Thackeray Turner's personal tastes,' and went on to state 'though I admit that its design has much historical significance as a revolt from Gothic in a fashionable neighbourhood, I feel

225

that the building deprived of its context, historically and local, might be more of a curiosity than a thing of beauty.'[19] Ultimately, re-erection was rejected, although elements of the building were used in a new St Anselm's, built at Belmont, Stanmore, designed by N.F. Cachemaille-Day.

Work in Surrey for the Powell family

Following Thomas Wilde Powell's involvement with York Street Chambers, in 1894, he commissioned his son-in-law to design a block of worker's apartments in Guildford, called the Wycliffe Buildings (**7.14**). The site was steeply sloping and an awkward triangular shape. Turner rose to the challenge to produce one of his most important buildings. Pevsner, in particular, praised the building noting that 'This is the style of the London County Council's (LCC) housing of *c.* 1900, but better done and earlier than the famous Millbank Estate. It is up to the best English (hence, at this time, European) work of the nineties.'[20] Like both York Street Chambers and Campden House Chambers, it was intended that the building would be used to encourage a community within the building. A communal dining room, laundry and reading room were all provided, together with a common room, which included an organ for entertainment.

The external design of the building reflects Powell's advanced artistic taste which freed Turner from the demands of his often pretentious Mayfair clients. The Wycliffe Buildings' elevations are devoid of decoration, relying on the scale and proportion of the design, combined with the beauty of the local Bargate stone, to achieve effect. The latter Turner achieved, without brick or other stone dressings, to an unusually rugged effect. His experience of working for the SPAB influenced the building's protective, castle-like appearance and monastic simplicity. The main doorway is deliberately understated and its rough-hewn appearance gives the impression of the entrance to a castle. This theme is continued with the staircases where the sophistication of the spiral design contrasts to the deliberate crudeness of the blackened adzed texture finish. The same understated Arts and Crafts approach was adopted for the design of Mill Cottage, built a year later, in the vicinity the Wycliffe Buildings.

The design of these two buildings can be placed in the same category as work created during this period by the young Arts and Crafts architects Sidney Barnsley, Alfred Powell and Detmar Blow. This trio was extensively engaged on SPAB projects under the direction of Philip Webb and Turner, often working on site with the tradesmen. As a result the SPAB became a school of 'rational building' in which the design of new structures was influenced by vernacular traditions and conservation techniques. This is very evident in Turner's work, particularly in his structural use of concrete and decorative use of clay tiles, both of which were specified by the SPAB in building conservation. The work by these and other SPAB architects represent the attainment of the Arts and Crafts ideal.

The death of Thomas Wilde Powell in 1897 and the significant inheritance bequeathed to his children resulted in a flurry of building activity. True to Powell's wishes, his children continued the tradition of building both for themselves and for the wider community. The first of these buildings was a new school in Dorking, to which Powell's eldest son, Thomas Edward Powell, generously donated £3,100, and recommended the appointment of Balfour Turner as architects. The building shows Turner's design at its understated best, simply proportioned and subtly detailed. The school gives the impression of a small country house, homely and inviting, rather than institutional. It was built in warm, natural-coloured render, beneath a red clay-tiled roof, dominated by three large chimney stacks. At the same time, Powell's eldest daughter Christiana Herringham commissioned Turner to design a weekend house and studio, adjacent to the entrance to the family home at Piccards Rough in Guildford. The house is built around an existing small cottage and the new building succeeds in creating the impression of there being three cottages that have evolved over a period of time. The eastern side of the house is built in white render, the centre section of red brick and red tile-hanging, while the stables to the west are built in purple brown bricks and dark coloured tile-hanging. The floors of the house are constructed in concrete and its design is full of Turner's idiosyncratic features and details. Several aspects of the house act as a prelude to the design of Turner's own house, 'Westbrook' (**7.15**).

Turner was always a countryman at heart, although his career had resulted in his living in London. At weekends, every opportunity was taken to escape to the country with his growing family, which now included three daughters. The purchase of a bicycle enabled him to explore the countryside and sketch vernacular buildings. In 1900, his wife's substantial inheritance enabled Turner to build a country house called 'Westbrook', and permanently move his family from London to Surrey. 'Westbrook' is considered to be his masterpiece, drawing on the diversity of his architectural experience for inspiration. Pevsner enthused: 'It is as comfortable and free from period allusions as anything Lutyens or Voysey were building at the time, with in addition a distinctive rough-hewn overtone which makes Lutyens seem a little fussy.'[21]

The house is located close to Godalming and situated high on a hill facing northwards across the River Wey Valley and the distant spires of

Chapter 7

7.15: 'Westbrook', Godalming, Surrey, 1900. Turner's own house and an important example of Arts and Crafts house and garden design. (*Author.*)

Charterhouse School. Its style follows the same rugged simplicity as the Wycliffe Buildings and is built from stone, quarried on site. For practical reasons, however, Turner chose to use the stones in large lumps lifted by crane, rather than following the local tradition of building with small pieces of stone. The structure of the building is also innovative, using concrete for the construction of the upper floors and steel for the roof structure. The main staircase is built from oak railway sleepers, which banishes the creaking normally associated with timber examples. The house was also designed to incorporate warm air heating (which his nephew John Mallory commented never worked) and electric lighting.

The front elevation of the house appears defensive and mysterious. The most prominent feature is a massive, rough-stoned, gabled entrance portico, supported on paired archaic Doulton stone columns. Above the portico is placed a horizontal band of windows providing the first-floor landing with panoramic views across the valley. By contrast, the garden elevations of the house are relaxed and inviting. On the south side the handmade clay-tiled roof is allowed to sweep down to just above ground-floor windows. The house is designed from the inside out, with windows sized and located to suit the individual rooms, or to capture particular views of the garden. Inside Laurence Turner contributed decorative plasterwork. Contemporary photographs show it to have been richly decorated in Morris & Co. wallpaper

Hugh Thackeray Turner (1853–1937)

making it a warm and appealing family home. Despite the rationale and logic of Westbrook's design, Turner typically could not resist the addition of a quirky idiosyncratic feature. On the first-floor front elevation is located a curious projecting, rendered gable feature. This serves no purpose and its appearance is at odds with the rest of the house, yet Turner placed it there to pay homage to the type of haphazard additions often seen on traditional buildings.

The design of the garden is integral to the design of the house. It consists of both formal and informal areas, with garden rooms created by the use of tall Bargate stone walls and hedges. Sheltered seating areas are placed within these garden rooms to enable the garden to be enjoyed at all times of the year. Gertrude Jekyll, a family friend, praised it and contributed a planting scheme for the sunken garden area. The house and garden were twice featured in *Country Life* and Jekyll devoted a chapter to the garden in her book *Gardens for Small Country Houses*, published in 1912. Here she wrote: 'When an architect of ripe experience and keen sensibility plans a house and garden for his own home, we may look for something more than usually interesting, and at 'Westbrook' one is not disappointed.'[22]

In 1901, Turner designed a country house in Dorking for his brother-

7.16: 'Goodwyns Place', Dorking, Surrey, 1901, continues the theme of using contrasting architectural features as previously used at Tygon Place. SPAB-influenced clay tiles form the quoins and balustrade. (*English Heritage/NMR*.)

Chapter 7

7.17: 'The Court', Guildford, 1902. A prelude to the architecture of the later Garden City Movement. Concrete was used for the floor construction, which, on the second floor, was extended externally to form the eaves. (*Author.*)

in-law Thomas Powell. Called 'Goodwyns Place' (**7.16**), the house adopts a different design approach to 'Westbrook', showing Turner developing further the concept of using contrasting styles, which he had used at Lygon Place. Unlike Lygon Place, where the different styles are confined to different elements of the building, at 'Goodwyns Place' the contrasting styles are combined on the same elevations. For instance, on its south side, three projecting gables use square-pane leaded light windows set in stone mullions; between the gables small pane sash windows are used; and set into the roof, the dormer windows use diamond pattern leaded lights.

Like the Powell Corderoy School, the principal external materials are natural-coloured render and plain clay roofing tiles. An unusual feature is the use of clay tiles for the quoins and some of the window details. Clay tiles are also used to form decorative trellis pattern balustrading both on the house and in the garden. This is likely to have been inspired by the SPAB's use of clay tiles in the repair of historic buildings. 'Goodwyns Place', like 'Westbrook', employed modern construction methods, using concrete floors and a steel roof structure. Here was the final example of Turner's use of contrasting architectural styles; his subsequent designs followed a more conventional approach.

A year later he completed a group of fifteen townhouses in Guildford called 'The Court' (**7.17**), commissioned by Miss Eleanor Powell. These were arranged around a grassed courtyard in a splayed 'C' shape, facing eastwards, towards the River Wey. Turner's design adopts a similar restrained design approach previously used for the Powell Corderoy School in which cream-coloured render is used for the upper storey, balanced against red brickwork on the ground floor. The second floor is contained within a large, plain clay-tiled roof. Horizontal emphasis is created by rows of small-pane casement windows, and subtle use is made of clay tiles to form a projecting string-course above the ground-floor windows, which gently curves over the front doors. Once again Turner used concrete for the construction of the upper floors, but this time it is taken a stage further by allowing the second floor to project, forming exposed concrete eaves. Just as the Wycliff Buildings were a prelude to the later work of the LCC, so The Court is a precursor to the style of the later Garden City Movement and in particular the work of Baillie Scott.

Final work in London

The succession of the 2nd Duke of Westminster in 1899 heralded a new era for the Grosvenor Estate, characterised by the increasing use of stonework for façades. An example of Balfour Turner's work for the estate during this period is 17 Upper Grosvenor Street, built in 1907, designed in an Arts and Crafts-influenced, late seventeenth-century Low Countries Classical style. The house features a prominent foliated stone frieze carved by Laurence Turner. Other work from this period includes the re-facing in stone of Wilton Crescent in 1908-12, evidence that Balfour Turner were capable of working within stricter Classical principles.

Through the connection of Eustace Balfour's wife, Lady Frances, in 1906 Balfour Turner were appointed to design their second church, a rebuilding of the Church of Scotland's, Crown Court Church, Covent Garden,[23] (**7.18**). It was proposed that it should seat 480 and include a school. The site, however, was very challenging, surrounded on three sides by buildings, with the only light available from Crown Court. Turner's solution was to locate the school at floor level and place the church above as a double-height space, using galleries around three sides to double the seating capacity. The building represented an early use of a structural steel frame, here encased in decorative timber. The church interior was free Jacobean stylistically, featuring extensive carving by Laurence Turner.[24] Externally, the Jacobean theme is continued, shunning any reference to ubiquitous Gothic. The design was both ingenious and innovative, a forerunner of several of the new multi-purpose, multi-storey, urban churches of today.

CHAPTER 7

7.18: Crown Court Church, London, 1906-9. The design features innovative planning and the use of a structural steel framework. The coat of arms was carved by Laurence Turner. (*English Heritage/NMR.*)

Eustace Balfour found that the 2nd Duke of Westminster's character ran contrary to his own, making it difficult to perform his role as the estate's surveyor. This situation was made worse by Balfour's increasing, alcohol-induced illnesses. In 1910 he resigned and on 14 February 1911, died. This effectively ended the practice's work in London.

Later work outside London
On moving to Godalming, Turner and his wife, immediately became involved with the local community and conservation issues, and in 1905 were involved in the acquisition of the Devil's Punchbowl, Hindhead, by the National Trust. A year later they bought 240 acres of land at Witley and Milford Commons to prevent them being developed, later, in 1921, given to the National Trust by Turner and his daughters.

In 1907, Turner suffered two severe blows, first with the death of his father, then the death of his wife (from pneumonia) leaving him to bring up three teenage daughters.

The deaths in 1911 of Eustace Balfour, and then John Kent, the Assistant

Hugh Thackeray Turner (1853-1937)

Secretary of the SPAB, had a major affect on Turner and he subsequently resigned from his position as Secretary. As his replacement, he recommended the appointment of A.R. Powys, an architect trained in SPAB conservation techniques by William Weir. Powys became an important figure in the continued success of the SPAB during the inter-war period. Within six months, Turner took Powys into partnership at Balfour Turner.

Turner continued to be involved with the SPAB, serving as Chairman, a position better suited to the more strategic role he was then performing with the society, particularly since the retirement of Philip Webb. Slightly earlier, in 1903, Turner had been involved in publishing the SPAB landmark conservation book, *Notes on the Repair of Ancient Buildings*. This summarised the techniques developed over the previous ten years by Webb and Turner, when working with Detmar Blow, Alfred Powell and William Weir. Turner is considered to have largely written the book, but did not take credit, perhaps because it recorded what had been the result of the society's combined initiatives.

Despite Turner's personal tragedies, he continued to be actively involved with the local community. In 1912, at the instigation of Gertrude Jekyll, he

7.19: The Phillips Memorial Cloister, Godalming, 1914, a collaboration with Gertrude Jekyll to commemorate Jack Phillips who lost his life as the wireless operator on the SS *Titanic*. (*Author.*)

CHAPTER 7

became involved with a proposal to build a memorial to Jack Phillips, the locally born wireless operator whose life had been lost in the sinking of the *Titanic*. Turner and Jekyll proposed that the Phillips Memorial (**7.19**) should take the form of a cloister, surrounding a planted pool. Jekyll described the design of the building as being inspired by west Surrey vernacular farm buildings,[25] in which Turner used traditional local buildings as an inspiration for a sophisticated and original design, rich in detail and interest. The oak timberwork uses details similar to those at Westbrook, and Turner made extensive use of red clay-tile features to provide a contrast to the local purple-coloured brickwork. An important element of the design is four large arched openings in the east elevation which are intended to frame views of the sky and distant hills. This effect was slightly diminished by the location of the memorial being changed, which altered Turner's preferred view from the memorial. Laurence Turner carried out the carving to the Bargate stone memorial tablet and drinking fountain.

During this period, another important commission was the design of Shottendane House, Margate (**7.20**), for Dr Arthur Rowe, a surgeon and well-known geologist. The house uses the same combination of natural-coloured render and tiled quoin details as had appeared at 'Goodwyns Place', but in a simplified form, using only leaded light casements. A prominent external feature is a unique dentil eaves detail formed in terracotta tiles. Internally, the house is designed in Turner's typical sixteenth-century inspired style. It is surrounded by an extensive, organically planned garden, although it is not known whether Turner was responsible for its design.

7.20: Stottendane House, Margate, Kent, 1910. The building uses similar render and clay tile details as 'Goodwyns Place' but is a much more straightforward design. (*Author.*)

It is likely that Turner's last design was a house for the Darnley family of Cobham Hall, in Kent. Construction began in 1914, but due to the First World War was not completed until 1923. It was a substantial house, simply, but assertively designed and built in local yellow stock brickwork with contrasting red-brick dressings. The wall construction is unusual, using a cavity, filled with mass concrete. Shuttered concrete is used to form elegant curved eaves to the roof. Internally, the oak joinery is simply designed, and in contrast to Shottendane House, does not use historic references. The design of the oak staircase is particularly impressive with the joints clearly expressed. An unusual feature is the plaster ceilings, which are subdivided by Japanese-style timber grid-work. Turner may have been influenced either by a visit to Japan earlier in the century by his eldest daughter, or perhaps by the work of Frank Lloyd Wright, which he would have known through his friend C.R. Ashbee.

On the completion of Pucklehill House, Turner retired from Balfour Turner, aged 70. Two years later, Powys took the SPAB architect John MacGregor OBE into partnership and changed the name of the practice to Powys MacGregor, which continued until Powys' early death in 1936. Turner continued his involvement with both the SPAB and the National Trust, until his death in 1937.

Turner's approach to architectural design is best summarised by the words on his memorial in Godalming Church: 'architect and artist in the craft of building.' Like the work of an artist, Turner's buildings reflect his own personality and its many contradictions, logical yet idiosyncratic, modern yet romantic, reserved yet flamboyant, sensitive yet inviting controversy. Like an artist, Turner experimented with numerous themes, exploring ideas until they reached a conclusion, typified by Goodwyns Place and 40-46 Brook Street. Buildings such as 'Westbrook' and the Wycliffe Buildings contain many of the ingredients which lie at the heart of the Arts and Crafts Movement. What links all Turner's buildings is their honesty, sincerity and commitment, qualities that transcend time and fashion.

Notes
1   F.H.W. Sheppard (ed.), *Survey of London*, 39, Athlone Press, 1977.
2   F.W. Troup, 'Thackeray Turner', *Journal of the Royal Institute of British Architects*, 10, 1938, 258.
3   G. Stamp, *An Architect of Promise: George Gilbert Scott Junior (1839-1897) & the Late Gothic Revival*, Shaun Tyas, 2002, 21.
4   Troup [n. 2], 258.
5   H. Thackeray Turner, account book 1878, 1881, unpublished, SPAB archive.
6   For Moore, see G.K. Brandwood, *Temple Moore; an Architect of the Late Gothic Revival*,

Chapter 7

Paul Watkins, 1997. Although Turner and Moore would have known each other, their careers took very different paths.
7. Scott's decline is discussed in Stamp [n. 3], 319-42.
8. S. Gray, *Edwardian Architecture*, Wordsworth Editions, 1985, 99-100. Lady Francis Campbell, later a prominent suffragist, was the daughter of the 8th Duke of Argyll; her brother, the 9th Duke, married Queen Victoria's daughter, Princess Louise.
9. 'Men Who Build, Number 49', *Builders' Journal & Architectural Record*, 24 Mar. 1897, 88.
1. Ibid.
11. A. Saint, *Richard Norman Shaw*, Yale U.P., 1976, 435, 440.
12. E. Crawford, *Enterprising Women, the Garrett's and their Circle*, Francis Boutle, 2002, 282-8.
13. 'News of the Week: Hugh Thackeray Turner', *Architect & Building News*, 17 Dec. 1937, 333.
14. W.R. Lethaby, *Philip Webb and his Work*, Oxford U.P., 1935.
15. *Builders' Journal & Architectural Record*, 24 Mar. 1897, 89.
16. Troup [n. 2], 258.
17. *Builders' Journal & Architectural Record*, 24 Mar. 1897, 89.
18. A. Beresford Pite, *Architectural Association Notes*, 10, 1896, 174.
19. F.H.W. Sheppard (ed.), *Survey of London*, 40, Athlone Press, 1980, 79.
20. I. Nairn, N. Pevsner & B. Cherry, *The Buildings of England: Surrey*, Penguin, 1971, 292.
21. Ibid., 259.
22. G. Jekyll & L. Weaver, *Gardens for Small Country Houses*, Country Life, 1912, 27-35.
23. J.B. Huffman, 'For Kirk and Crown: the rebuilding of the Crown Court Church, 1905-1909', *London Journal*, 17, 1992, 56.
24. Ibid., 65.
25. *Surrey Advertiser & County Times*, 30 Sep. 1912.

Notes on the Contributors

Dr Stewart Abbott has taught architectural history at Reading and Southampton Universities and currently teaches in the School of History at Queen Mary, University of London. He contributed 'Urban meets Rural: a study of three eighteenth-century retreats on the Isle of Wight' in *Rural and Urban: Architecture between Two Cultures* edited by Andrew Ballantyne, published in 2010 by Routledge. He is interested in representations of architecture in image and text and is working on a study of English speaking visitors' diaries and travel notes made during tours of southern Italy since the seventeenth century.

Professor James Stevens Curl has many books, reviews, scholarly papers, and articles to his credit. He has held chairs in architectural history at two universities, was twice Visiting Fellow at Peterhouse, University of Cambridge, is a member of the Royal Irish Academy, and a fellow of the Societies of Antiquaries of London and Scotland. He has acquired an enviable international reputation for thoroughness of research, impeccable scholarship, and lucidity of style, and has not been afraid to venture into realms unfrequented by those of more timid disposition. Now in his eighth decade, his acerbic wit, intellectual curiosity, and fluency of expression remains undiminished.

Professor Hilary J. Grainger is a dean of London College of Fashion, University of the Arts London. An architectural historian, she is the leading authority on the work of the late Victorian architect Sir Ernest George and the architecture of British crematoria. Her books *Death Redesigned: British Crematoria History, Architecture and Landscape* and *The Architecture of Sir Ernest George* were published by Spire Books in 2005 and 2011 respectively. She is Chair of the Victorian Society and a council member of the Cremation Society of Great Britain.

Joseph Sharples worked as a curator at the Walker Art Gallery, Liverpool, from 1990 to 2001. He is the author of the *Liverpool* volume in the Pevsner Architectural Guides series (Yale University Press, 2004), and has published and curated exhibitions on various aspects of Liverpool architecture. He is currently a researcher at Glasgow University, where he is working on a new study of the architecture of Charles Rennie Mackintosh.

Robin Stannard is a historic building surveyor who works for the architectural practice, ADAM Architecture. He began his conservation career with the SPAB architect David Nye, and then went on to work for English Heritage. He has a special interest in the Arts and Crafts Movement and has spent several years undertaking research on the life and work of Hugh Thackeray Turner with the aim of producing a monograph.

Christopher Webster is an architectural historian who has published widely on the late Georgian and early Victorian periods. He is particularly interested in post-Waterloo stylistic debates, the development of the provincial profession in this period, and the early work of the Cambridge Camden Society. His *R.D. Chantrell (1793-1872) and the Architecture of a Lost Generation* was published in 2010, and in 2011 he edited *Building a Great Victorian City: Leeds Architects and Architecture, 1790-1914* and *Episodes in the Gothic Revival: Six Church Architects*.

Picture Editor

Ruth Baumberg read mathematics at Somerville College, Oxford and spent her working life in the computer industry. She has an interest in late Victorian art pottery and has published articles on Burmantofts pottery. She is a member of the Victorian Society, enjoys looking at buildings and has always had an interest in photography.